THE CHICAGO BOARD OF TRADE, 1859–1905

THE CHICAGO BOARD OF TRADE
1859–1905

The Dynamics of Self-Regulation

by JONATHAN LURIE

UNIVERSITY OF ILLINOIS PRESS
URBANA, CHICAGO, LONDON

Publication of this book has been made possible in part by grants from the Research Council of Rutgers University and the W. McNeil Kennedy Securities Law Memorial Fund of the Chicago Bar Foundation.

FRONTISPIECE: A detail of the Pit
from an illustration in *Harper's Monthly*, July 1886.
Courtesy Historical Pictures Service, Inc., Chicago

LIBRARY OF CONGRESS CATALOGING IN PUBLICATION DATA

Lurie, Jonathan, 1939–
The Chicago Board of Trade, 1859–1905.

Bibliography: p.
Includes index.
1. Chicago. Board of Trade. I. Title.
KF1087.C55L87   346′.73′092   78–20881
ISBN 0–252–00732–8

For Maxine

in memory of Nanny

Contents

Preface

I T HAS LONG BEEN ACCEPTED that the nineteenth century, particularly the years between 1820 and 1890, represented a period of rapid change in American history. At the same time, however, and with no awareness of internal inconsistency, public policy encouraged a stable atmosphere within which change could occur. Willard Hurst has written that "the nineteenth century United States valued change more than stability and valued stability most often where it helped create a framework for change."[1] The inevitable tension between these two forces had its effect, in different ways, upon the course of both modernization and industrialization.

Confronted with limited governmental resources, American public policy recognized, from an early period, the usefulness of the corporate charter—granted originally with great selectivity and only in special circumstances—as a means for promoting change within a stable context. Yet, by the middle of the nineteenth century, corporate charters had become no longer the exception but rather the rule. Their proliferation indicated that the modernization of American society was proceeding at a faster rate than that to which public policy could respond. For a time this policy attempted to stay in tandem with what Hurst aptly called "the release of energy."[2] Ultimately, however, the forces of modernization pulled ahead, and the results were devastating in immediate effects as well as in long-range planning.

In the heady atmosphere of the Jacksonian era, state after state indulged in a rash of internal improvements, all designed

1. Willard Hurst, *Law and the Conditions of Freedom in the Nineteenth Century United States* (Madison, 1964), p. 24.
2. Ibid., pp. 3–32.

to facilitate change. Grandiose schemes, including the construction of turnpikes and canals, the improvement of harbor facilities, and the building of railroads, were all replete with generous state charters that offered both state aid and public credit. These ventures, hastily conceived, often poorly executed, and almost always inadequately financed, were ill-prepared to withstand the severe economic dislocation and panic of the late 1830s. Few ever reached fruition. The reaction of the states to these events was clear. By the time of the Civil War, virtually every state had erected its own rigid constitutional barriers against further state involvement in such projects.

Typical of this experience, during the 1830s the State of Illinois launched "the most stupendous, extravagant, and perhaps ruinous folly . . . that any civil community perhaps ever engaged in."[3] The legislature voted to spend about $20 million to construct a vast program of railroads, turnpikes, and river and harbor improvements. It is not clear whether the finished projects would have benefited the state, but the scheme ultimately failed to survive the general economic collapse.

In the aftermath of this ambitious plan, more than $14 million had to be raised, completely from taxes, to pay off the debt incurred. According to *Hunt's Merchant Magazine*, "Among all the states of the Union, none had more canvas spread, or so little ballast, as that gem of the West, Illinois."[4] Indeed, by the summer of 1841, Illinois had defaulted on her interest payments and was blacklisted "by every financial center in the United States and western Europe."[5] When the state adopted a new constitution in 1848, one of its provisions enjoined the use of the state's credit in any manner for the "aid of any individual, association or corporation."[6]

Although the number of states that had been hurt by the failure of internal improvement schemes could only have dampened support for future state involvement, other factors discouraged such policies as well. Traditionally, popular acceptance of the concept of limited government is credited to the influence

3. George H. Miller, *Railroads and the Granger Laws* (Madison, 1971), p. 50.
4. Ibid.
5. Ibid.
6. Ibid., p. 51.

of such late nineteenth-century writers as Spencer, Sumner, and Cooley. Actually, however, this concept had been widely accepted by the middle of the nineteenth century, before the ideas of these men received popular circulation. Perhaps because American public policy was too firmly anchored to the post-revolutionary Madisonian concepts of power balance and limitation, it tended to make government a passive, supervisory force. Given this tendency and the economic collapse of the 1830s, a public policy resulted that had neither the means nor the inclination to involve itself actively in any economic rationalization beyond the granting of charters and the formulation of liberal laws of incorporation.

But the forces of market expansion and economic change could not be halted by a relative absence of state involvement. Inevitably, therefore, the task of reconciling change with stability had to be undertaken by private groups. While the political system retained its revolutionary legacy of limited government and decentralization, of necessity it placed responsibility for market rationalization in the private sector. The growth of the American market during this period is well known. In no other sector of American society was the pressure for growth and expansion so strong and the need for an ordered, stable framework in which it could occur so great. This was especially true of that extremely volatile component of the market, the American grain trade.

One outgrowth of the pressure exerted upon the grain trade was the establishment of state-chartered private associations, which could reconcile the need for market predictability with a desire for economic growth and gain. Such organizations, although private in origin and practice, gradually received and exercised important regulatory authority. They were, therefore, well equipped to resolve, in the name of public policy, tensions arising from the clash between change and stability. The quest for success in this endeavor is exemplified by the Chicago Board of Trade, the largest and most controversial of these organizations and the subject of this study.

An analysis of the Chicago Board of Trade as it functioned during the late nineteenth century offers important insights into the ways in which Americans "valued stability . . . where it helped create a framework for change." By studying this institution over a period of years and in various stages—in its relation to its members, to the trading public, and to the legal system—one can discern what Robert Wiebe has called "the search for order."[7] One can see how complex this search for stability—its desire for reform mingled with a longing for monopoly and its conflicts of interest mingled with consensus—became during this period. Finally, one can see the changing concepts of internal and external regulation, the process by which Americans sought to reconcile their new world of urban centers, corporate enterprise, and vast industry with the practices and values of an earlier time.

These are the major themes that link the following chapters together. However, it is not sufficient to examine the commodities exchange solely in the context of what Louis Galambos has called "the organizational synthesis."[8] Because the exchange acted as a quasi-public regulatory agency, its development must be seen as an important part of an emerging body of legal doctrine that has been relatively unexplored by historians: the growth of American administrative law. By placing the study within this dual framework, it becomes possible to raise (and, I hope, to answer) questions that bring these themes into clear focus.

The book's emphasis on internal regulation is intentional. In recent years scholarship on governmental regulation has focused almost exclusively on two alternative models: (1) the "public interest" model and (2) the "captured by the regulated interests" model.[9] A case can certainly be made for either or both of these approaches when studying the activity of a particular regulatory agency during a particular period. These models alone, however, do not suffice as historical explanations. Regulation in the American environment had other characteristics as well. One of the most important and neglected of these characteristics, especially during the late nineteenth century, has been self-regulation. Whereas lawyers, sociologists, political scientists, and economists are becoming increasingly at home in dealing with aspects of modern administrative theory, the evolution of the private asso-

7. Robert Wiebe, _The Search For Order_ (New York, 1967), passim.

8. Louis Galambos, "The Emerging Organizational Synthesis in Modern American History," _Business History Review_ 44 (1970):279–90.

9. Thomas K. McCraw, "Regulation in America: A Review Article," _Business History Review_ 49 (1975):159–83.

ciation with quasi-public regulatory powers is a study better suited to historical analysis.

It is my hope that this book will make a contribution toward a better understanding of the administrative process. In spite of the plethora of public regulatory agencies that have appeared since the 1930s, the basic fact remains that the vast majority of American legal arrangements are in the area of private ordering. I hope this study will be a valuable addition to the existing literature and will open up the self-regulatory role of law as a subject for scholarly inquiry among historians.

Much of this book was submitted to the University of Wisconsin as a doctoral dissertation. Here again I repeat my grateful acknowledgment to all those who are listed therein. I also acknowledge my debt to Cameron Allen and the staff of the Law School library at Rutgers University, and to Stanley N. Katz and Alfred Chandler, Jr., for perceptive advice and criticism. I am especially grateful to Dean Albert Sacks and Professor Harold Berman, both of the Harvard Law School, for making it possible for me to study there in 1973–74 as a visiting Liberal Arts Fellow in Law and History. The financial assistance of both the Social Sciences Research Council and Rutgers University in making my leave of absence possible is deeply appreciated. Professor Archibald Cox willingly dicussed aspects of administrative law and internal regulation with me in some detail, as also did Dean Sacks, whose permission to quote from and cite the unpublished Hart and Sacks materials on the legal process is warmly acknowledged. Frank Williams and Rita Zelewsky of the University of Illinois Press and the anonymous critic who examined an earlier draft of the manuscript have also been of great assistance.

My colleagues at Rutgers, especially Elliot Rosen, Norman Dain, and Frederick Russell offered valuable suggestions. To Gerald Grob of Douglass College and Louis Galambos of Johns Hopkins goes my deep gratitude. Their critical suggestions and encouragement were vitally instrumental in bringing the manuscript to completion. Morton Horwitz of the Harvard Law School gave freely of his time, suggestions, and materials, with a generosity for which I remain very grateful. Professor Thomas McGraw, who was himself working on historical aspects of American regulation, made beneficial suggestions concerning the introductory chapter. The Research Council of Rutgers University, in addition to contributing toward the publication costs of this study, has consistently supported my long-range research work in American legal history. I am deeply indebted to the Council, as well as to the American Philosophical Society, for financial assistance.

Excerpts from the following chapters first appeared in *Agricultural History*, the *American Journal of Legal History*, the *Bulletin of the Missouri Historical Society*, and the *Rutgers Law Review*. I am grateful to the editors of these journals for their permission to reprint portions of my earlier articles.

Finally, I acknowledge the affection and support of my wife and family—of my father especially, who has waited for this book longer than both of us like to admit.

Abbreviations

CBT *Rules*	Chicago Board of Trade, *Rules,* Chicago Board of Trade Papers, University of Illinois, Chicago.
D.P.	*Directors' Papers,* Chicago Board of Trade Papers, University of Illinois, Chicago.
D.R.	*Directors' Records,* Chicago Board of Trade Papers, University of Illinois, Chicago.
Report of the Directors	*Report of the Directors.* Preface to Chicago Board of Trade *Yearbook* (Chicago, various dates 1874–1905).
Report on the Grain Trade	Federal Trade Commission, *Report on the Grain Trade,* 7 vols. (Washington, D.C., 1920–26).
SB	Citizen's Association of Chicago, comp., *Scrapbooks,* Chicago Historical Society, Chicago.

THE CHICAGO BOARD OF TRADE, 1859–1905

CHAPTER ONE

A Framework and Overview

I

A COMPREHENSIVE HISTORY of American administrative law has yet to be written. Indeed, the subject matter that should properly be included in any such undertaking is so vast that a general synthesis may be impossible. Colonial administration, early federal administrative actions concerning land, Indians and veterans, the development of post-Civil War federal commissions, and the proliferation of modern administrative agencies since the New Deal all present legitimate areas of historical inquiry. However, even more would need to be considered. Early state administrative growth paralleled, and in many cases preceded, federal actions. The interplay between state, local, and federal administrative action in a historical context warrants analysis. Finally, and for the purposes of this study most important, there is the field of non-public administrative action undertaken by private groups (voluntary associations) that wield considerable power in the name of public policy.

Clearly, a general all-inclusive study of the history of administrative law that could do justice to all of these areas (which in themselves are by no means complete) would not be feasible. Yet, as has been shown in the field of American legal history, it is possible to work within a narrower range of inquiry, producing "installments" of a complete historical analysis.[1] It is

1. See, for example, Oscar and Mary Handlin, *Commonwealth: A Study of the Role of Government in the Economy* (Cambridge, Mass., 1969); Willard Hurst: *Law and the Conditions of Freedom in Nineteenth-Century United States* (Madison, 1956), *Law and Economic Growth* (Cambridge, Mass., 1964), *Legitimacy of the Business Corporation in the Law of the United States* (Charlottesville, Va., 1970); Leonard Levy, *The Law of the Commonwealth and Chief Justice Shaw* (Cambridge, Mass., 1957); Harry Scheiber, *Ohio Canal Era: A Case Study of Government and the Economy* (Athens, O., 1969). See also *Perspectives in American History*, vol. 5, ed. Donald Fleming and Bernard

hoped that this book will be the first of several such installments dealing with a systematic historical treatment of American administrative law.

The recognition that a viable conceptual framework within
a narrower scope is feasible and desirable does not in itself
completely resolve the problem. This study focuses on the development of a regulatory institution. If one is to analyze this process historically, it is not sufficient merely to delineate the actual
regulatory course of one specific institution over a period of
time. This procedure must be viewed in relation to several other
questions. How does one measure the effectiveness or success of
specific regulatory actions? What were some of the underlying
assumptions behind the growth of economic regulation, public
and private, during the late nineteenth century? Were there
certain societal values held in common by both those who sought
to regulate and those upon whom such constraints were imposed?
To phrase the question in this way may be of value in narrow-
ing the gap between the writers who argue that the regulatory
process has been, for the most part, merely an incestuous relationship between those who regulate and those whose interests
are regulated and the other writers who claim that governmental administrative regulation has been effective and beneficial to
the "public interest."

Viewed thus, the problem seems to have generated merely
controversy and not enlightenment. History is often as much
what we believe happened as what actually did occur, and this
famous generalization applies with particular force to the area
of governmental regulation. One can argue, in the tradition of
Solon Buck, John Hicks, and others, that the public outrage at
abuses committed by the railroads and other powerful corporate
enterprises spawned federal regulation in the late nineteenth
century.[2] Or one may be more convinced by the alternative view,

Bailyn (Cambridge, Mass., 1971). This volume is devoted entirely to law in
American history. See, in particular, the essays by Morton Horwitz, Stanley Katz,
and Harry Scheiber. It should be noted that Lawrence Friedman attempted a
general synthesis in *A History of American Law* (New York, 1973). Although
the book is an important contribution to the literature, its conceptual difficulties
appear to demonstrate conclusively that a more narrow approach to American
legal history, including administrative history, is essential. See this author's review of Friedman's book in *Rutgers Law Review* 27 (Winter 1974):354–63.

2. John D. Hicks, *The Populist Revolt* (Minneapolis, 1931); Solon J. Buck,
The Granger Era (Cambridge, Mass., 1913).

exemplified by such writers as Gabriel Kolko or Louis Kohlmeier, that federal regulation arose merely as an exercise in collusion between the interests involved and the federal government, thereby rendering the so-called American Progressive tradition more fraudulent than factual.[3] Both of these viewpoints, which are not necessarily mutually antagonistic, are irrelevant to this study.

It is an error to discuss regulation in isolation or the regulators as being merely pawns of the regulatees. The inherent structure of the industry or institution involved shapes the regulatory process applied to it. Historical inquiry and examination should be given to each area of regulation, in an effort to understand the values and goals that were implicit both in support of and in opposition to its enactment. Once such research has been completed, it may be that the Hicks-Buck school is essentially correct, or that the alternative critique is more accurate, or (as this writer thinks likely) that private mercantile regulation was more effective in the late nineteenth century than has generally been assumed. Perhaps the most important result of such research is that a firmer historical foundation will be gained, upon which to generalize.

It is extremely difficult to ascertain how much evidence and documentation are needed to arrive at valid historical generalizations, as is well illustrated by the Hicks-Buck and Kolko examples just cited. It should be acknowledged that we simply do not know enough about the development of regulation in American political-legal history to generalize as they do. These two viewpoints owe more to the ideological convictions of their exponents than to the existing state of historical knowledge. Both suffer from a tendency to produce history that vindicates certain previously formed and deeply felt convictions of the writers. Perhaps no historical analysis can ever be totally free from bias, but historians can be aware, at least, of the dangers, especially in subject areas that have not yet been adequately researched.

Another essential fact that must be accepted is that most, if not all, of the major historical writing that has been offered in

3. Gabriel Kolko: *The Triumph of Conservatism* (Glencoe, Ill., 1963), *Railroads and Regulations* (Princeton, 1965); Louis Kohlmeier, *The Regulators* (New York, 1969). See also Irwin Unger, "The 'New Left' and American History," *American Historical Review* 72 (July 1967):1237–63.

this field deals with official federal or state regulation. This trend may be due in part to the growing extent of government regulative action in the last eighty years. Furthermore, as administrative agencies have expanded and multiplied, so have their records, along with legislative hearings, debates, and similar materials. The increasing availability of these sources has made possible some extremely important studies on governmental regulation. I. L. Sharfman's classic work on the I.C.C. comes immediately to mind as also do the monumental volumes on American political administration by Leonard White.[4] However, the value and distinction of these and other volumes should not obscure the fact that it would be a gross error to assume that the regulatory process inherent in administrative law and absolutely vital to any study of its history must be limited to official governmental bodies only.

One of the theses of this study is that unofficial regulation should be explored in much greater detail, with particular emphasis placed upon the growth of private nonprofit voluntary associations and the interplay between private regulatory action and public policy as it developed. There are sound reasons for this suggested emphasis. In the first place, it accurately reflects our legal history, which has demonstrated that in the American experience private ordering has been "the primary process of social adjustment within the dynamics of a legal system."[5] American legal history reveals an unmistakable tendency toward the encouragement of private activity, including, of course, economic growth and its resultant private regulation. We tend to lose sight of this fact, because critical attention is so often called to the official regulatory agencies. Contemporary concern with the effectiveness or ineffectiveness of these agencies has been matched by a popular obsession with formal and official dispute-settling mechanisms. Whoever heard of Perry Mason or any one of his numerous counterparts settling a case out of court? Actually, the great majority of all cases filed in the courts are settled

4. I. L. Sharfman, *The Interstate Commerce Commission* (New York, 1931–37); Leonard White: *The Federalists* (New York, 1948), *The Jeffersonians* (New York, 1951), *The Jacksonians* (New York, 1954), *The Republican Era* (New York, 1958).

5. Henry Hart, Jr., and Albert Sacks, *The Legal Process* (Cambridge, Mass., 1958), p. 183.

prior to trial. Indeed, the problems that "private orderers are able to solve never reach officials at all," and "most of the problems which do reach officials take their shape from the successes and failures of prior efforts at private adjustment."[6]

In the second place, study of the role of private ordering raises questions that ought to be considered if we are to better understand the regulatory process in light of the themes noted earlier. What, in fact, has been the role of private decision-making in the direction of American society since the middle of the nineteenth century? What have been its characteristic advantages and disadvantages? How far has private ordering been permitted to proceed so as to make the most of its virtues while curbing possible abuses? Henry Hart has noted that a fundamental purpose of "official law" is "guiding and channeling the processes of private autonomy and adjustment so as to release to the utmost the enormous potential of the human abilities in the society—its ultimate and most significant resource."[7] In what circumstances then can the effective regulation of private ordering create conditions, as in a free market, that are favorable to the interplay of competing interests? Finally, what has been the appropriate role for direct, official regulation of private decisions in prescribing duties and conditions for the effectual exercise of private power; and what part did the courts and/or the legislature play in such activity?

Conviction that the subject of private ordering represents a fertile field for study within American administrative law does not automatically insure immunity from the difficulties cited at the outset of this chapter. The subject of private ordering, as with its parent field of administrative law, is vast in its dimensions. A viable answer to an inquiry into the types of private ordering and the extent to which they can be discussed may lie in the extended discussion of an example that has sufficient historical significance to offer insight into the questions raised previously. Such an example can be a private, voluntary, nonprofit association that developed in growth and influence during the late nineteenth century; that, though private in composition, was

6. Ibid.
7. Henry Hart, Jr., "The Relations Between State and Federal Law," *Columbia Law Review* 54 (1954):489–90.

public in result if not in purpose; that wielded considerable formal and informal disciplinary power over its members; and that held regulatory powers subject to periodic judicial and (to a much lesser extent) legislative scrutiny. The Chicago Board of Trade eminently fulfills all of these criteria.

This study traces the evolution of the Chicago Board of Trade from its beginnings as a sort of private club to its later function as a quasi-public regulatory agency. The Chicago Board of Trade has been used as a case study for two reasons: (1) it appears to be the only major commodities exchange to have preserved its records and papers (the collection that forms the basis of this study); and (2) as one of a number of similar institutions that emerged during the middle of the nineteenth century, it shared with others of the same genre virtually identical functions and similar mercantile procedures. Hence, a study of the Chicago Board of Trade can be of great value in resolving questions like the following, which go beyond the experience of a single institution.

What were (and are) the functions of the commodities exchange? What part has internal regulation played in its development, and why has internal regulatory power been so important in its growth? Are the types of activities that the exchange sought to regulate and control comparable to those facing railroad leaders, bankers, and other businessmen? Why did the external legal order (the courts and the legislature) permit the commodities exchange such a large measure of self-regulation? Finally, does the experience of the exchange offer any insights into the nature of internal regulation; that is, are certain kinds of institutions and activities inherently easier to police and rationalize than others?

In answering these questions, the following chapters treat the Chicago Board of Trade both as a private voluntary association and as a quasi-regulatory body. The institution's development can be better understood by placing it within a general framework of modern administrative law. As will be seen, the potential of administrative law concepts for research in American legal history is exciting and promising. These chapters then represent not a general history of an institution but a historical exploration into the growth and effectiveness of a private regulatory agency. They are less concerned with the Board as a marketing institution than with its use of power over the membership, the success or failure of its rulemaking authority, and the interplay between its organization and the courts. Here again the importance of administrative law for this kind of analysis will be obvious.

II

Although modern administrative law exerts a heavy emphasis upon contemporaneity both in the issue and formation of policy, the basic definitions involved are readily adaptable to historical inquiry. Administrative law is, simply, that body of rules and doctrines which deals with the powers and actions of administrative agencies.[8] An administrative agency, Kenneth Davis states, is an organization "other than a court and other than a legislative body, which affects the right of private parties through either adjudication, rulemaking. investigating, prosecuting, negotiating, settling, or informally acting."[9] The administrative process can thus be identified as "rule making when not done by the legislature and adjudication when not done by the courts."[10]

Two characteristics inherent in these definitions should be noted. In the first place, there is an obvious mingling of functions. The administrative organizations are not either legislative or judicial or executive in function; rather, they combine all three attributes in varying degrees. As will be seen, the Chicago Board of Trade ultimately undertook all of the actions that Davis listed in his definition. It acted like a legislature in passing certain rules and regulations that were binding upon its members as law. It acted like a judge when it heard complaints, issued penalties, and tried to mediate disputes. In enforcing the rules it adopted, the Board demonstrated executive authority. Of course, the Board was not always uniformly successful in fulfilling these various functions, and its slow development from a private club into a quasi-public regulatory agency marks one of the important themes of this study.

8. Ernest Gellhorn, *Administrative Law and Process* (St. Paul, 1972), pp. 6–7.
9. Kenneth C. Davis, *Administrative Law Treatise,* 3d ed. (St. Paul, 1972), pp. 1–5.
10. Louis L. Jaffe and Nathaniel L. Nathanson, *Administrative Law: Cases and Materials,* 3d ed. (Boston, 1968), p. 4.

   This intermingling of functions is not new and, of course, has not been limited to modern administrative agencies. In 1781, for example, the colonial legislature of Maryland empowered justices of the county courts to license the local ferry service. The judges were to

> ascertain in current money the price of ferriage [sic] for passengers and horses, and the several kinds of carriages . . . , at every ferry by them licensed; and the said justices shall direct how many and what kind of boats shall be kept, and what number of able bodied and skillful hands shall be employed in the boats at every ferry by them licensed, . . . and if any licensed ferry-keeper shall ask or receive, directly or indirectly, more than the price allowed for ferriage, he shall, for every demand or receipt, forfeit twenty shillings current money.[11]

The regulatory character of nonjudicial role given the judges is striking. Sitting as a quasi-regulatory commission, these judges "held in their hands the power to determine who could enter business; the charges which might lawfully be made for services rendered, and the standards of performance and personnel imposed on those engaged in transporting the public."[12]

   The Chicago Board of Trade, likewise, in determining who would have access to its trading floor by limiting its membership, to some extent controlled access to the commodities markets. Furthermore, by setting specific commission rates and regulating the mercantile conduct of those engaged in the grain trade, the Board acted as an administrative agency. Again, the organization's (slowly) growing awareness of its public responsibilities in this area is delineated in the following chapters.

   In the second place, there is the element of delegation. The administrative agency receives its powers from the legislature and is thus enabled to act in the name of public policy. The matter of delegated authority is important to a regulatory agency. Although basic policy formulation traditionally rests with the legislature, its episodic nature and the variety of demands made upon it render the legislature unsuited to seek out the facts and information necessary for the basic regulation involved. Similar-

11. 1781 Md. Laws (Nov. sess.), ch. 22.
12. Walter Gellhorn, *Federal Administrative Proceedings* (Baltimore, 1941), pp. 3–4.

ly, the courts are better equipped to resolve a particular case or controversy; they are not intended "to engage in consistent determination of policy or to maintain steady contact with a general and continuing problem."[13] It will be seen that these same policy considerations apply with equal force in explaining the Chicago Board of Trade's exercise of the authority delegated to it via a charter issued by the legislature and its quasi-judicial power for adjudication and dispute settlement.

It has already been noted that administrative law involves the intermingling of executive, legislative, and judicial activities. This pattern, although necessary, raises serious problems with delegation. Just as too much power may be dangerous when lodged in one office, it may be equally dangerous when concentrated in one agency. A good case may be made for keeping the lawmaking process confined to the most representative branch of the government; this representativeness in the legislative body may well help to increase public acceptance of its work. Most important, however, excessive delegation by the legislature may lead to a loss of legislative independence and initiative, and legislature may become too dependent upon the agency experts. Although a great deal of further research must yet be undertaken, the questions may at least be raised whether delegation leads to a gradual erosion of the capacity of the legislature to legislate and whether this has, in fact, been the case with commodities exchange regulation.

Effective administrative regulatory procedure can ideally supplement both the legislature and the courts. It is clear that, between these two branches and aside from the initial legislative policy determination, the courts are of paramount importance in evaluating the functions of an agency. Indeed, it is the courts that have had to set specific limits on permissible agency action within a broad legislative delegation of authority. This tendency has resulted in (1) increased authority for the agency through expansion of the delegation doctrine, and (2) increased court interest in agency activities. Both of these conclusions apply to the Chicago Board of Trade.

The courts, in theory, appear to have looked with suspicion

13. Walter Gellhorn and Clark Byse, *Administrative Law: Cases and Comments*, 5th ed. (Brooklyn, 1970), p. 3.

upon the delegation of powers, permitting it only within narrowly drawn limits. As late as 1892, for example, the Supreme Court stated flatly: "that Congress cannot delegate legislative power . . . is a principle universally recognized as vital to the integrity and maintenance of . . . government ordained by the Constitution."[14] In fact, with the court's blessing, the legislature has delegated extensively. Indeed, the thrust of modern administrative law has been toward more and more delegation. Five years before the court decision just quoted, Woodrow Wilson observed that "large powers and unhampered discretion seem to me the indispensable conditions of responsibility. . . . There is no danger in power, if only it be not irresponsible. If it be divided, dealt out in shares to many, it is obscured; and if it be obscured, it is made irresponsible."[15]

Writing in 1887, Wilson emphasized that· "Self-government does not consist in having a hand in everything, any more than housekeeping consists necessarily in cooking dinner with one's own hands. The cook must be trusted with a large discretion as to the management of the fires and the ovens."[16] The future president's plea for adequate delegatory powers was based upon an awareness of the realities of American governmental regulation. He stated candidly in 1887 what the Supreme Court still refused to admit in 1892: that "the practical necessities of modern government demanded delegation of law-making authority."[17] Whatever the courts might hold, it was, in fact, increasingly difficult to delineate clearly the line between legislative authority to pass statutes and administrative power to enact regulations. Although the courts could limit the doctrine of delegation by insisting on evidence of a clear, "reasonable standard" and proper procedure, the years since 1887 have shown Wilson, in this area at least, as a perceptive prophet.

Courts have traditionally been reluctant to reverse agency decisions. This tendency is all the more pronounced in areas of agency expertise. However, "if this view were carried to its

14. Field v. Clark, 143 U.S. 649, 692 (1892).
15. Woodrow Wilson, "The Study of Administration," *Political Science Quarterly* 2 (1887):213–14.
16. Ibid., p. 214.
17. E. Gellhorn, pp. 14–15.

logical conclusion, judicial review would be a nullity."[18] In fact, if there is one important link between judicial intervention within a private association during the nineteenth century and judicial monitoring of administrative action today, it is the presumption of judicial review. Louis Jaffe states the point concisely: "In our system of remedies, an individual whose interest is acutely and immediately affected by . . . administrative action presumptively has a right to secure at some point a judicial determination of its validity. This is . . . the teaching of our history and tradition. It is our common law, and . . . a corollary of our constitutions."[19]

Jaffe's conclusion points to a very real tension between the Wilsonian paradigm of administrative power free from undue interference and the presumption of review. How closely should the court monitor an agency's function? At what point should it intervene? Should the court delay until both the informal and regularized processes of negotiation and decision-making within the organization have been exhausted? Should it respond promptly to a party's request for judicial relief whenever such request is filed? These questions apply with equal force whether the agency is a public regulatory agency or a private association with quasi-public regulatory powers. The answers to these problems are by no means unanimous, as any modern textbook in administrative law will indicate.

Thus, total resolution of this tension is probably impossible and, indeed, may well be undesirable. But a somewhat pragmatic reconciliation has evolved in administrative law in the doctrine of primary jurisdiction. The term means, essentially, that the initial determination or regulatory action must first come from the agency involved. The courts generally will not intervene until there *is* something to review. The administrative organization is thus assured a relatively unimpeded first attempt at dealing with its assigned subject matter. Primary jurisdiction also implies that, while the courts may review and thus undo, they will not restrain in anticipation of a supposed wrong. The usual pattern is for the courts to decline injunctive relief before the agency acts. The experience of the Chicago Board of Trade

18. Ibid., p. 124.
19. Cited by W. Gellhorn and C. Byse, p. 112; E. Gellhorn, p. 245.

will also be examined to see whether or not this pattern is common to the cases that arose between it and an aggrieved party during the late nineteenth century.

Closely related to the doctrine of primary jurisdiction is the matter of administrative expertise. Indeed, one of the justifications for primary jurisdiction is the argument that the courts may "take advantage of whatever contribution the agency can make within its area of specialization."[20] Administrative law relies heavily on the assumption that "it is the agency, not the court which is the legislatively designated expert, and the agency is thought to know what effective regulation needs."[21] Of course, at some point the courts must resolve how much credence they will give to the "experts." In matters of complex economic regulation where administrative expertise is probably greater than that of the judges, the courts will be more inclined to accept the action of the agency. Again, the experience of the Chicago Board of Trade will be examined in an attempt to ascertain whether or not this tendency also existed in those late nineteenth-century disputes over mercantile rules or actions to which it was a party.

The same danger of undue reliance on delegation also exists in the relationship between judicial review and the administrative agency. A too heavy reliance upon judicial review will block the effective functioning of the agency. In general, courts limit judicial review of administrative action to three questionable areas: (1) has the agency exceeded its statutory or constitutional authority, (2) has it properly interpreted the applicable law, and (3) has the agency conducted a fair proceeding, avoiding the capricious, as well as the unreasonable?[22] Thus, any relief available through judicial review may be very limited. The doctrine checks agency abuses, not agency actions. It does not in itself assure a "correct" result, and "the possibility of judicial review has at most but a limited impact where review is not sought —the practical result in most cases."[23] Here, also, the experience of the Chicago Board of Trade may be useful in providing either

20. E. Gellhorn, p. 56.
21. Ibid., p. 124.
22. Ibid., p. 46.
23. Ibid., p. 49; Glen O. Robinson and Ernest Gellhorn, *The Administrative Process* (St. Paul, 1974), p. 33.

confirmation or refutation of the supposition that judicial review of private regulatory actions may have been subjected to similar considerations during the late nineteenth century.

Questions concerning delegation, judicial review, and administrative discretionary jurisdiction are especially important in a study of the historical evolution of an institution like the Chicago Board of Trade. These issues ultimately focus on the exercise of power. An analysis built around them reveals that private lawmaking does not stand "in absolute contradiction to the traditional process and conditions of lawmaking; it is not incompatible with the conception of law. It exposes and brings into the open, it institutionalizes a factor in lawmaking. . . ."[24] That the Board was a "voluntary association" does not change the fact that as an exchange it exerted "under the forms and sanctions of law enormous powers of determining the substance of economic . . . arrangements in large part irrespective of the will of particular individuals."[25]

III

Although the immediate context within which the Chicago Board of Trade and kindred exchanges developed is presented briefly in another chapter, this introductory overview would be incomplete without some discussion concerning the legal framework for private mercantile law as it had evolved in Western Europe and, later, in the United States prior to the Civil War. Law is primarily a responsive mechanism to various pressures in the

24. Louis L. Jaffe, "Law Making by Private Groups," *Harvard Law Review* 51 (1937):210–53.

25. Ibid., pp. 220–21. In this context the words of A. F. Bentley are instructive. Although he was writing about the Minneapolis Chamber of Commerce, his comments typify a viewpoint that is widely held concerning all major exchanges, including the Chicago Board of Trade. Bentley noted that the Minneapolis Chamber "is a body maintaining its own courts with what are substantially extra territorial rights for its own citizens; and if a final issue arises, the state courts merely enforce its decrees—*not only as against its own members, but incidentally and indirectly as against all non citizens of the Chamber* [emphasis added]." Arthur F. Bentley and Sidney Ratner, eds., *Makers, Users and Masters* (Syracuse, N.Y., 1969), pp. 103–13. See, in particular, the reference in Bentley's note 6 on page 113. I am indebted to Sidney Ratner, emeritus professor of history at Rutgers College and editor of this edition, for calling Bentley's insights to my attention.

particular environment around it. As the nineteenth-century American legal system responded to economic growth and technology by accepting as legal various merchant practices (such as futures trading, bills of lading and exchange, and negotiable instruments of title), so too an earlier system had evolved, between the thirteenth and eighteenth centuries, which facilitated economic intercourse between merchants all over Europe. The rise of the *lex mercatoria* (law merchant) resulted from the growth of cities and towns, as well as from the establishment of merchant and trade guilds. The law merchant was similar in characteristic and function to the later exchanges.

The main source of doctrine concerning the law merchant was mercantile custom. These customs often extended well beyond state boundaries and were, in reality, transnational. In 1473, for example, the chancellor of England referred to the law merchant as "the law universal of the world."[26] An early study of the law merchant published in 1622 described it as "a customary law approved by the authority of all kingdoms and commonweals, and not a law established by the sovereignty of any prince."[27] Blackstone, in his Commentaries, wrote about the *lex mercatoria* "which all nations agree in and take notice of, and it is particularly held to be part of the law of England which decides the causes of merchants by the general rules which obtain in all commercial matters."[28] The universal custom of this type of law was the primary characteristic of the law merchant.

Among the customs accepted by the law merchants as binding were the validity of bills of exchange and the rule that informal agreements could be legally binding. Mercantile custom is intimately related to mercantile expertise, and acceptance of a particular market practice by the merchant community could become for the courts the imprimatur of legitimacy, whatever

26. These paragraphs on the English law merchant are based in part upon the unpublished manuscript "The Western Legal Tradition" by Professor Harold Berman. This material was made available to me by the author and is cited with his permission. See also *Cambridge Economic History of Europe* (1952), 2:168–251, and the bibliographical notes; ibid. (1963), 2:42–280, and the bibliographical notes; Harold Berman, *Western Legal Tradition* (Cambridge, Mass., 1972), p. 271.

27. Berman, *Western Legal Tradition*, p. 272.

28. Ibid.

the state of the written law might be.[29] This fact will be considered in greater detail in the chapter dealing with futures trading and the law. But here it is sufficient to cite the remarks made by Emery Storrs, a distinguished Chicago attorney, at the dedication of the new Chicago Board of Trade building in 1885: "This Board, directly or indirectly has settled legal questions of the largest importance to the producing and financial interests of the country. It has demonstrated the fact that those customs which, for the convenience of business, merchants have established among themselves, are stronger than any mere legal technicalities, and that to those customs, when among merchants they become uniform, universal and well established, the law must bend, and if it does not it will break."[30] The continuity between his statement and the practice of the law merchant of hundreds of years earlier is noteworthy.

A second characteristic of the law merchant was that its courts were administered not by professional judges and lawyers but by other merchants. As early as 1154, a law of Milan authorized the establishment of *consules mercatorum* (consuls of merchants). These men were empowered to settle disputes between merchants; and the demand of Italian traders that they be judged by their own laws and their fellow merchants led to the establishment of consuls in the major ports—the background of the commercial consul of modern times.[31] The practice of confining mercantile disputes within the exchange and settling them through internal procedures wherever possible, without outside legal or judicial action, continues to the present day.

Closely connected with the practice of settling disputes internally was the speed and informality with which mercantile disputes were resolved, a third characteristic of the law merchant. This attribute stands in sharp contrast with the formalistic pro-

29. Thus, in deciding a case involving a cargo of sugar expropriated by the Cuban government, Judge Dimock stated: "The choice lies between Cuban and New York law. I find it unnecessary to make a choice of law. The principle involved is one of the law merchant common to civilized countries, and hence I shall presume that the law of Cuba is the same on the present issues as that of New York." Banco Nacional de Cuba v. Sabbatino, 193 F. Supp. 375 (1961). The case is briefly discussed by Berman, *Western Legal Tradition*, pp. 273–74.

30. Chicago Board of Trade, *Opening Ceremonies of the Chicago Board of Trade Building* (Chicago, 1885), p. 42.

31. Berman, *Western Legal Tradition*, p. 275.

cedural mechanizations of the English writ system that was evolving at the same time. Bracton emphasized that there were certain classes of people "who ought to have swift justice, such as merchants."[32] At the height of the legal development of the law merchant apart from the common law, special informal merchant courts of Pepedrous, later called Piepowder, were common. Indeed, as late as 1692 in the colony of New York, a law authorized the establishment of "pypowder" courts "in each fair or market in the cities and counties throughout the province." Two years before the outbreak of the Revolution of 1775, these provisions were extended to new counties and to additional fairs and markets authorized in newly settled parts of the colony.[33]

The vast increase in commercial transactions during the nineteenth century made the modern exchange extremely important as a device for the speedy and informal settlement of disputes. Indeed, the custom, common to most exchanges, of forbidding participants in mercantile disputes to have assistance of outside legal counsel is directly descended from the old merchant piepowder courts. This custom will be discussed further in a later chapter; but the interesting question arises here of the extent to which the Chicago Board of Trade was able to combine its quasi-judicial functions with appropriate safeguards of procedural due process.

By the eighteenth century two important developments affecting the English law merchant had occurred. The court of chancery at first assumed much of the jurisdiction in mercantile cases but lost it to the more aggressive courts of King's Bench and Common Pleas (the common law courts) under the leadership of Sir Edward Coke, who became chief justice in 1606, and his successors. Coke claimed that "the law merchant is part of the law of this realm."[34] In cases where the plaintiff or defendant was a merchant, the issues were submitted to a jury with instructions to decide "according to the usage and customs of merchants." With the triumph of the common law courts assured by events that occurred between the Protectorate and the Glorious Revolution, the law merchant became a part of the customary law of England.

32. Ibid., p. 276.
33. Ibid., p. 288.
34. Ibid., p. 282.

But the England of Coke was not the England of the eighteenth century, replete with an overseas empire. Customary law as argued by merchants and found in jury verdicts, in fact, no longer met the needs of a commercial power. Harold Berman observes that "from the point of view of the individual merchants, there was a need for the law to be more clearly defined; and from the point of view of national policy, there was a need for the law to be developed officially and not merely informally by commercial experience."[35] The second development of the law merchant came in response to these needs. In 1765 Lord Mansfield, chief justice of the King's Bench, held that the rules of the law merchant were questions of law (not fact) to be decided not by juries but by courts; that such rules applied to all persons, not only merchants; and that, indeed, the law merchant was a part of the common law of all nations (*jus gentium*). In one famous decision, Mansfield made the law merchant part of English common law.[36]

Although no coherent body of commercial legal doctrine that was virtually complete in itself developed in the colonies as it had in Europe, certain aspects of the law merchant were reflected in American commercial practices between 1750 and the Civil War.[37] The settlement of private disputes through arbitration and reference was widespread; it was far less expensive than litigation, generally easier, and invariably took less time. John Watts, a New York merchant, refers time and time again in his letters to the delays inherent in legal proceedings. In 1762 he described arbitration as "the most speedy and just determination, rather than be put to the expense of two or three lingering Law suits, that may be spun out for Years in the way the law is here."[38] In another letter, written the next year, Watts mentioned "a number of vexatious Suits, that no Mortal can see thro' or know when or where they will end."[39] In 1764 Watts characterized the "legal" method, "where the inexplicable Law is to puzzle a suit, Any Empirick [sic] can throw more difficul-

35. Ibid., p. 283.
36. Ibid.
37. The material in these paragraphs is based upon sources suggested by Professor Morton Horwitz; it draws in part upon his collection of unpublished materials on American legal history and is cited with his permission.
38. John Watts, *Letter Book* (New York, 1928), p. 108.
39. Ibid., p. 114.

ties in the way than Solomon & all the wise Men of the East put together can move."[40]

Implicit in Watts's biting tone is, perhaps, the most important justification for the private settlement of disputes. By this means merchants were enabled to avoid what Morton Horwitz aptly calls the "pre commercial mentality" prevalent among "Lawyers and other Officers of the Courts, who grow Rich on the Ruins of their Neighbors . . . [and] who never trade."[41] Watts, writing in 1762, objected to a "Mungrell Commerce," concerning which "no two Courts pursue the same Measure." The resulting inconsistencies were inconvenient and frequently expensive. "A Stranger to form a judgment from them would imagine that the Nation in its Jurisdiction had neither Rule Law or probity and yet the Evil is suffer'd to go on without any determination, [and] Subject is tore to pieces by Robbers, Lawyers and all sorts of Vermin."[42]

The American proclivity for avoiding the common law settlement of mercantile disputes duplicated the English law merchant period in the one hundred and fifty years before Lord Mansfield became chief justice (1758). However, Mansfield had brought mercantile custom within the common law, thus making it the domain not of the merchant but of the court. Much the same transformation took place in the United States during the first half of the nineteenth century. After 1800, the traditional deference by judges to the reports of arbitrators lessened dramatically. In 1801, for example, the New York Supreme Court ruled that it would no longer refer any mercantile dispute to arbitration when it appeared to involve a question of law.[43] This holding effectively nullified the most important reason why merchants sought arbitration in the first place, the presumed familiarity of the referee with commercial law.

The next year, in a book that probably was the first American treatise on *lex mercatoria* (commercial law), George Gaines ar-

40. Ibid., p. 229.
41. Morton Horwitz, Cases and Materials in American Legal History (Harvard Law School, 1973), p. 272; Stuart Bruchey, *The Colonial Merchant* (New York, 1966), pp. 83–84.
42. Watts, p. 27.
43. De Hart v. Coverhaven, 2 Johns. Cas. 402 (1801). See Horwitz, Cases and Materials in American Legal History, p. 275.

gued that an arbitration agreement (in this case part of an insurance contract) would not in itself bar further legal action
"because the tribunals of the land are not, by the contracts of
individuals, to be thus ousted of their jurisdiction."[44] In 1805
the Massachusetts Supreme Court held that a private corporation could not coerce its members.[45] Although the case did not
involve arbitration, the implication for private lawmaking and
dispute settlement was clear. Private associations would be unable to coerce, enforce, or settle without some internal agreement based upon contractarian principles.

In part, the explanation for these changes can be found in
the growing self-consciousness of an American legal profession,
including bench and bar, understandably hostile to the old anti-
legalism prevalent among merchants during the eighteenth century. But there was more to this hostility than merely, as one
critic observed, the Bar's desire for "augmentation of professional
emolument."[46] The trend against extralegal dispute settlement
reflected both an effort to unify and confine lawmaking functions to the judiciary and an extremely significant change in judicial attitudes toward commercial ventures. The nineteenth-century judges were certainly anything but opposed to economic
growth and exansion. With remarkable frequency they accom-
modated the law to promote mercantile development, demon-
strating the flexibility, creativity, and predictability so important
to commercial progress.[47] Hence, merchant justification for re-
sorting to extralegal tribunals lessened, because at the same time
as the courts demonstrated hostility toward them, they dramatically molded the law to satisfy the needs of a burgeoning commerce that was becoming increasingly national in scope.[48]

Thus, judicial coolness toward competing sources of law must
ultimately be seen as indicative of a new instrumental vision of

44. Morton J. Horwitz, *The Transformation of American Law* (Cambridge,
Mass., 1977), p. 150.
45. Horwitz, Cases and Materials in American Legal History, p. 435. The
case is Ellis v. Marshall, 2 Mass. 269 (1897).
46. Horwitz, *Transformation of American Law*, p. 154.
47. Levy, *Law of the Commonwealth and Chief Justice Shaw*; Hurst, *Law
and the Conditions of Freedom.*
48. Morton Horwitz, "The Transformation in the Conception of Property in
American Law, 1780–1860," *University of Chicago Law Review* 40 (1973):
248–90. See, in particular, pp. 270–90.

legal change.[49] Law became much more than a mechanism for settling disputes. It was transformed into a vigorous, dynamic means for both social control and release of economic energy.[50] Judicial attitudes during the nineteenth century reflected an active and growing interest in economic affairs.

Within this new legal framework, which was molded by contractarian principles favorable to a market economy, private lawmaking did not disappear. On the contrary, the proliferation of associations so typical of the nineteenth century, together with the growing complexity of modern market transactions, made delegated legal power absolutely essential.[51] But this delegation of power would be under the auspices of the law and not in addition to it. Furthermore, it would follow judicially approved standards and would, in theory at least, be subject to judicial examination if not intervention. Within this framework mercantile organizations like the Chicago Board of Trade were established.

49. Morton Horwitz, "The Emergence of an Instrumental Conception of American Law, 1780–1820," *Perspectives in American History* 7 (1971):287–326. See, in particular, pp. 309–26.

50. Morton Horwitz, "The Historical Foundations of Modern Contract Law," *Harvard Law Review* 87 (1974):917–56.

51. Gerald N. Grob, "The Political System and Social Policy in the Nineteenth Century: Legacy of the Revolution," *Mid America* 58 (1976):5–19.

CHAPTER TWO

Early History and Rule Development
of the Chicago Board of Trade to 1880

I

THE OUTSTANDING LOCATION of Chicago as the nexus for new railroad and Great Lakes shipping routes made the city's growth as a dominant economic center inevitable. This conclusion was justified as early as 1848, the year in which the Chicago Board of Trade was founded. By that time interstate telegraph service had reached the city; so also had the first chartered railroad line in Illinois, with its first shipment of grain. In the same year the stockyards in the city were opened, and the federal district court began its work. Indeed, even as the Age of Jackson came to an end, the key components of a modern system of commodities trading were in place, in such cities as Chicago, Milwaukee, Buffalo, and St. Louis.

Innovations in transportation and shipping were accompanied by the increasing availability of land, as well as improvements in mechanized farming. In 1831 Cyrus McCormick invented the reaper. Within three years the mower and the threshing machine appeared, to be followed in 1836 by the combine. By 1850 the time required to harvest one acre of wheat had been cut from twenty-seven hours to eleven and a half.[1] These developments resulted in a vast expansion of grain planting and harvest. From 1873 to 1882, wheat acreage in the United States rose from 29 million to 41 million, production from 368 to 555 million bushels.[2]

1. James S. Schonberg, *The Grain Trade: How It Works* (New York, 1956), pp. 8–10.
2. Morton Rothstein, "America in the International Rivalry for the British Wheat Market, 1860–1884," *Mississippi Valley Historical Review* 47 (1960): 410–18.

At harvest time, literally tons of grain arrived in the port cities by wagon, barge, or railroad car. This vast influx inevitably created a glutted market and forced prices to decline sharply. Moreover, the lack of suitable storage space caused considerable damage to the grain as natural elements rendered many thousands of bushels worthless. During the off seasons, on the other hand, available grains were in very short supply and were widely sought. Prices were inflated, as commission men and merchants tried to procure the grain that was needed by millers for production of the flour required by an increasing population. In addition to the inconveniences caused by this imbalance of supply and demand, distribution of the available grain left much to be desired. Uniform standards of grading were nonexistent, causing the quality of grain to vary from sack to sack. The absence of standardized amounts and grades rendered dealings between buyer and seller (often conducted at great distance) uncertain and often resulted in inconvenient and expensive litigation. To a society growing increasingly more oriented toward the market and commercial gain, these conditions were intolerable.

From the late 1840s through the 1880s, a sophisticated system of grain marketing evolved. It included: futures trading, whereby one might buy or sell for future delivery and thereby eliminate the usual imbalance between supply and demand; grain inspection and the standardization of grades and amounts; increased warehouse and elevator facilities; and the acceptance of bills of lading and warehouse receipts as negotiable instruments of title.[3] Neither did these changes occur all at once, nor did their introduction follow any preconceived policy. They represented a pragmatic response that was initiated by millers, merchants, shippers and grain dealers and was ultimately accepted by the legal order—all striving for both greater profit and pre-

---

3. Morton Rothstein: "American Wheat and the British Market, 1860–1905" (Ph.D. diss., Cornell University, 1960), pp. 92–97, "The International Market for Agricultural Commodities, 1850–1873," in *Economic Change in the Civil War Era* (Wilmington, Del., 1965); Julius B. Baer and Olin G. Saxon, *Commodities Exchanges and Futures Trading* (New York, 1949), pp. 1–137; G. Wright Hoffman, *Futures Trading on Organized Commodity Markets in the United States* (Philadelphia, 1932); Henry C. Emery, *Speculation on the Stock and Produce Exchanges of the United States* (New York, 1896), Studies in History, Economics and Public Law, no. 18, pp. 289–512; Julius B. Baer and George Woodruff, *Commodity Exchanges* (New York, 1935), pp. 21–45.

dictability in a market-oriented age. The key to the success of this new system lay ultimately in the establishment of boards of trade. Thus, one should take note of the founding of the Buffalo Board of Trade in 1844, the Detroit Board three years later, the Chicago Board in 1848, and the Milwaukee Chamber of Commerce the next year.

In the 1840s, however, the primary purpose behind the founding of the Chicago Board of Trade appears to have been less a desire to rationalize the grain trade than a plan to provide some sort of general meeting place in which businessmen and merchants could discuss and resolve issues of mutual concern, including controversies over fulfillment of contracts. Indeed, among the twenty-five members of the Board's first directorate, almost half were in occupations other than the grain trade. Included were a druggist, a bookseller, a tanner, a grocer, a coal dealer, a hardware merchant, and a banker.[4] Furthermore, the first act of incorporation that was granted to the Chicago Board stipulated: "Any number of persons not less than twenty, residing in any town or city, may associate themselves together as a Board of Trade."[5] Although many of the Board records dating prior to 1871 appear to have been lost in the Great Fire, there seems little doubt that for about the first decade of its existence the Board did not function as an exchange, and that it enforced few if any rules upon the members. Actually, the organization appears to have had some difficulty in attracting members at all.[6] By 1853 Board attendance was so poor that it had to be encouraged by free lunches.[7]

4. Edwin O. Gale, *Reminiscences of Early Chicago* (Chicago, 1902), p. 261.
5. *Charter: An Act for the Incorporation of Boards of Trade and Chambers of Commerce* (1849 Ill.), p. 1 (in the archives of the Chicago Historical Society). For the early history of the Chicago Board of Trade, see Charles H. Taylor, *History of the Board of Trade of the City of Chicago* (Chicago, 1917), 1:135–274; Leon T. Kendall, "The Chicago Board of Trade and the Federal Government" (Ph.D. diss., Indiana University, 1956), pp. 8–36; *Commodity Trading Manual* (Wilmette, 1966), pp. 9–13; *The Development of the Chicago Board of Trade* (Chicago, 1936), pp. 5–30; Peter B. Carey, *The Rise of Exchange Trading* (Chicago, 1933), pp. 1–4. See also the relevant chapters in Alfred T. Andreas, *History of Chicago*, vol. 3, *1871–1885* (Chicago, 1886); and Bessie Pierce, *A History of Chicago* (New York, 1937–), vol. 3, *1871–1893: The Rise of a Modern City*.
6. Taylor, p. 166.
7. Guy A. Lee, "History of the Chicago Grain Elevator Industry 1840–1890" (Ph.D. diss., Harvard University, 1938), p. 59.

Events between 1854 and 1865 forced the Chicago Board of Trade to alter this rather innocuous lifestyle. The growth of the grain trade during these eleven years was so swift that a chaotic market often resulted.

TABLE 1
CHICAGO WHEAT SHIPMENTS, 1854–64

	Bushels Received	Bushels Shipped
1854	3,038,955	2,306,925
1855	7,535,097	6,298,155
1856	8,767,760	8,364,420
1857	10,554,761	9,846,052
1858	9,639,614	8,850,257
1859	8,060,766	7,166,696
1860	14,927,083	12,402,197
1861	17,385,002	15,835,953
1862	13,978,116	13,808,898
1863	11,408,161	10,793,295
1864	12,184,977	10,250,026

Source: Chicago Board of Trade, *Yearbook* (Chicago, 1910). These figures appear in virtually every yearbook of the Board after 1880.

After several joint meetings between the major Great Lakes exchanges during this period, standardized grades of grain and the widespread use of the "to arrive" contract (also known, and hereafter referred to, as the futures contract) came into common practice. Uniform standards for grading grain made it possible to undertake a commercial transaction by telegraph, without the need to send samples ahead before a contract could be finalized. Furthermore, the acceptance of uniform standards and amounts added an extremely important element of predictability to the burgeoning commodities market.

Futures trading had several advantages for both the buyer and seller of commodities. The ability to buy in the present for delivery in the future greatly lessened the problem of glut or scarcity noted earlier. Moreover, as the price of grain and the quality of the commodities were known in advance as a result of standardized grades, credit needs were sharply reduced and prices tended to be stabilized. Because futures trading "stretched out the period during which the sale and delivery of the crop occurred, [it] thereby reduced the time lag between purchase by the processor and sale to the ultimate consumer."[8] Finally, futures trading served as a legitimate outlet for speculative capital, attracting buyers and sellers on a daily basis to a market usually "able and willing to absorb at any time during the trading day all transactions, regardless of volume, without serious disruption of prices."[9]

In short, by the late 1850s, this new and sophisticated market system had become reality. Uniform contracts, standardized grades of inspection, weighing and quality of grain produced both uniformity and efficiency in commodities trading, contributing in turn to that predictability so necessary in large-scale market transactions and so desired during the late nineteenth century.[10] However, futures trading required a competitive market; and standard grades meant little without a means to impose them on the trading community and to provide for their enforcement. Thus the Chicago Board of Trade recognized a need for organizational continuity and basic powers of sanction.

In 1859 the Chicago Board sought and received from the Illinois legislature a charter that, with only minor changes, still remains in effect today. The charter differed from the Board's original general act of incorporation in three key ways. (1) It empowered the Board to establish such rules "for the management of their business and the mode in which it shall be transacted, as they may think proper." (2) It clothed any award made by a Board committee of reference or arbitration with the same authority as "if it were a judgment rendered in the Circuit Court." (3) It gave the Board the right to appoint inspectors and weighers of grain; stated that the resulting certificates would be evidence between buyer and seller of quantity,

8. Thomas Odle, "Entrepreneurial Cooperation on the Great Lakes: The Origins of the Methods of American Grain Marketing," *Business History Review* 38 (1964):439–55. See, in particular, p. 452.

9. Baer and Saxon, pp. 31–32.

10. The interplay between the quest for economic predictability and late nineteenth-century political and economic change is discussed in Robert Wiebe's excellent analysis, *The Search for Order* (New York, 1967). See also Willard Hurst, *Law and the Conditions of Freedom in the Nineteenth-Century United States* (Madison, 1964), and Samuel Hays, *The Response to Industrialism* (Chicago, 1957).

quality, and grade; and ordered that determinations by the inspectors would be binding upon Board members.[11]

One is struck by the potential for strong regulatory powers inherent in the 1859 charter. While an outsider could always appeal a decision from the Circuit Court, Board rules—which every member gave his word to accept and honor—made the final results of arbitration binding. Appeal was virtually impossible. Upon becoming a member of the Chicago Board of Trade, a person had to sign the following "solemn compact": "We . . . hereby mutually agree . . . with each other, and with the said corporation, that we will in our actions and dealings with each other, and the said corporation, be in all respects governed by and respect the Rules, Regulations and By-Laws of the said corporation, as they now exist, or as they may be hereafter modified, altered or amended." The significance of this agreement concerning litigation between exchange members and the institutions themselves is very important, as will be seen in later developments. In most cases it placed an all but insuperable burden on the member seeking adjudicative relief. By his signature to such an agreement, the member brought himself within the purview of a contractarian relationship, which by the mid-nineteenth century had become a legitimizing basis for private coercive power.

Although it is beyond the scope of this study to explore this point in any great detail, the great latitude given the Board through legislative charter is striking and can best be understood when placed in an appropriate historical context. As was shown in the preface, the numerous private acts of incorporation so prevalent between 1820 and the Civil War were symptomatic of a larger redefinition of the domestic political system. Anchored too firmly to the post-Revolutionary Madisonian concepts of power limitation, the political order responded to the nineteenth-century need for modernization by making government a more passive, supervisory force. The vehicle for this transformation was extensive delegation of power, often to quasi-autonomous public and private regulatory agencies. While the political system thus retained the revolutionary legacy of limited

11. Chicago Board of Trade, *Board of Trade Report*, 1877, appendix, pp. v–viii.

government and decentralization, it also inevitably placed responsibilities for economic rationalization and innovation largely in the private sector. This was especially true in the commodities markets.

II

The new rules adopted by the Chicago Board of Trade after its 1859 incorporation gave the membership power to elect the three executives (two vice presidents and a president), the arbitration committee, the appeals committee, and the board of directors. The arbitration and appeals committees each consisted of ten members, five elected each year for a two-year term. The arbitration committee heard all cases involving business disputes that members wished to place before it.[12] From the arbitration committee's findings a member could go before the appeals committee. If he remained unsatisfied after its verdict, the chances for further relief were exceedingly remote. Although in theory the member could go into civil court and, indeed, most judges would probably have upheld the right to a judicial hearing, this was in fact not a practical alternative. The member who went into court invariably placed himself in bad repute with other members of the Board, if not in actual violation of agreements concerning membership and arbitration. For breaking these agreements, the member was liable to receive Board penalties, including suspension and/or expulsion. This

12. The exchanges differed among themselves concerning compulsory arbitration. The Chicago Board of Trade made submission to arbitration voluntary but required that once the step had been taken the parties bind themselves to "fulfill the final award or finding which shall be made touching the matter submitted, without recourse to any other court or tribunal." On other exchanges, such as the St. Louis Merchants' Exchange or the Milwaukee Chamber of Commerce, arbitration was mandatory and "in case either party shall refuse to submit to arbitration . . . or . . . shall neglect or refuse to perform the award, such neglect or refusal shall, in either case, be cause of suspension or expulsion." CBT *Rules*, 1865, p. 13; Milwaukee Chamber of Commerce, *Rules*, 1890, p. vi; Federal Trade Commission, *Report on the Grain Trade* (Washington, D.C., 1920), 2:218–19. As will be seen in chapter 3, the problem of compulsory arbitration troubled the courts, and for good reason. What was true in 1801 held even greater relevance for the late nineteenth century—i.e., that "the tribunals of the land are not, by the contracts of individuals, to be thus ousted of their jurisdiction." See above, ch. 1, n. 44.

consideration, as well as the understandable reluctance of the courts to interfere with an arbitration finding even when they did grant a hearing, may explain why the appeals committee generally served as a court of last resort.

In terms of policy making, the rules placed ultimate responsibility for the operation of the Board of Trade in the directorate, which was elected at the same time and in the same manner as the other two committees. The authority of the directors extended to all financial and business concerns of the association. The directors appointed such administrative officers of the Board as the secretary, treasurer, and attorney. They selected the various inspectors, weighers, and similar functionaries. The directors also had responsibility for hearing, investigating, and resolving all complaints and charges of business misconduct brought against any Board member by another. The disciplinary authority of the directors over the members ranged from extremely serious matters of unmercantile conduct, such as falsifying prices or gambling on fictitious market sales, to incidents of lesser gravity.

One of the less serious incidents occurred in St. Louis on February 9, 1888. The floor manager of the St. Louis Merchants' Exchange filed a complaint against J. O. Linebarger, claiming that he had used "abusive and insulting language to your floor manager," whom he had called "a d - - d liar, also said other people said he was getting to be a bigger d - - d s - - t ass every day."[13]

Another such incident took place in January 1875 when the King of Hawaii was escorted onto the floor of the Board of Trade during a visit to Chicago. He received what the official historian of the Board described as "a boisterous reception" that included a loud rendition by some of the younger members of a song entitled "King of the Cannibal Islands." The Mayor of Chicago did not help matters when he introduced the royal guest by saying, "I have the honor of escorting into your midst the king of the Can. . . ." Although the mayor apologized during the resulting hilarity, the king was evidently offended

13. Merchants' Exchange Collection, February 9, 1888, Missouri Historical Society, St. Louis.

and soon left the chamber; whereupon two Board members presented a song and dance routine, including the use of a black mask. The directors of the Board expressed shock and outrage at this occurrence and devoted an entire meeting to the incident."[14]

To handle efficiently the numerous matters coming before it, the directors adopted (and still use) a system of internal committees. Usually the president appointed these committees to serve concurrently with his term. Over the years, the number of directors' committees ranged from fifteen to twenty, covering such areas as rules, warehouses, market reports, rooms, legal advice, and membership. Matters that came before the directors would be referred to the appropriate committee, frequently with "power to act." Sometimes the committee reported back to the parent body asking for directorate approval of its decision. Each committee normally consisted of three directors, although this could sometimes vary. In addition, the directors occasionally appointed other Board of Trade members to these committees. Each director served on several committees at the same time.

The chief avenue of official communication between the directorate and the membership was the petition. Petitions ranged in subject matter from a request that the directors set aside a room to be used as a gymnasium for the members to proposed changes in the rules governing the Board of Trade. Sometimes petitions were tabled by the directorate, but more often the directorate referred them to the appropriate committee. The directors frequently ordered that a particular question be submitted to the membership for approval or rejection. Less frequently they rejected the petition outright. The rules required that when the directorate rejected a petition to change the rules, a new petition with one hundred signatures would automatically cause the question to be submitted to the membership for a vote.

14. *D.R.*, January 18, 1875, pp. 90–92; Taylor, p. 515. It might be noted that the problems of decorum on the floor of the Board of Trade were not confined to the late nineteenth century. On October 25, 1921, the vice-president of the Rogers Grain Company complained to the directors about "the disgraceful conditions existing" on the floor. The trading area is congested by "a hundred boys and young men." Nearly every day "they can be seen in the middle of the floor wrestling, fighting, cursing, playing and everything else that is unseemly." *D.P.*, October 25, 1921.

The membership could override a decision of the directors on the adoption of a particular rule, although it rarely did so. The directory thus used this policy-making power with moderation. The nature of Board discipline required that a rule, once adopted, must have the sanction of the Board behind it. The rule would have to be either enforced or repealed; if it were not, the entire disciplinary structure of the Board would be weakened. Petitions and letters to the directors often emphasized this point. A strongly phrased rule that could not be enforced would weaken the prestige of the Board.

However, the directors were not powerless against the membership. A basic purpose of the Board was to facilitate profitable economic activity by the members, so the directors had to sense with some accuracy how far they could go in the areas of rule enforcement. If rules were enforced too harshly, board members could either ignore them or decline to remain in the organization. Yet another primary purpose of the exchange was to rationalize the commodities market through efficient and effective regulation, and the efforts of the directors to reconcile this inherent tension between private economic activity and an ordered national market represent a recurring theme throughout the remaining chapters of this study.

The rules of the Board made the decision of the appeals committee final and binding in all disputes that members submitted to it. But the members were not compelled to bring their cases before the arbitration and appeals committees, even though many did. A member could take his grievance to the directors and ask that they hear the matter. All trials and/or hearings over business disputes and charges of mercantile misconduct took place before a quorum or better of the entire directorate. When dealing with a complaint or dispute between two members, the directors heard both sides, questioned witnesses, and announced a decision. Sometimes they listened to part of the case and then urged that the two sides submit the dispute to the arbitration committee, or they recommended that one of the parties settle in favor of the other. On occasion they postponed hearing of the dispute, urging that the parties settle it among themselves. Not infrequently they dismissed the case entirely. Whenever possible, the directors tried to avoid making a definite finding in these cases, utilizing the options just mentioned.[15] In some cases, however, most notably those involving the refusal of one member to pay a certain sum in settlement of market transactions to another, the directors almost always found for one side or the other.

One basic policy that the Chicago Board of Trade and other exchanges enforced was the rule that business transactions had to be settled equitably. If a Board member made a valid contract in accordance with the rules and then either refused to pay or admitted that he could not pay, he faced suspension by the directorate until such time as he settled the obligation. Neither did the amount of money involved make any difference. Thus, the Board sought a predictable, efficient, and regulated market framework within which the members could deal.

When the issue involved an official charge of misconduct brought by the directors against a Board member, the directorate assumed responsibility for the prosecution. If, for example, the matter involved market reports, the committee on market reports would handle the prosecution. In cases involving mercantile misconduct, directors participating in the prosecution did not vote when the time came to decide the problem. With one very important exception, the internal trials adjudicated by the Board of Trade were similar in procedure to courts of general jurisdiction. The president of the Board acted as presiding officer, but he could be overruled by the other directors. Board rules gave the directors authority to compel members to appear and testify at hearings, trials, and investigations. If a member refused to appear or if he appeared and declined to answer "any question which may, by a majority vote of the said Board of Directors . . . be declared proper and pertinent to the case in hearing," the directors could suspend the individual from all Board privileges "for such time as said Board may determine."[16] But the rules also protected the membership from arbitrary and unreasonable interference by Board officials. No witness could be "compelled to answer any question which shall incriminate himself; nor shall any testimony be admitted which, in the opinion of the committee or other tribunal, is irrelevant to the case in hearing." Fur-

---

15. The alternatives available to the directors through these options illustrate again the pervasiveness of private "unofficial" dispute settlement within the association.

16. CBT *Rules*, 1881, p. 16.

ther, no member could be disciplined "without an examination of the charges against him . . . nor without an opportunity to be heard in his own defense."[17] The defendant also had the right to question all prosecution witnesses and to call upon his own.

Moreover, Board rules distinguished between the member guilty of mercantile misconduct, who was punished by either suspension or expulsion, and the member unable to meet his debts simply because of unexpected vicissitudes of the trade. Seeking always to maintain a balance between an ordered though active market and encouragement of private commercial activity, the rules provided that a Board member suspended for failure to fulfill a business obligation could make application for reinstatement. If, after due notice had been given, no further claims were filed against the individual, and if the directors "shall be satisfied that such failure was merely from financial inability or misfortune, such member, having so adjusted or settled such outstanding obligations *shall* be reinstated." Like bankruptcy proceedings, the reinstatement "shall hereafter serve as a bar to any further discipline" by the Board "on account of claims maturing at a date prior to the reinstatement of said applicant."[18]

The important exception was the rule that forbade any member of the association to have outside counsel in any internal hearing. However, members involved in a trial could have another member of the Board assist them: a member of the directorate, a member who had been a lawyer, or a member who had an acquaintance with the law. That the Chicago Board of Trade has kept this rule in effect from its early years to the present[19] can probably be explained by the nature of the organization.

One of the basic purposes for organizing the Board of Trade was to provide a means of settling commercial disputes within

17. Ibid., p. 17. Most of these detailed rules for due process in hearings and trials before the directors were adopted after the famous Sturges case of 1874. For an example of court pressures on Board officials to make them conform to proper procedure, see Brine v. Board of Trade, 2 Am. Law Rec. 268 (1873).

18. Ibid., pp. 14–15; CBT *Rules*, 1898, p. 13.

19. Rule 4 § 16 (1877) states: "In investigations before the Board of Directors, or before any committee of the Association, no party shall be allowed to be represented by professional counsel." Rule 160 (1967) states: "No member of the association shall have a right to be represented by professional counsel in any investigation or hearing before the Board or any Standing or Special Committee." Although the change of wording is interesting, the general thrust of the rule has remained constant over the years.

the commercial community quietly and quickly. These disputes, involving business matters, should be resolved by businessmen. The picture might only be confused by the unnecessary legal jargon of an outside lawyer and irrelevant legal procedure. The concept of a self-regulatory, self-disciplined association seemed to rule out the use of professional counsel. Indeed, to have to rely upon outside counsel in a hearing before the directors would have been tantamount to admitting distrust of the Board's machinery for resolving the internal disputes that came before it.

When the directorate meted out punishment, it had four options: to fine, to reprimand, to suspend, or to expel. The charter explicitly limited to five dollars the amount of a fine the Board could impose upon its members.[20] Thus, it is not surprising that the directors rarely invoked this penalty. The reprimand was frequently used for minor offenses committed on the trading floor, such as provoking disorder, pushing, cursing, throwing sample bags of grain, and similar actions. Sometimes these reprimands were solemnly recorded in the minutes, and notice of them was posted for all other members to read.

Suspension from trading privileges represented a far more serious form of discipline. Only Board members were permitted to buy and sell upon the floor. A member who was deprived of this privilege even for one day could easily suffer great financial hardship. Expulsion was the ultimate penalty, one the directors rarely invoked. In addition to the loss of trading privileges, this action further involved possible loss of the money invested in Board membership.

The directors tried "to make the punishment fit the crime." That they did not find it easy to punish is clearly demonstrated by the many votes that often had to be taken at the conclusion of the trials. More often than not the directors were lenient. Not infrequently they remitted the penalty before it had been entirely served. Sometimes they responded favorably to petitions submitted by members on behalf of the accused, asking some sort of clemency on the grounds of financial need or other reasons.

---

20. The maximum amount of fine that could be imposed by an exchange varied widely. The Merchants' Exchange of St. Louis, e.g., could impose fines of up to $500 for violation of its rules. *Articles of Association*, p. 4. For a discussion of litigation involving a fine levied by the Merchants' Exchange, see ch. 3 below.

The directorate reflected the larger membership from which it was elected. The antennae of the directorate appear to have been tuned with real accuracy toward the sentiments of the Board as a whole. One reason for this awareness is the fact that the directors were also active members of the Board. They participated in the daily trading sessions—yelling, jostling, gesticulating with all the rest; and they were subject to the same strains and weaknesses as the rank and file. On more than one occasion in the period covered by this study, a director was guilty of what the Board sought to punish in other members. Participating in the activities of the Board, listening each morning to the market gossip on and off the floor, it was not always possible to dissociate one's self from these experiences upon entering the directors' room for a board meeting. Louis Jaffe writes that one important characteristic of the American administrative regulatory process is that government agencies are able to make decisions in the area of management, but do not have to accept managerial responsibility for their actions.[21] As a quasi-regulatory organization, the directors of the Chicago Board of Trade did not have this "luxury." On the contrary, they had to accept full responsibility for the results their decisions and rule making might have upon the membership.

These facts help to explain the Board's slow and often contradictory progress in internal discipline. Had the directors been isolated from the sounds and pressures of the markets, their disciplinary record might have been more impressive. But they were an integral part of the trading world, and isolation was impossible. Thus the not infrequent remission and modification of penalties becomes understandable; yet the Board's growth in self-discipline over a thirty-year period becomes impressive.

III

In recent years sociologists and political scientists have explored the subject of what Seymour Lipset calls "the politics of private government."[22] Using Robert Michels's classic study *Political*

21. Louis L. Jaffe, "The Effective Limits of the Administrative Process: A Reevaluation," *Harvard Law Review* 67 (1954):1127.
22. Seymour M. Lipset, *Political Man* (New York, 1960), pp. 357–99.

Parties and the Oligarchical Tendencies of Modern Democracy as a starting point, scholars have analyzed such private associations as the American Medical Association, the American Bar Association, and various trade unions in an effort to explain the oligarchic nature of these "democratic" organizations.[23] Grant McConnell has further noted two characteristics that set private associations apart from "public governments." He claimed that generally "there is little conception of checks and balances as a system" within the association. Even more important is the absence of a bill of rights or its equivalent. In constitutions of private associations, "it is possible to cull a list of membership duties which could stand as obligations, but almost never a comparable list of members' rights of the order of importance of those in the first few amendments to the Federal Constitution."[24] Even though all this literature is focused on present day organizations, the conceptual scheme employed has relevance for this study. It may help us to understand why the Board of Trade, a fairly large private association with power vested in a very small group of men, did *not* (at least in the late nineteenth century) appear to operate as an oligarchy.

Michels laid down the dictum that "Who says organization, says oligarchy."[25] Seymour Lipset accepts Michels's "law," noting that "at the head of most organizations" can be found a small number of men who have held high office in the organization for

23. Robert Michels, *Political Parties*, intro. Seymour M. Lipset (New York, 1962), p. 16n; Oliver Garceau, *The Political Life of the American Medical Association* (Cambridge, Mass., 1941); Jack Ladinsky and Joel Grossman, "Organizational Consequences or Professional Consensus: Lawyers and Selection of Judges," *Administrative Science Quarterly* 11 (1966):79–106. See, in particular, p. 81, n. 4, and pp. 104–5, n. 36.

24. Grant McConnell, "The Spirit of Private Government," *American Political Science Review* 52 (1958):754–70. McConnell has enlarged upon themes discussed here in his book *Private Power and American Democracy* (New York, 1966). A stimulating collection of essays on the voluntary association may be found in J. Roland Pennock and John W. Chapman, eds., *Voluntary Associations* (New York, 1969). See, in particular, the essays and commentaries by Lon Fuller, Willard Hurst, and McConnell. Valuable insights into the nature of groups and their effect upon the political system can be found in Arthur F. Bentley's *The Process of Government* (Cambridge, Mass., 1967). See pp. 272–97 and 434–46 for his treatment of law and his analysis of different groups. By far the best summary of the very extensive literature on the voluntary association is Constance Smith and Ann Freedman, *Voluntary Associations: Perspectives on the Literature* (Cambridge, Mass., 1972).

25. Michels, p. 365.

lengthy periods without being seriously challenged by any internal opposition.[26] Whether or not the membership has a basic right of control through annual elections makes no difference; the real authority, Lipset claims, rests with those who hold the highest leadership positions. This is possible because the leaders possess several advantages not shared by the general membership. The leaders have superior knowledge in that they have access to the records, documents, and material not usually seen by the membership. They control the formal means of communication between the leadership and members, such as the organizational press. They possess what Lipset calls "skills in the art of politics," being far more competent than the rank and file in speech making, writing, and organizing functions.

All of these advantages rest upon a base of what Michels calls the "incompetence of the masses." Lipset claims that membership influence requires active involvement in the affairs of the organization, attendance and participation at meetings, and an awareness of the problems confronting the organization. In actuality, he maintains, these qualities are seldom found in party or union members. Work, leisure activities, a family, all limit the time an average person will invest in membership or political activities. Finally, lower interest and participation are a result of the membership's having "less education" and general sophistication than the leadership."[27]

The Chicago Board of Trade centered around an active, everchanging market. New members were admitted regularly, as other members died, moved away, or failed. The frequent turnover of seats on the Board helps to explain the constant number of new names appearing on the lists of officers. One-third of the directory changed each year, and each year the directors' committees were formed anew. Sometimes the committees contained completely different members. Sometimes, however, a director might be reappointed to a particular committee, even serving as long as three years on that committee. The record for the twenty-year period under analysis seems clear, however: with few exceptions the committees changed each year. An oligarchy is not

26. Seymour Lipset, Martin Trow, and James Coleman, *Union Democracy* (Glencoe, 1956), pp. 4–13.
27. Michels, intro., pp. 16–17.

characterized by a yearly turnover of newly elected officials who wield important decision-making powers.

The requirements for holding office in the Board of Trade were minimal: one had to be a member and reside in the Chicago area. The level of member interest in the annual elections fluctuated from year to year. In some years there were several candidates for president; in other years only one. Any member could run for office, and there were no complicated nominating procedures. Usually an informal caucus open to all members might present a slate for the election; but, occasionally, competing tickets were put forth and the bitter campaigns that ensued often resulted in a very narrow margin of victory. The number of members voting in the annual elections varied widely. In one year 44 percent voted, in another 67 percent, and from 1898 to 1900 between 70 and 73 percent voted.[28]

The rules of the Board gave the membership ample opportunity to overrule the directors. As has been noted, the Board was solicitous for the due process rights of members, particularly those involved in internal proceedings. Also, the leaders of the Board did not possess the several advantages cited by Lipset; there were no formal means of communication for them to control. While the directors did have access to papers and documents not shown to the membership, the minutes of the Board meetings were open to inspection by any member of the Board.

The gap in education and sophistication cited by Lipset does not appear to apply to the Board of Trade. The directors came from the membership at large and reflected interests and weaknesses found there. In addition, there is little evidence to indicate lack of interest on the part of the membership in matters taken up by the directors. Virtually all the important issues confronting the directorate were placed before it by the members. As noted earlier, the directors seemed to be very much in tune with prevailing sentiment.[29]

28. These figures are compiled from the annual reports of the Chicago Board of Trade.

29. Michels, pp. 22–23. In making the claim that the Chicago Board of Trade *in the years studied* does not appear to have been an oligarchy, it is not asserted that Lipset and other scholars are necessarily wrong in their analysis, but only that their framework does not fit the Board. Further, I do not extend this claim to cover other exchanges, such as the Merchants' Exchange of St. Louis or the Milwaukee Chamber of Commerce; the data is much too incom-

The relatively small size of the Board of Trade as contrasted with a large industrial union is another reason for the absence of oligarchic Board control. Moreover, the nature of the business of the Board of Trade differed widely from an organization like the American Medical Association or a large trade union. The Board met every day, in the same place, and at the same time. The directors were all a part of the daily activities. This is far different from a union, which might execute an important contract once every three years; or the A.M.A., whose members, drawn from all parts of the country, come together once a year, leaving the affairs of the association largely in the hands of a professional bureaucracy.

IV

Under its 1859 charter, the Chicago Board of Trade adopted rules and regulations in two general areas. One such area, which might be called "secondary rules," set up machinery for arbitration procedures that made possible the resolution of internal business disputes quickly, quietly, and without the need for expensive, time-consuming litigation. These rules also covered the settlement and clearing of contracts made in the exchange. The word "secondary" is applied to these regulations, because they dealt with transactions *after* they had taken place.

A more important group of regulations set forth the initial conditions under which a person might transact business upon the exchange at all. These "primary" rules concerned who might trade on the floor of the exchange; when, where, and what kind of market transactions could take place; and how much commission and/or margin would be required. We are largely concerned with the particular area of the "what, when, and where." For it was here that the exchange undertook to confront and reconcile an inherent tension between the individual member's pursuit of commercial gain, often through speculative risk, and the greater need for efficiency and predictability in the

plete. On the basis of what has been assembled in appendix 1, it may well be that the Milwaukee organization in particular was oligarchic in character. It might be noted, too, that lack of participation ought not to be automatically equated with lack of interest, as Lipset seems to imply.

national market. Furthermore, in this capacity the exchange functioned as an administrative regulatory agency, using quasi-legislative, judicial, and executive actions to further these occasionally antagonistic if not irreconcilable goals.

During the expanded trading that accompanied the Civil War, many Board members protected their futures contracts by dealing in privileges at the same time, thereby gaining an option or privilege whether or not to make delivery, depending upon the state of the market. Trading in privileges or, as it was also known, dealing in "puts and calls" refers to a market practice common on exchanges. A trader could obtain the privilege of either buying or selling a given quantity of grain at a given price, paying a small fee, such as one dollar per thousand bushels, for this privilege or option.

Normally such an option was valid for the following market day only, but this could vary. Suppose, for example, that on one day the market closed at 61¢ for wheat, and a trader bought a "call" for 63¢. If on the next market day the price of wheat went to 65¢, the trader had the "privilege" of either taking it at 63¢ or doing nothing at all. If, on the other hand, the price of wheat declined to 59¢, he had the "privilege" of doing nothing, of letting his option lapse, while the seller benefited by the fee paid for the privilege in the first place, one dollar per thousand bushels.

In the 1865 rules, however, the Board required delivery (or some form of delivery) and thus rejected privileged trades. The last section of rule XI stated that "privileges bought or sold to deliver or call for grain . . . by members of the Association shall not be recognized as a business transaction by the Directors or Committee of Arbitration."[30]

In this early period of internal regulation by the Board, the directors tended to resolve the market tension in favor of the individual member. The wording of this section well illustrates the point. Because dealing in privileges did not contemplate actual delivery, it appeared to be little more than gambling. This was sufficient grounds for condemnation by the Board. Yet privilege trading represented a widely accepted market practice. The solution was to frame the statement in the rules so as to per-

30. CBT *Rules*, 1865, p. 6.

mit privilege trading but not under Board auspices. As worded, the section was not a rule. It set no policy for members to follow, forbade no practices, and provided no penalties. It was in reality a warning that Board officials would not recognize dealing in puts and calls as a legitimate basis for complaint against a member. Members were perfectly free to deal in privileges at their own risk. If neither party objected, well and good. But if one of the parties got hurt financially and sought redress through the Board, the directors would neither take up his case, nor grant him relief.

This tendency to frame a rule so as to permit a maximum of private economic activity is also revealed by the Board's actions concerning when members could transact business. In 1873 the Board voted on two rules relating to the hours of trade. On the surface this seems a rather unimportant topic. One traded when the market was open and stopped when it was closed. This elementary logic broke down when confronted with an active, often frenetic, market, where fortunes could be made or lost in a matter of minutes. A buyer could always find a seller, and one could easily consummate a transaction off the floor as well as on it. Being practical men, the directors wished to avoid making the daily trading period too short. If this were the case, the membership (over sixteen hundred in 1873) probably would ignore it. For the same reason, the directors wanted to avoid prohibiting trading before or after certain hours. Yet there had to be definite limits to the times of trade, if only to provide that ordered and rational market for which the Board of Trade had been established in the first place.

The chief reason for restricting the hours of trade was to promote the greater efficiency and accuracy of the futures market as a price-setting mechanism. Long hours of trade permitted traders to wander in and out of the pits, leaving the way open to rigging and manipulation. By concentrating the influences and competition of differing factors and opinions bearing on the price of futures at a particular time and market, the resulting prices tended to "reflect more truly actual and prospective conditions, and the general opinion of the trade."[31]

The wording of the rule adopted by the association in April

31. *Report on the Grain Trade,* 5:145–46.

1873 was reminiscent of the privilege statement adopted in 1865. It stated that any commodity purchased or any sale made before or after a certain time "shall not be recognized as legal or binding by the . . . directors . . . upon complaints made for the non fulfillment of contract."[32] As in 1865, the Board did not deem it necessary to prohibit what it desired to prevent. Members could and did continue to trade before the opening and after the close of the daily market session, but at their own risk. No penalties needed to be specified, because, as worded above, trading before or after hours did not violate the rule.

In October 1873 the Board changed the rule, but its wording still remained ambiguous. The members added a section stating that "no property shall be tendered by members of the Board on any day on which the Board shall hold no business session." Again recognizing the realities of the market world, the rule went on to add that any trades made "on any such day" would not be considered as binding.[33] Now, presumably, a member trading when the Board held no session violated the rules and could be liable for disciplinary action at the option of the directors.

Although several additional resolutions concerning privilege trading were adopted by the Board, they all reflected a bias in favor of the individual member. In April 1876, for example, the directors resolved that privileged trading was forbidden by statute in the State of Illinois, also that such dealings were not recognized by the Board as legitimate transactions. The resolution prohibited dealing in privileges "in the open market of the exchange rooms." Any members so trading were to be suspended from admission to the exchange.[34]

It is doubtful, in spite of the strong language used, that this resolution was designed to eliminate privileged trading in its entirety. Rather, it was intended to end the more flagrant and obvious deals in puts and calls that were carried on in the open, right on the floor, during regular trading hours. Nothing in this resolution prevented privileged trading at the curb outside the building or in the corridors. Indeed, the rule that dealt with hours of trade did not forbid curb or corridor trades when the Board was in session.

32. *D.R.*, April 19, 1873, p. 308.
33. Ibid., October 18, p. 339.
34. Ibid., April 10, 1876, pp. 346–47.

On October 22, 1877, a director "called attention to the extensive trading going on in puts and calls daily."[35] The directors voted to refer the matter to the rules committee for investigation and to report some plan "to accomplish the suppression of this species of trading." One week later "a numerously signed petition" was submitted to the directors, asking for "such proper action as would check and if possible entirely suppress" puts and calls.[36] At the meeting of November 5, the committee reported the Board attorney had advised that the directors could refuse to entertain for complaint any contract growing out of a privileged trade. The committee urged the directors to adopt such a policy.[37] However, the directors had adopted such a rule in 1865, and they had readopted much the same rule in April of 1876, all to no avail.

Nevertheless, at the meeting of the directorate held on November 12, yet another resolution dealing with privileged trading was adopted. This latest effort stated that puts and calls were contrary to the statutes and that contracts based upon them were liable to be declared null and void by the courts. The resolution then declared that the directors would not accept any such contract as legitimate under the rules of the Board and that "any member transferring to an innocent party a contract known by him to be based upon a privilege shall be deemed guilty of fraud, and shall be liable to the penalties prescribed for fraud or bad faith."[38]

These actions indicated the unwillingness of the Board to adopt a flat rule that prohibited privileged trading. Board members in a very real sense lived to take risks; for many, it was their business. It should be emphasized again that a buyer could always find a seller. Ironically the integrity expected between members in their dealings with each other allowed them to violate the spirit of the rules. Rarely in the vast numbers of puts and calls did members ever seek the aid of the Board in settling a contract. They resolved it among themselves. Thus it made very little difference for the directors to declare solemnly that they would not recognize any such trades. They were hardly ever given the opportunity to consider them at all! Here, too, may be

---

35. Ibid., October 22, 1877, p. 77.
36. Ibid., October 29, p. 80.
37. Ibid., November 5, p. 82.
38. Ibid., November 12, pp. 99–100.

seen an example of the pervasiveness of private ordering within an autonomous organization. Indeed, by refusing to recognize puts and calls rather than simply forbidding the practice outright, the directors encouraged private settlement between the membership. What it required under the November resolution was that both parties to the privileged contract understand the nature of the transaction. In reality, during this period the Board asked nothing more.

V

The Board's "liberal" construction of its rules dealing with puts and calls and irregular trading reflected a practical awareness that economic gain should result from participation in its mer-

TABLE 2
CHICAGO AGGREGATE ANNUAL RECEIPTS, 1868–79

	Barrels of Flour	Bushels of Wheat	Bushels of Corn	Bushels of Oats
1868	2,192,413	14,772,094	25,570,494	16,032,910
1869	2,218,822	16,876,760	23,475,800	10,611,940
1870	1,766,037	17,394,409	20,189,775	10,472,078
1871	1,412,177	14,439,656	41,853,138	14,789,414
1872	1,532,014	12,724,141	47,366,087	15,061,715
1873	2,487,376	26,266,562	38,157,232	17,888,724
1874	2,666,679	29,764,622	35,799,638	13,901,235
1875	2,625,883	24,206,370	28,431,150	12,916,428
1876	2,955,197	16,574,058	48,668,640	13,030,121
1877	2,691,142	14,164,515	47,915,728	13,506,773
1878	3,030,562	29,713,577	63,651,518	18,839,297
1879	3,369,968	34,106,109	64,339,321	16,660,428

Source: Yearbooks of the Chicago Board of Trade.

cantile activities. If such were not the case, the association would have found it difficult to survive. However, the Board could only go so far in encouraging individual speculative effort. While the association could not operate without an economically active membership, it also could not function if the members were able to rig and distort the market by artificial manipulation of prices.

By the 1870s the erratic increase in volume of the Chicago grain market, with the accompanying increase in natural price fluctuation, encouraged many speculators to run corners. A corner existed when one speculator controlled nearly all the available wheat (or any other commodity) on the market, thus forcing other speculators, who had to obtain the grain to settle their own trades, to buy it at very high prices.

The most important characteristic of the corner, as distinguished from a natural shift in price direction, was the intentional manipulation of the market, generally by one individual. These efforts invariably disturbed the system of grain distribution. In the first place, corners injured many traders who were caught short, occasionally through no fault of their own. More serious was the effect corners had on the price of grain to the public. There was "a general loss to the community because the normal direction and rate of flow of grain" became distorted, and the terminal market was clogged with grain that was actually needed elsewhere but was diverted to cover the corner.[39]

As early as 1868 the directors had taken a tentative step toward opposing corners when they resolved that "the practice of 'corners,' of making contracts for the purchase of a commodity, and then taking measures to render it impossible for the seller to fill his contract, for the purpose of extorting money from him, has been too long tolerated by this and other commercial bodies in the country to the injury and discredit of legitimate commerce; that these transactions are essentially improper and fraudulent, and should any member of this Board hereafter engage in any such transactions, the directors should take measures for his expulsion."[40] Yet the resolution was ineffectual, because the directors made little effort to enforce it, choosing again not to interfere with members' market activity. But the increasing number of such corners aroused much criticism against the Board, particularly in the downstate areas, where these manipulations caused sharp fluctuations in the value of grain sold by the farmers. Indeed, in the spring of 1874, the Illinois legislature passed an "anti-corner" statute.[41] However, the corners kept coming, and

39. *Report on the Grain Trade*, 5:323.
40. Ibid., 2:110.
41. This statute and various court decisions involving it are discussed in the following chapter.

"A Flurry in Wheat." *Harper's Weekly*, October 1880. Courtesy Historical Pictures Service, Inc., Chicago.

from June through September 1874 William Sturges attempted to run a spectacular corner in corn.

Sturges, who was a former director of the Board and was popularly known as "King Jack," forced the price of corn upward on July 28. The price advanced even further on the next day. A short time later, he sold large quantities of corn, causing prices to fall and encouraging many other traders to sell on the presumption that the corner had not been successful. When these traders sought to buy the corn needed to cover these sales, Sturges promptly forced the price up again, much higher than before. In the resultant squeeze, those who were caught short (and many were) "suffered severely."[42]

While he controlled the market, Sturges appeared to be "a ruling power . . . a temporary seeming dictator of the fortunes of the less wily."[43] The use of "temporary" here was accurate; for, as often happened in these operations, by September Sturges had gotten himself into a corner! Later he refused to pay the settlement price of the claims against him. A group of Board members, who claimed (1) that Sturges owed them money and (2) that his actions were "unmercantile" and thus tended to bring the Board of Trade into disrepute, filed a complaint with the directors of the Board; much of October and November 1874 was spent dealing with the case. After protracted arguments, the directors referred the matter to the full Board "for their consideration and action."[44] Corners were not uncommon in the 1870s, and they were generally settled by a directorate committee that fixed a "fair" settlement price for all parties concerned, a price all had to accept. However, the Sturges case had special ramifications.

The years 1869 to 1876 represented the flood tide of "Grangerism" in Illinois. By 1874 important warehouse and railroad acts had already been passed. Also, the Illinois legislature had enacted an anticorner statute even as Sturges began his manipulations; and at the height of the squeeze in the summer of 1874, the new law was in effect.

To make matters worse, Sturges did more than run a corner and defy the legislature. He gloried in his actions, and after his

42. Taylor, p. 504.
43. *Chicago InterOcean*, August 1, 1874, p. 12.
44. *D.R.*, November 4, 1874, pp. 51–52.

operations failed, he defied the Board as well. Corners were a simple fact of life to the men of the Board. But there were certain rules, some of them unwritten, by which one played the corner game. King Jack may have been guilty of doing nothing more than what any other good speculator would have done under similar circumstances. His "crime" from the Board's point of view probably lay as much, if not more, in his conduct after the corner failed as in running the corner in the first place.

According to many Board members, Sturges refused to play the game according to the rules. He declined to settle at the agreed upon price and to accept arbitration and findings of the Board. He did this at a time when, as the directors noted in the annual report for 1874, members believed "that the Board has lost its power of discipline."[45] To a number of directors it appeared that "the very existence" of the Board of Trade was involved and that in confronting Sturges the association had "reached a crisis in its history."[46]

There is no doubt that certain Board rules were being violated with impunity. In March 1874 the *Chicago InterOcean* reported on the "speculative business transacted on the street today among grain dealers." The fact that the Board was not open and that the trades concluded "were not in conformity with the rules" made no difference.[47] Late in the same year the paper noted that the Board did, indeed, have a rule to prevent curb trading but that "so far it has met with but indifferent success, speculators being willing to trade among themselves on their honor." In addition, the directors were aware that the actions of Board members like King Jack had contributed to the legislation of 1874.

It thus becomes understandable why many observers, both on and off the Board, felt that the Sturges case had to be resolved with the Board of Trade as the winner. "The question," the *Inter-Ocean* declaimed, "is now fairly up [to] whether or not the Board is competent to protect its honor and, if need be, purge its membership of those who seek its privileges, but defy its established

---

45. *Report of the Directors, 1874*, p. xxiii. The report discussed no fewer than ten lawsuits in progress or recently settled between the Board and members who had been either suspended or expelled.

46. *Chicago InterOcean*, November 8, 9, 1874, p. 4.

47. Ibid., March 31, p. 7.

regulations and authority." The alternative would be "to sink into commercial anarchy and public disgrace."[48]

When the Board membership ultimately voted to expel Sturges, he elected to fight the action, and the ensuing dispute dragged on for five years.[49] The case resulted in two Illinois Supreme Court decisions, both favorable to the Board; but Sturges persisted.[50] Finally in 1879 the battle between the Board and King Jack concluded with an agreement to drop the entire proceedings, with Sturges to withdraw his suits and the Board to restore him to membership.[51] Although the case was legally inconclusive, it was significant in two respects: (1) it revealed the Board's recognition that the economic institutional need for predictability in the market could take precedence over a member's private business affairs; and, more important, (2) caused the Board to adopt detailed rules for self-regulation.

VI

As the 1870s drew to a close, the Chicago Board of Trade had already developed both its basic trading practices and a general administrative framework—procedures that would remain nearly unchanged for the next thirty years. In this period, total membership fluctuated between 1,830 and 1,930 individuals, with a little over half that number involved in the grain trade, the others in professions such as transportation, milling, stocks and bonds, meat packing, and brewing.[52] Yet, as the previous pages have indicated, the Board remained something of a private club, its basic purpose to provide its members with a market facility conducive to economic gain. Indeed during the late 1860s the Board

48. Ibid., November 9, p. 4.

49. Ibid., November 21, p. 12, November 24, p. 8, November 25, p. 8; *D.R.*, November 24, 1874, pp. 16–17. A printed copy of the charges and supporting evidence filed by the directors against Sturges has been preserved in the library of the Chicago Historical Society.

50. Sturges v. Board of Trade, 86 Ill. 441 (1878), 91 Ill. 81 (1879). On the continuing efforts by Sturges to gain readmittance to the Board, see *D.R.*, 1878: April 16, p. 170; April 23, pp. 173–76; May 7, p. 182; June 4, pp. 200–201; September 3, pp. 240–41.

51. Ibid., 1879: September 17, pp. 415–16; September 19, p. 417.

52. This statement is based on a tabulation of Board members' occupations as compiled every ten years over a fifty-year period.

had found itself caught in the middle, with elevator and warehouse interests on the one side and numerous commission merchants on the other, in a bitter feud over abuses perpetrated by the railroads and elevators upon farmers and dealers who were attempting to move their grain to or through Chicago. Because many of the antagonists on either side were members of the Board, effective internal resolution proved impossible, and the Board had openly joined other Chicago businessmen in appealing to the state to enact legislation to curb the railroad and warehouse operators rather than tighten up its own rules.[53]

To conclude that by the beginning of the 1880s the Board had become the tool of its members misses the point. It had never really been anything else, even though the potential for effective regulation had already been recognized, as was indicated by the newspaper commentary concerning the Sturges case. It was one thing for the Board to join others in calling upon the state to deal with abuses within the grain trade; it was quite another for the Board itself to be included by many among the perpetrators of these abuses. Indeed, between 1874 and 1894 different pressures upon the Board to attain effective internal regulation mounted. One obvious source of these pressures was the courts, which by this period had ruled extensively on both the Board's transactions and its authority over members.

53. See ns. 1 to 5 for the following chapter, particularly n. 3.

CHAPTER THREE

Futures Trading, the Exchanges, and the Law: Legal Developments in Illinois, 1874–86

THE Chicago Board of Trade, in taking the initial steps during the 1870s toward effectiveness as a regulatory administrative body, did not operate in a vacuum. Court decisions in two distinct areas also helped to mold what transpired on the Board floor. One of these areas was the legality of futures trading and settlements; the other was the extent to which the institution's disciplinary and rulemaking authority would be permitted to operate. Since the majority of Illinois cases dealing with the first category arose after the 1874 statute mentioned in the last chapter, this discussion begins with an analysis of the enactment and subsequent litigation. Cases dealing with the second category are then briefly summarized.

I

The Act of 1874 dealing with corners and options was only one result of agrarian agitation prevalent in Illinois after the Civil War. The rapid growth of Chicago during the war as a major grain center contributed to an increasingly profitable relationship between the burgeoning elevator interests and the railroads. By 1869–70 this "unholy alliance" had established a virtual monopoly of grain traffic in and out of Chicago. A storage charge of two cents was levied on every bushel entering the city "whether or not the grain was placed in a warehouse." To make matters worse, farmers were compelled to place the grain in one of the favored elevators because "the railroads assessed an additional charge of eight to ten cents on each bushel sent to warehousemen who did not belong to the ring."[1] In addition, the Board of Trade lacked any effective means to force the railroads and elevators to conform to the standards for grain grading and inspection.[2] In 1870, the Board president stated, the "genius of our country and of our age is . . . freedom from tyranny and monopoly," and he urged the Board to destroy without a delay "a monopoly highly deterrant [sic] to every interest in the city."[3] The *Chicago Tribune* asserted, "The name of a Chicago warehouseman has become a synonym with that of a pirate in the agricultural districts and there has been ample justification thereof."[4]

This ill-concealed collusion between elevator interest and the railroads was not the only grievance held by the farmers. They objected to the manipulation of prices by gamblers and speculators through dealing in "fictitious and spurious receipts."[5] Further, the great expansion of available farming lands caused an increase in crops and a decrease in their market value. Prices in wheat, for example, fell from \$1.52 in 1866 to \$1.08 in 1868. The fact that farmers in Illinois were at this time almost totally dependent on wheat and corn made their position even worse.[6]

The agarian discontent found expression in the Illinois Constitutional Convention of 1869–70. Numerous resolutions hostile to "Boards of Trade or other commercial organizations" were introduced, and the convention ultimately provided for effective state regulation of both railroads and warehouses.[7] In 1871 the

1. Kendall, p. 23.
2. Benjamin F. Goldstein, *Marketing: A Farmer's Problem* (New York, 1928), pp. 26–29.
3. Harold Woodman, "Chicago Businessmen and the 'Granger' Laws," *Agricultural History* 36 (1962):16–24; Dale E. Treleven, "Railroads, Elevators and Grain Dealers," *Wisconsin Magazine of History* 52 (1969):205–22.
4. Kendall, p. 24. According to Goldstein, p. 29, "Five railroads and warehouse operators" controlled "fourteen out of eighteen elevators, aggregating 9,000,000 bushels capacity out of a total of 10,000,000 bushels in the Chicago district." The relations between the Chicago Board of Trade and the elevator-warehouse interests have been analyzed in some detail by Guy A. Lee, "History of the Chicago Grain Elevator Industry," cited above, ch. 2, n. 7. See also his summary article "The Historical Significance of the Chicago Grain Elevator," *Agricultural History* 11 (1937):16–32.
5. Kendall, p. 26.
6. Goldstein, pp. 30–31; Roy V. Scott, *The Agrarian Movement in Illinois* (Urbana, 1962), pp. 5–9.
7. Kendall, pp. 27–28.

legislature enacted laws giving effect to this provision, but the railroad statute was declared unconstitutional by the Illinois Supreme Court in 1873.[8] Organizations reflecting agrarian discontent multiplied rapidly. There were eight Granges throughout the state in 1871. By 1873 the number had reached more than 500. Indeed, in January 1873 the members of various local farmers clubs joined with the Grange to form a statewide organization, and within six months the new Illinois State Farmers' Association had over 1,000 local branches.[9]

Even as the State Farmers' Association organized early in 1873, the legislature convened in Springfield. Through the media of mass meetings, petitions, and memorials, the agrarians denounced the "agencies, institutions and practices" that were supposedly hostile to the interests of rural Illinois. Complaints were levied against the railroads, the Board of Trade, grain elevator men, grain commission merchants, and the lawyers who controlled the legislature, in that approximate order of importance.[10] Besides gambling in nonexistent grain, members of the Board were criticized for the numerous corners being run during the early 1870s. In 1872 the *Chicago Tribune* noted the effects a

8. Roy V. Scott, "Grangerism in Champaign County, Illinois, 1873–1877," *Mid America* 43 (1961):139–63; Buck, pp. 123–58. In a unanimous opinion, the Illinois Supreme Court held that the 1871 railroad law violated the "spirit" of the state constitution, although it admitted the power of the legislature to regulate railroad franchises. The decision was an early example of "due process" used to strike down state regulation. The law was ruled unconstitutional because "it does not prohibit unjust discrimination merely, but discrimination of any character, and because it does not allow the companies to explain the reason of the discrimination, but forfeits their franchise upon an arbitrary and conclusive presumption of guilt to be drawn from the proof of an act that might be shown to be perfectly innocent." Chicago and Alton Railroad v. People, 67 Ill. 11, 22–23, 27 (1873). For a similar case, wherein the judges upheld the statute, see Minnesota v. Chicago, Milwaukee and St. Paul Railway, 38 Minn. 281 (1888), reversed in Chicago, Milwaukee and St. Paul Railway v. Minnesota, 134 U.S. 418 (1890). On the significance of these cases for the development of the administrative law doctrine of delegation, see Jaffe and Nathanson, pp. 33–47. The Illinois legislature also passed a warehouse law in 1871. A long series of court suits ultimately resulted in the United States Supreme Court upholding the law in the famous case of Munn v. Illinois, 94 U.S. 113 (1877). By the time this case was decided, Ira Munn, a former president of the Chicago Board of Trade, had already been expelled by that body for dishonest mercantile conduct. Taylor, pp. 466–67.

9. Goldstein, pp. 70–71.

10. Howard A. Merritt Papers, n.d., n.pag., State Historical Society of Wisconsin Archives, Madison.

corner could have upon an innocent party: "A man in White-
side, Illinois sold 15,000 bushels of his own oats on the Chicago
market before the [Chandler oats] corner started, at 38 cents a
bushel to be delivered in June. The blockade of the railroad and
warehouse facilities made it impossible for him to make the actual delivery, and he was forced to buy from the manipulators at
43 cents to settle his contract. When his oats reached market,
after the corner ended, they sold for 31 cents a bushel. So, he lost
12 cents a bushel on his own oats."[11]

The legislature quickly responded with a more stringent railroad measure that became law on May 2, 1873.[12] A House committee, consisting primarily of rural legislators, favorably reported a bill to prevent gambling in grain. The bill lay pending
as the session of 1873 ended. When the General Assembly reconvened in January 1874, with the main order of business a revision and enlargement of the state criminal code, one of the
proposed new sections submitted by the Joint Committee of
Revision dealt with option trading. It stated that anyone who
contracted for the sale of grain for future delivery, "except when
the seller is the owner, or agent of the owner thereof, and in actual possession of the same," would be fined not more than one
thousand dollars and imprisoned for not more than one year. All
such contracts were to be considered gambling contracts and,
thus, were void at law.[13]

On its face, the proposed law would have rendered illegal most
contracts made on the Board of Trade, even though it did permit
futures trading when the seller had actual possession. However,
the purposes of futures trading were to provide a constant market, always open to buyer and seller regardless of harvest time,
and to insure a means by which one might protect oneself from
price fluctuations between the time of purchase and delivery. Thus,
it is not surprising that the Board of Trade very strongly opposed
the measure. Although the Board made its opposition known,
how it did so is not clear. The proposed law does not appear to
have been discussed in the minutes or papers of the directors. The
vice president of the Board did point out that if grain could
be sold only when in possession, the market would be glutted

11. Kendall, p. 45.
12. Buck, pp. 146–49.
13. *Chicago Tribune*, January 21, 1874, p. 2.

during harvest times and that then manipulators could buy grain accumulated to such levels that the price would be minimal. Such activity, he felt, would lead to corners and much lower prices for farmers and small dealers.[14]

After some debate, in which several senators expatiated on the wickedness of the Chicago Board of Trade and the way in which the country innocents were fleeced, the Senate struck out the entire section by a vote of 32 to 5. Apparently a majority felt that the proposed bill would not prevent the "pernicious" practice of grain gambling without seriously damaging legitimate commerce.[15] In its place, the Senate adopted, without a roll call, a statute supposedly prohibiting four separate market abuses: option trading, forestalling the market by spreading false rumors to influence the price of commodities, cornering the market, and attempting to corner the market. The most important section of the statute provided that "whoever contracts to have or give to himself or another the option to sell or to buy at a future time any grain or other commodity" was to be fined and/or imprisoned similar to the earlier version.[16] Early in February 1874 the Senate approved the revised criminal code, and the House concurred.

On its face, the new law seemed ambiguous. Did the statute forbid all futures trading entirely, or did it merely render privileged trading (puts and calls) illegal? In the leading case of *Porter v. Viets* (1857), a Federal court ruled that the contract at issue was an absolute one, calling for delivery at a future date. "Whatever doubts may have existed," lack of a commodity on the part of a contractor at the time he contracts to deliver it at a future date, will not in itself vitiate the contract. Such "must now be considered the settled law, both in England and this country."[17] The agreement was not a contract for a future sale. It is this very subtle distinction that the 1874 statute may have sought to clarify. The statute did not appear to bar futures trading if

14. Taylor, p. 501.

15. *Chicago Tribune*, January 21, 1874, p. 5; *Chicago Times*, January 21, 1874, p. 3.

16. *Ill. Rev. Stat.* (1874), ch. 38, § 130, p. 1295.

17. Porter v. Viets, 19 F. Cas. 1077, 1078 (1857). For a penetrating analysis of the relationship between futures contracts and the development of modern American contract law, see Horwitz, "Historical Foundations of Modern Contract Law." See, in particular, pp. 936–46.

such activity took the form of binding agreements for delivery within a specified period of time. Various decisions of the Illinois Supreme Court handed down between 1875 and 1887 confirm this conclusion.

The 1875 case of *Sandborn v. Benedict* concerned a contract made between a farmer and a grain dealer while the corn dealt in was still growing in the field. Sandborn, the dealer, later refused to pay on the grounds that by not having the required amount of grain at the time of making the contract, Benedict had "perpetrated a fraud" and should not be allowed to recover. Echoing *Porter v. Viets,* the Illinois Supreme Court rejected Sandborn's contention, noting that "to say a man perpetrates a fraud by contracting to sell that which he has not in present possession, is saying too much, and, if admitted, would put a stop to much of the trade and commerce of the country."[18]

The case of *Wolcott v. Heath,* also heard in 1875, involved a similar time contract, which was, again, upheld by the court. "The obligation was to deliver the grain at all events, but it was the seller's option to deliver it at any time before the closing of business on the last day of the month." There was nothing illegal in this kind of contract. The first sentence of the 1874 statute was intended to bar the privilege "to deliver . . . or not, at the seller or buyer's option."

> Time contracts, made in good faith, for the future delivery of grain . . . are not prohibited by the common law nor any statute of this State, nor by any policy beneficial to the public welfare. Such a restraint would limit commercial transactions to such a degree as could not but be prejudicial to the best interests of trade. . . . What the law prohibits . . . is speculation in differences in market values, called, perhaps, in the peculiar language of the dealers, "puts and calls," which simply means a privilege to deliver or receive the grain, or not, at the seller or buyer's option. It is against such fictitious, gambling transactions we apprehend the penalties of the law are leveled.[19]

18. 78 Ill. 309 (1875). See, in particular, pp. 315–16.
19. 78 Ill. 433, 437 (1875). See also Cole v. Milmine, 88 Ill. 349 (1878); Barnett v. Baxter, 64 Ill. App. 544 (1896); Bailey v. Bensley, 87 Ill. 556 (1877); Schneider v. Turner, 130 Ill. 28 (1889). On a legal definition of puts and calls, see Woods v. Bates, 126 Ill. App. 180 (1906), affirmed in 225 Ill. 126 (1906).

Three years after the statute had become law, the court further distinguished between present sale and future delivery (legal), and future sale and/or delivery (illegal). In the case of *Logan v. Musick & Brown*, a unanimous court again confirmed that the 1874 statute "does not prohibit a party from selling or buying grain for future delivery." Selection of a day within a limited period on which the party was to receive the grain was perfectly lawful, because this was not an optional sale. An option within limits of a delivery date "does not fall within the statute, for the reason that it does not render the sale optional."[20]

In 1879 the Illinois Court of Appeals made the distinction even more obvious. Deciding the case of *Tenney v. Foote*, the decision emphasized that to fall within the ban of the statute, a contract must be one "to have to one's self, or to give to another, an option to buy or sell some commodity at a future time." Further, the court defined *option* as "a stipulated privilege to a party in a time contract, of demanding its fulfillment on any day *within the specified limit*" (emphasis added). However, the word *option* as used in the statute "means a mere choice, right or privilege of selling or buying; and it is the contracting for such a choice, right or privilege of selling or buying at a future time [that] the statute was intended to prohibit, as contradistinguished from an actual sale, or purchase, with the intention of delivering and accepting the commodity specified."[21]

The question arises concerning the kind of contract that did come within the prohibitions set out in the statute. In 1875 the Illinois court rejected a contract to be settled at maturity without any delivery of grain. The court called the agreement a "privileged" contract, in which "the seller had the privilege of delivering or not . . . and the buyer the privilege of calling or not . . . for the grain, just as they chose. . . . Being in the nature of gambling transactions, the law will tolerate no such contracts."[22] The next year the court enlarged the scope of the statute, placing contracts settled by differences within its prohibition. Such contracts, "where neither party intends to perform them, but simply to cancel them before or at their maturity, and pay differences,

---

20. 81 Ill. 415, 419 (1876).
21. 4 Ill. App. 594, 598–99 (1879).
22. Pickering v. Cease, 79 Ill. 328, 330 (1875).

are as injurious to trade and fully immoral as are the sale of options. Neither belongs to fair and legitimate trade."[23]

This decision caused some concern among the directors of the Board. It was one thing to be against privileged trading. The Board did not recognize such contracts, and during the 1870s made frequent if ineffective attempts to bar the membership from dealing in puts and calls. But it was common practice to make contracts with every intention of delivery and then, because of changes in the market, settle them before delivery time had arrived. The matter of settling by differences, however, was a completely different issue. Suppose a party to a contract for future delivery changed his mind and decided to settle before the contract had matured. Was this illegal under the court's opinion? If this was an illegal practice, most of the contracts made upon the floor of the Board were also illegal.

The basic problem for the court, in dealing with contracts made by Board members, was delivery. The courts uniformly insisted that delivery had to take place to have a legitimate contract. However, it was common knowledge and Board officials openly admitted that there was no actual delivery of grain in more than ninety percent of the contracts. How then could the courts uphold these agreements? The solution lay in how one defined "delivery." By the 1880s several basically similar methods for fulfilling contracts without actually handling the grain had evolved that were accepted by the courts. (A small portion of Board contracts were, of course, fulfilled by actual delivery or through exchanging warehouse receipts.)

An order for a commodity could be transferred through various traders to its ultimate purchaser, each intermediate trader signing the order and passing it along in succession. In this way "all the trades between the original seller and the last in line are wiped out by each of the pairs of buyers and sellers paying each other 'differences' as compared with the settlement price established each day."[24] Always, it was claimed, the intent of delivery

23. Lyon & Co. v. Culbertson, Blair & Co., 83 Ill. 33, 39–40 (1876). See also Carroll v. Holmes, 24 Ill. App. 453 (1887); Kennedy v. Stout, 26 Ill. App. 133 (1888); Miles v. Andrews, 40 Ill. App. 155 (1891); Colderwood v. McCrea, 11 Ill. App. 543 (1882).

24. Albert C. Stevens, "Futures in the Wheat Market," *Quarterly Journal of Economics* 2 (1887):37–63.

existed; and had any of the parties involved so desired, delivery could and would take place.

An alternative practice was indirect settlement, or delivery by "clearing the contracts." By this method, for example, a merchant who had sold 10,000 bushels of wheat and had just received a different order to buy 10,000 bushels could go to the man to whom he had sold the grain and buy it back. The two transactions would thus cancel each other out, and the entire transaction would be done without touching any grain at all.

The courts also accepted settlement by "ringing." A dealer might sell, for example, 10,000 bushels of wheat for future delivery to an exporter, who might in turn sell it to a miller, who might in turn proceed to sell it to a speculator, and so on until the number of individuals involved was large. At this point the original dealer might again need to buy, for a completely different transaction, 10,000 bushels of wheat for future delivery. The contracts could be settled through the "ring" created by the series of trades. "Would it make the method of settlement any more legitimate if A actually turned over his wheat to B, and B passed it on to C, and this was kept up until [the last buyer involved] received it, and handed it over to A again?"[25]

An average market session involved hundreds of dealers, all buying and selling at the same time, dealing in contracts that could be freely substituted one for the other. On the legality of clearance by substitution, see *Oldershaw v. Knoles*, 6 Ill. App. 325 (1880) and affirmed in 101 Ill. 117 (1881). This case is a good example of the difficulty some judges had in accepting established methods for settlement of Board contracts.

Before the trial court, the defendant offered to prove that in settling certain contracts through clearance by substitution he had followed accepted Board custom. The trial judge refused to hear the evidence, and the Illinois Appellate Court reversed the decision. In ordering the judge to hear the proof, the court noted that there was nothing unlawful in such settlements. At the next trial the judge heard the proof but promptly ordered the jury to disregard it on the grounds that the practice of substitution was contrary to public policy and thus was void. This time the Appellate Court sternly rebuked the judge for not following its

25. Ibid.

decision, and it again upheld the custom of settlement by substitution, as did the Illinois Supreme Court.

Like other observers then (and now), the trial judge may have found it difficult to understand how one could settle a contract in which delivery was mandatory without delivering. With transactions of this kind, where the grain (or, in reality, the rights to the grain) changed hands countless times each day, actual delivery of the commodity was impossible, and the courts did not appear to insist upon it. Rather, they emphasized intended delivery or the willingness and ability to deliver if desired.[26]

In 1876 the Illinois Supreme Court declared certain contracts void because the parties involved had expected to settle on the basis of differences "without either performing or offering to perform" the agreed upon contract. When the parties dispense with the performance (or delivery) "or at least an offer, or readiness to perform, then they render the contract obnoxious to the law."[27] Similarly, a federal court in 1878 held that when the parties *intended* actual delivery "a subsequent mutual settlement . . . which took the place of actual performance, cannot have the retroactive effect of making [the contracts] void for illegality."[28]

II

The emphasis of the courts on the *intent* of delivery insured that most of the futures contracts litigated before them would be upheld, as indeed they were. Board of Trade rules, it was true, required delivery.[29] But it was very easy for a commission merchant and broker to "intend" delivery, make a contract, change their minds, and settle between themselves. The parties could always

26. On the legality of settling by "ringing up," see Wolcott v. Reeme, 44 Ill. App. 196 (1892).

27. Lyon vs. Culbertson, at pp. 38, 40.

28. Clark v. Foss, 5 F. Cas. 955 (1878). A perceptive statement of the "intent" theme may be found in a Michigan case, Gregory v. Wendell, 39 Mich. 337, 340–41 (1878).

29. Indeed, the trading fraternity frowned upon trying to escape one's contract by claiming in court that it grew out of either gambling, privileges, or irregular trading. To so claim was contemptuously described as "pleading the baby act."

claim they had intended to deliver all along. The judges could not help being aware that one might easily gamble on prices, using the form of a futures contract, always stating an intent to deliver. They also could not help recognizing realities of the market-oriented society. While public policy did, indeed, encourage punishment for gambling, it also supported an open market: competitive, relatively unrestricted, and expanding.

The courts acknowledged that different customs for dealing in commodities had evolved, and that some of them, such as "ringing up" were "legitimate, though very difficult to trace through and explain."[30] For the most part, the justices made little if any effort to "trace through and explain." In 1878 a federal judge candidly admitted, "The truth is, men are speculative creatures as certainly as they are eating and sleeping ones." Granting that harm does result from overspeculation, he doubted that "the world would be better off without speculators; or, if it would be, that the law can do much in abolishing them." To rule that settling contracts by clearance was illegal would be to hold that "a great part of the banking and clearing-house transactions in our great commercial centers are illegal also," and to so decide "would be entrenching too severely upon the business of the commercial world, without any corresponding benefit to be derived from it." In general, he concluded, "commercial transactions must be left to be regulated by the higher and more inexorable laws which govern the trading world." The judge's reasoning is a good example of judicial delegation if not abnegation. It reflects both a sense of market reality and awareness that judicial expertise in this area was irrelevant. The Supreme Court of Wisconsin made the point succinctly: "The law aims to be practical, and to favor what is practicable."[31]

Perhaps the apparent inconsistency between the courts' requirement of delivery and the admitted infrequency with which it took place bothered the judges. They realized that gambling contracts might be difficult to discover, especially when the parties involved sought to evade the law "by assuming the livery of legitimate commerce."[32] Once the courts had determined to their

30. Wolcott v. Reeme; Clark v. Foss.
31. Ibid.; Guinard v. Knapp-Stout and Co., 95 Wis. 482, 487 (1897).
32. Beveridge v. Hewitt, 8 Ill. App. 467, 482 (1881).

own satisfaction that a contract *was* a gambling transaction, they condemned it in judicial language not susceptible to misinterpretation.

In the case of *Webster v. Sturges*, the Illinois Court of Appeals found the contract at issue to be forbidden by the statute and, as such, "a contract from which no rights could spring, but whose baleful and poisonous influence must necessarily taint and corrupt every other contract into which it was allowed to enter."[33] The Illinois Supreme Court, in its description of gambling contracts, emphasized that the law "has not sanctioned pernicious practices that are injurious to its votaries, and are demoralizing in their tendencies."[34] In 1888 the same court described settling by market price fluctuations as a crime against the state, the general welfare and happiness of the people, religion, morality, and all legitimate trade and business. Even worse, it found: "This species of gambling has become emphatically and pre-eminently the national sin. . . . In its pernicious and ruinous consequences it is simply appalling. . . . It submits to no restraint, and defies alike the laws of God and man."[35]

Implicit in these and similar opinions are several themes. The justices seem to agree that, in a market-centered society, gambling was wrong in itself, because it produced nothing for the market, no commodity that changed hands. The courts did not exist to endorse this type of activity, even when a gambling contract "may upon its face purport to be an absolute contract for the sake of the sale or purchase of such a commodity for future delivery."[36] Kent's *Commentaries on American Law* notes that "the law has been thought to descend from its dignity when it lends its aid to recover the fruits of an idle and frivolous wager."[37] More than this, gambling in stocks and/or commodities was wrong because it disrupted that creative market expansion so important to the late nineteenth century, luring away important funds and seducing hard-earned capital.

---

33. 7 Ill. App. 560, 564 (1880).
34. Lyon v. Culbertson, at p. 40.
35. Cothran v. Ellis, 125 Ill. 501 (1888).
36. Coffman v. Young, 20 Ill. App. 76, 79 (1886).
37. James Kent, *Commentaries on American Law.* 12th ed. (Boston, 1874), 3:227. See also Joseph Chitty, *Treatise on Law of Contracts*, 11th ed. (New York, 1874), 1:376.

In 1876 the Illinois Supreme Court held that if gambling transactions were permitted, the results would "engulf hundreds in utter ruin, disrange and unsettle prices, and operate injuriously on the fair and legitimate trader in grain, as well as the producer, [as well as being] pernicious and highly demoralizing to the trade."[38] Deciding a case in 1885, the Court concluded, "Considerable fortunes secured by a life of honest industry have been lost in a single venture in options."[39] Perhaps the best judicial synthesis of these themes came from the Pennsylvania Supreme Court in 1872, even before the Illinois statute had been passed. The court did not deny the importance of legitimate speculation. Gambling in differences, it found:

> represents not a transfer of property, but a mere stake or wager upon its future price. . . . [and causes] men of small means to enter into transactions far beyond their capital, which they do not intend to fulfill, and thus the apparent business in the particular trade is inflated and unreal, and like a bubble needs only to be pricked to disappear; often carrying down the bona fide dealer in its collapse. Worse even than this, it tempts men of large capital to make bargains of stupendous proportions, and then to manipulate the market to produce the desired price. . . . Such transactions are destructive of good morals and fair dealing, and of the best interests of the community. If the article be stocks, corporations are crushed and innocent stockholders ruined to enable the gambler in its price to accomplish his ends. If it be merchandise, *e.g.* grain, the poor are robbed, and misery engendered.[40]

In 1916 Mr. Justice Holmes observed, "Every question of construction is unique, and an argument that would prevail in one case may be inadequate in another."[41] His point is especially apt in explaining the Illinois Court's interpretation of the 1874 statute. Handing down opinions at a time of tremendous economic activity and market expansion, the court demonstrated flexibility in its decisions. The courts tended to uphold the vast majority of

38. Lyon v. Culbertson, at p. 38.
39. Pearce v. Foote, 113 Ill. 228 (1885). "The evil is all the more dangerous from the fact that it seemingly has the sanction of honorable commercial usage in its support. It is a vice that has in recent years grown to enormous proportions." Ibid., p. 239.
40. Kirkpatrick & Lyons v. Bonsall, 72 Penn. 155, 158–59 (1872).
41. United States v. Jin Fuey Moy, 241 U.S. 394, 402 (1916).

futures contracts litigated before them, even though actual delivery was rarely accomplished, if at all envisaged, past opinions to the contrary notwithstanding.

The court's acceptance of the intent test reflected an awareness that in the late nineteenth century it was both necessary and desirable for men to be encouraged to take risks in the interests of market expansion. "The law should not lightly add risks of its own creation to those inherent in the business situation."[42] Perhaps this was one reason for upholding so many of these contracts. Certainly their findings do not appear to have dampened speculative enthusiasm for dealing in commodities during this period. In the cases where a contract for future delivery was challenged as illegal, the courts uniformly placed the burden of proof upon the party claiming that the contract was invalid. Unless proven to be gambling or in some other way contrary to public policy, the courts assumed the contract to be valid. Again, this attitude reflected judicial awareness that there were already sufficient risks in entrepreneurial activity without the law adding any more.

The court's action seemed to result in a discrepancy between the written statute and the court's interpretation of it. The justices' unwillingness (or inability) to draw a clear line between valid futures contracts and contracts that were in reality gambling wagers created judicial cloudiness rather than clarity. In one such federal case heard in 1882, the judge upheld the purchases and contracts of a defendant who intended to deal in time contracts and to settle the differences so as to avoid paying for and carrying the commodities bought. The court, in its opinion, stated:

> He may have contemplated dealing wholly in differences to such an extent as to make the transactions such as have been construed by the courts of this state to be wager contracts. . . . But he did not, I am satisfied, intend that his brokers should make for him such contracts as are expressly illegal by the Illinois statutes, but, at most, they were to be transactions where it was not intended that any commodity should be actually received or delivered, but that he was to deal in differences only, coming

42. Hurst, *Law and the Conditions of Freedom*, p. 20.

perhaps within the rule laid down by the supreme court of this state.

The court held these transactions to be valid, because the party had dealt in differences on regular futures contracts, instead of on option or privileged contracts.[43] The fact that the defendant had admitted to no intent to deliver at all, as the court acknowledged, apparently made no difference!

III

When one examines the Illinois courts' attitude toward disciplinary authority of the Chicago Board of Trade, there is little evidence of the judicial confusion just noted. With striking frequency, the Illinois Supreme Court supported the Board's enforcement of its rules upon the membership.[44] Although the justices were willing to hear a case, judicial relief did not result. The usual pattern, as evidenced from the cases between 1860 and 1887, was for a member who had been suspended or expelled to file a petition for mandamus, which was immediately followed by a bill for an injunction against the directors pending the outcome of the mandamus proceedings.[45] Yet the court consistently ruled that injunctive relief would not help one who had already been penalized, and mandamus was also inappropriate, unless the Board's actions had been irregular in terms of due process.[46] The decisions invariably noted that "when the appellant became a member of the Board of Trade under and subject

43. Jackson v. Foote, 12 Fed. 37, 40–42 (1882). The Illinois Supreme Court in Lyon v. Culbertson placed all trading in differences, subject to the intent test, under the ban of the 1874 statute.

44. Sturges v. Board of Trade, 86 Ill. 441 (1878), 91 Ill. 81 (1879); People ex rel. Page v. Board of Trade, 45 Ill. 112 (1867); Fisher v. Board of Trade, 80 Ill. 85 (1876); People ex rel. Rice v. Board of Trade, 80 Ill. 134 (1876); Baxter v. Board of Trade, 83 Ill. 146 (1876); Chase v. Cheney, 58 Ill. 509 (1872).

45. A mandamus was a court order that certain action be undertaken, whereas an injunction was a court order that certain action be forbidden.

46. I have been able to discover only one such recorded case, a proceeding in the Cook County Circuit Court, where the trial judge issued a mandamus against the Board. See Brine v. Board of Trade. However, the Illinois Supreme Court, in a companion case that grew out of the same market transactions, sustained the Board. See People ex rel. Rice v. Board of Trade.

to the articles and conditions of its charter, and by signing an agreement to be governed by the rules . . . passed in pursuance of that charter he, of course, became such [a] member under and subject to the rule."[47] As early as 1876, ten years before the decision just quoted, the court had held that the Board "is only a voluntary organization, which its charter fully empowers it to govern in such mode as it may deem most advisable and proper. It has adopted its by-laws, provided a forum for their enforcement . . . , and the court will not interfere to control its action."[48]

Even the Board's procedures for settlement of corners, themselves subject to dubious judicial regard, were affirmed by the Illinois Supreme Court in a case that well illustrates the extent to which judges supported the organization in its administrative role of private ordering. Board rules provided that when a member defaulted on his contract, that is, when—as in a corner—he was unable to procure grain that he had to buy in order to settle his trades, a committee of "discreet and reputable" members was to be appointed by the president. The group was to take evidence and then arrive at a settlement price, which "shall be accepted and recognized . . . as final" by members and officials of the Board.

In March 1882 such a committee fixed a price for wheat that apparently was highly favorable to those who had run the corner. Other members accused the committee of violating the spirit, if not the letter, of the rules by not imposing a more equitable settlement. Led by Abner Wright, who later became Board president, they submitted a new rule dealing with malfeasance in office. It provided that any Board officer or committee member "who shall neglect or refuse to execute or enforce any rule . . . in conformity with its true intent, spirit and meaning" or who shall "pervert, misconstrue or distort any rule . . . thereby making [it]

47. Pitcher v. Board of Trade, 121 Ill. 412, 420 (1887). See also Dickenson v. Chamber of Commerce of Milwaukee, 29 Wis. 45, 51 (1871): "And the plaintiff, after having voluntarily connected himself with the association, is bound to observe the rules and regulations adopted by it to secure the objects of its creation." See Farmer v. Board of Trade of Kansas City, 78 Mo. App. 557, 566 (1899): "The offending member must submit himself to the sentence of the tribunal provided for by the rules which he has signed and contracted to abide by."
48. People ex rel. Rice v. Board of Trade, p. 137.

inoperative or oppressively unjust" shall be guilty of the crime of malfeasance in office and shall be expelled from the association. On March 29 the directors voted to disapprove "this monstrously absurd proposition," and on March 31 the membership rejected it—364 against the rule, 98 for it.[49]

A few months later, as yet another committee arrived at a settlement price for a different corner, some twenty-four Board members, including Abner Wright, filed suit against the Board of Trade. Wright alleged that the Board committee appointed to settle the value of wheat had fixed it at an "extortionate" price; that the directors did not have the power to appoint such a committee, authority in these areas being limited to cases *voluntarily* brought before it; and that the committee was biased in the matter. He also claimed that the members interested in the success of the corner had threatened to seek Board disciplinary action unless he adjusted his contracts in conformity with the settlement price. Stating that the appointment and action of the committee were contrary to the Board charter, Wright asked the court to enjoin the Board "from recognizing it or giving it any validity, and from taking any action based thereon" against him.

The court held Wright was wrong on every point. It noted that the Board is a voluntary organization and one not established "for direct pecuniary gain," and that as long as it keeps within its charter, "it is completely self governing." There could be no doubt that the Board had power under the charter to adopt the rule setting up committees to fix prices in disputed transactions. This power was completely separate from the authority to set up committees of arbitration. Members who voluntarily joined agreed by joining to abide by the rules. If Wright believed the corner in grain was wrong and the committee's action illegal, he could prove it in a court of law. "Hence [he has] no right to resort to equity for relief." Injunctive action was inappropriate.

The opinion concluded with a few piquant observations about commodity exchange activities. Mr. Justice Walker noted that Wright & Co. had held Board membership for many years and had claimed the privilege of membership was lucrative, yielding some $15,000 a year. In view of that longstanding membership,

---

49. *D.R.*, 1882: March 29, p. 259; March 31, p. 260.

he stated, "it is not a violent presumption to suppose that they have derived a large portion of their gains by the force of this [settlement] rule in breaches of similar contracts . . . settled or adjusted as it is proposed to be against them." Wright was no novice. His firm was well "aware of the hazards incurred under the rules when they entered into these contracts, and it is but fair that they submit to the losses as they have exacted them from others under similar circumstances." The court used a variation of the famous "clean hands" test for an equity action to deny Wright his relief. Because he lost, or was placed in a position to lose, Wright could not now seek an injunction to block operation of the rules, especially when he had gained from them in the past.[50]

This decision particularly incensed Henry Demarest Lloyd, who was then writing an article about the abuses of commodities speculation. He objected both to the Board of Trade maintaining conditions conducive to corners and, especially, to the Illinois Supreme Court's "complete abdication of all the rights of the State to exercise any judicial supervision over this corporation, though created by it." Lloyd found it "incredible that this should be law in any civilized community." Paraphrasing Dante's famous words, he observed: "On the threshold of the Board of Trade . . . is inscribed: 'your rights resign within these walls.'"

Even though Wright lost the case, Lloyd's comments caused John Jewett, a distinguished Illinois attorney and one of Wright's lawyers, to complain that such statements "do not state correctly the issues or the facts, and are therefore calculated to produce a wrong impression." Lloyd's response echoed the tone of his earlier article. "If there has been any misrepresentation of the case," he wrote, "it has been due to the inability of counsel to present it properly." Perhaps the final word was held by a commission firm based in Milwaukee, which noted that the Board's "already unenviable record for rascality and imbecility" had increased. Indeed, "when a commercial body voluntarily prostitutes itself, as the Chicago Board of Trade has done, to a level with bunko steerers and confidence men, we may well wonder

50. For the background of the corner litigation, see *Nation* 35 (1882):214. Wright v. Board of Trade, Ill. Sup. Ct. (March 29, 1883). This case does not appear in the Illinois reports, but it is on file in the office of the Clerk of the Illinois Supreme Court.

what the standard of commercial honor will be with the coming generation."[51]

While the pattern of the Illinois Supreme Court's affirmative support for the Board is clear, other exchanges had more difficulty in convincing the appropriate judges that these organizations were acting within proper legal boundaries. The cases were few in number, but they seem to reveal a greater judicial concern with disciplinary power than was demonstrated by the Illinois courts. This tendency was especially true in cases involving compulsory arbitration—a problem the Chicago Board of Trade avoided by not making the practice compulsory. In 1875, for example, the Georgia Supreme Court affirmed a mandamus against the Savannah Cotton Exchange, ordering the restoration to membership of certain indivduals who had been suspended for refusal to submit a matter to arbitration. Granted that the Exchange did have power to arbitrate, "its decisions and awards are subject to be reviewed and examined, so far as the legal rights of the parties are concerned, by the judicial tribunals of the state, in the same manner as the awards of other arbitrators are reviewed and examined."[52]

The difficulties the courts confronted in accepting both compulsory arbitration and the admitted right to an external judicial inquiry are aptly illustrated by two decisions of the Missouri Court of Appeals that cannot be reconciled. In 1876 the court held compulsory arbitration on the Merchants' Exchange of St. Louis illegal. Again, there was no question of the legality of arbitration in general. Indeed, the law encourages "these domestic tribunals, although they may, if they choose, disregard the rules of law in their decisions." But the courts "will not have persons coerced into waiving their strict rights if they choose to insist upon them." Hence, was it not illegal for the Exchange to "compel every respectable merchant of the city . . . to submit every controversy arising in the course of trade to a tribunal which is

51. Henry D. Lloyd, "Making Bread Dear," *North American Review* 137 (1883):130–32; John Jewett to Henry D. Lloyd, August 14, 1883, and Lloyd to Jewett, August 16, 1883, Henry Demarest Lloyd Papers, State Historical Society of Wisconsin Archives, Madison; *D.P.*, November 21, 1882. See also Jonathan Lurie, "Henry Demarest Lloyd: A Note," *Agricultural History* 47 (1973):76–79.
52. Savannah Cotton Exchange v. State ex rel. Warfield and Wayne, 54 Ga. 668, 670 (1875).

not bound by legal rules, and which may, if it so choose, utterly disregard, in forming its decisions, every ruling of the courts and every legislative enactment?" The judges unanimously found the rule requiring arbitration "unreasonable in the legal and technical sense of that term."[53]

This decision meant very little, because the courts uniformly agreed that when one voluntarily joined an exchange and signed the usual agreement to abide by the rules, failure to do so was grounds for disciplinary action. Thus it made no difference if the exchange enforced the compulsory arbitration rule or, instead, the penalty for violating a rule of the exchange. The result was the same. Twenty-three years later, the Missouri court, without mentioning its earlier decision, unanimously agreed.[54] The judges affirmed again that "parties can not by agreement to arbitrate future differences, oust the courts of jurisdiction." This conclusion, however, did not bar the Kansas City Board of Trade from adopting a rule "requiring all differences between members to be settled by arbitration and to impose expulsion as a penalty for disobedience of such a rule." The exchange could not enforce the "agreement to arbitrate," but it could, indeed, enforce the penalty for refusal to arbitrate in the first place! "For the refusal is a violation of its rules which the member has agreed to obey."[55]

Another Missouri decision, this one dealing with the Merchants' Exchange disciplinary authority as opposed to an arbitration proceeding, reflected an attitude toward the organization different from the affirmative support consistently given by the Illinois courts to the Chicago Board of Trade. The case involved a rule against smoking on the floor during trading hours. In 1888 a member of the Merchants' Exchange was fined fifty dollars for violating this rule; and, upon his refusal to pay the fine, he was suspended from membership. After being refused admission to the floor, the member, C. H. Albers, filed a bill for an injunction to restrain the directors from interfering in his rights as a member. Counsel for the Exchange responded with what, in Illinois at least, appeared to be sound law. They argued that mandamus and not injunction was the proper remedy, as the

53. State of Missouri ex rel. Kennedy v. Merchants' Exchange, 2 Mo. App. 96, 99, 100, 102 (1876).
54. Farmer v. Board of Trade of Kansas City, 78 Mo. App. 557 (1899).
55. Ibid., pp. 566, 567, 568.

latter could not prevent what had already transpired. Further, the Exchange anticipated the reasoning of the court in the Kansas City Board of Trade case just discussed. It emphasized that the refusal of Albers "to pay the fine, thus lawfully imposed upon him for corporate misconduct, was in itself corporate misconduct, for which he was rightfully, after due hearing, suspended pending such refusal to pay."[56]

The Missouri Court of Appeals affirmed a circuit court decision against the Merchants' Exchange. The judges stated that they entertained "great respect for the decisions" of the Illinois Supreme Court but noted that "on this question its decisions seem to be contrary to reason." If the act of suspension was illegal, it followed that "the plaintiff has never, in contemplation of law, been suspended." Hence injunction was proper as a remedy to restrain the directors from interference with Albers' rights as a member. Further, when Albers argued that the directors did not have legal authority to impose this fine and he thus refused to pay it, "such a refusal cannot . . . be deemed misconduct within the meaning of the charter provision." Although the directors had the undoubted power to regulate smoking on the exchange floor, to use suspension from membership and its privileges as a penalty for not paying a fine of doubtful legality "was a summary method . . . not authorized either by the charter or the rules and regulations, and prohibited by the principles of the common law."[57]

Not content with his token victory, Albers proceeded to sue the directors of the Merchants' Exchange for $50,000 damages, on the grounds that they had "acted recklessly, willfully, and maliciously, and with design to injure and oppress plaintiff." Surprisingly, the judge ordered the jury to find for the plaintiff and to award damages in the sum of one cent. Both Albers and the Exchange appealed to the Missouri Supreme Court, which unanimously reversed the lower court's decision and, in support of its findings, cited earlier decisions by the Illinois Supreme Court that affirmed the Chicago Board of Trade's authority to act as a "corporate court."[58]

56. Albers v. Merchants' Exchange of St. Louis, 39 Mo. App. 583, 584–85 (1890).

57. Ibid., pp. 591, 597, 598. See also Lysaght v. St. Louis Operative Stonemasons' Association, 55 Mo. App. 538, 547 (1893).

58. Albers v. Merchants' Exchange of St. Louis, 138 Mo. 140 (1897).

IV

While the exchanges were not usually direct parties to the contract cases discussed earlier in this chapter, they had a vital interest in the outcome. In virtually every Illinois case, for example, the contracts at issue, including those contracts declared illegal by the courts, were made by members of the Chicago Board of Trade or a kindred exchange. The point that many of these contracts had been consummated under Board rules was irrelevant for the justices in determining their legality, as the Illinois Supreme Court specifically stated.[59] Perhaps these facts indicated judicial awareness that the Board had not yet successfully resolved the tension between individual speculative activity and the greater institutional need for dependability and order within the national market.

In the discipline cases in which the exchanges were actual litigants, the courts demonstrated less uniformity in delineating limits to exchange authority over its members. Yet it would be unwise to overemphasize these differences. The Illinois Supreme Court, for all its affirmative decisions on Board disciplinary authority, was far from ready to grant the organization additional regulatory powers that it sought, as will be seen in the next chapter.[60] The differences between the courts lay more in judicial approach than in doctrinal substance. The Missouri court decisions did not seriously restrain the Merchants' Exchange, just as the Illinois verdicts did not grant the Board of Trade anything approaching unbridled power.[61] Failure to resolve the primary market tension just mentioned necessarily implied failure to resolve its corollary—reconciling the requisite amount of organizational authority with the basic goal of unrestricted private

59. Pardrige v. Cutler, 168 Ill. 504 (1897).

60. Indeed, the proclivity of some of the Chicago trial judges to grant preliminary writs of either mandamus or injunction, even though invariably the Illinois Court sustained the Board of Trade, bothered the directors. They noted in their report for 1874 that such action "has tended to paralyze discipline [by placing] the party who has been . . . guilty of a violation of the rules, back upon the Board, with even more privileges than other members, because [he is] not subject to discipline during proceedings in court. The tendency of such cases has been demoralizing, in giving license to a defiance" of the Board's authority over its members. *Report of the Directors*, 1874, p. xxv.

61. See, for example, Goddard v. Merchants' Exchange, 9 Mo. App. 290, 295–97 (1880).

economic ventures. This was the thrust of the courts' message to the exchanges as the nineteenth century drew to a close.

However, the evolution of private mercantile associations between 1840 and 1900 has further implications concerning the nature of the regulatory process in general. The role of private decision-making in this period was crucial to the industrial and economic growth so much in evidence. Exchanges such as the Chicago Board of Trade evolved largely as a response to the need for an effective market mechanism. Similarly, public policy mandated private regulation because the nineteenth-century administrative framework was unable to guide effectively economic and industrial modernization—of which the exchanges were but one symptom. Hence, railroads proliferated, corporate enterprise matured into trusts and combinations, and commodities markets and exchanges developed, all virtually free from interference by the legal order. Not until these organizations had become institutionalized did the legal order respond, seeking to impose some sort of external regulation upon structures already mature and powerful. At that point, as much of our past regulatory history may well demonstrate, the challenge of regulating effectively a vast, well-established mercantile system had become extremely difficult, if not impossible.[62]

62. Portions of this chapter originally appeared in *Rutgers Law Review* 28 (1975):1107–40. See Jonathan Lurie, "Commodities Exchanges as Self Regulating Organizations in the Late 19th Century: Some Perimeters in the History of American Administrative Law."

CHAPTER FOUR

The Chicago Board of Trade
and the Bucket Shops, 1879–89

I

From its inception the Chicago Board of Trade has always been a private organization. Indeed, during the 1880s the association had barely begun to recognize that it had public responsibilities. The general public could not trade on the floor directly, although an individual could deal through a broker or commission merchant who was a Board member. There were other obstacles that a prospective speculator faced even after he had obtained a member to trade for him. Members could deal only in standard amounts of a commodity, such as 5,000 bushels of grain. The trades could be made, supposedly, only on the floor and during specific market hours. Delivery was mandatory, and the minimum rate of commission a member might receive for his services had been fixed by Board rules since 1878. The cost of membership formed another barrier to some who sought to speculate directly on the floor. By 1882 the initiation fee, once the proposed member had been cleared by a committee and a majority vote of the directorate, stood at $10,000. All these conditions insured that persons of small means would not be involved in speculative ventures on the Chicago Board of Trade, and this was in keeping with the purposes of the Board.

However, the lure of the market was as strong then as it is today. "With us," wrote a penitent but perceptive practitioner of gambling in 1890, "life is restless, and we can find recreation only in excitement. It is this feature of our national character that inclines us to gaming and speculation in a far higher degree than any other people."[1] Those who wanted to speculate and could not afford to or did not wish to adhere to the restrictions on exchanges like the Chicago Board of Trade found their solution in the bucket shops. It is not known exactly when these shops arose, but in 1879 the *Chicago Tribune* noted, "This year has witnessed the successful establishment of institutions which bear the euphonious and expressive title of 'bucket shops'."[2]

A bucket shop was a gathering place where wagers could be made in the form of orders or options at current prices for commodities (or securities) without any intention to purchase or deliver. Here an individual could indulge his speculative whims free from the troublesome restrictions of the legitimate exchange. The bucket shops kept longer hours. Any person with a few dollars to spend, "man or woman, boy or girl, white, black, yellow or bronze," could patronize them. There one could sell in much smaller quantities than was standard on the Board of Trade, bucket shops often charged less for commission than could Board members, and no delivery or receipt of the commodity bought or sold was usually intended as was supposed to be the case on the Chicago Board of Trade.[3]

The bucket shops had no connection with the national market, and they used the quotations purely in a gambling sense. An individual might bet that the price of grain would go up or down. Whichever position he took, the bucket shop operator would take the other side, and the loser would pay the difference as reflected in the everchanging quotations. The shops attracted the public, because they clothed an illegitimate activity (gambling) with the raiment of a lawful practice (speculation). Indeed, in outward appearance, most bucket shops appeared to be merely smaller models of commercial exchanges, and the shop proprietors tried to pose as legitimate brokers. A minor number

1. John Philip Quinn, *Fools of Fortune* (Chicago, 1890), p. 597. The author wrote from the perspective of one "who has tasted all the joys of a gambler's career and drained [to] the dregs the wormwood which lurks at the bottom of the cup of illusive, hollow happiness." In presenting his confessions of a reformed swindler, Quinn noted that he "modestly, yet with sincerity, tenders to the world what he hopes may extenuate his twenty-five years of gaming and systematic deception of his fellow men."
2. Taylor, p. 586. For the background of the term "bucket shop," see John Hill, Jr., *Goldbricks of Speculation* (Chicago, 1903), p. 39.
3. Taylor, pp. 586–87.

of bucket-shop patrons probably assumed that their money would be used in standard market transactions. However, the great majority of customers had no doubt that in patronizing a bucket shop they were gambling.

John Quinn well described the typical bucket shop of the 1880s:

> Clerks, artisans, merchants and men about town mingle in a sort of temporary companionship, truly democratic. Beardless youths sit side by side with men whose heads have grown bald and whose step has become feeble in a vain chase after a phantom, a chimera, a will-of-the-wisp, always just within the grasp, yet ever eluding the clutch. Here may be met the confidential clerk, who sees nothing wrong in following, at a respectful distance, the example of his employer, who ventures his thousands upon the floor of 'Change. Here one jostles against the decrepit old man, once a millionaire, but who having sunk his fortune in the maelstrom of some great Board of Trade, now passes his waking hours before these blackboards, reckoning that a red-letter day upon which he wins five dollars. And here, too, may be encountered the successful business man, keen of eye, quick of step, alert of perception, who has been drawn hither partly through a desire for speedy wealth, partly through an inordinate craving for the excitement which is not to be found in the legitimate walks of trade. . . . In the bucket shops, the attentive observer may sometimes hear the heavy sigh of despair from the young man who has been tempted to risk his employer's money, as he perceives the last dollar of his margin swept away by an unlucky turn of prices; or witness a senile smile of satisfaction momentarily gleam upon the face of the feeble old man who sees himself about to be provided with the means of keeping soul and body together for another day. O, wretched picture of sordid greed, of fallacious hopes, of blank despair! O, sad illustration of the sadder truth that in the contact for the mastery of the heart of man, the evil too often outstrips the good!"[4]

The facility with which a person could "invest" his money in a bucket shop also attracted some members of the Chicago Board of Trade who, if they did not actually patronize a shop, did "bucket" certain orders for their customers. Instead of executing an order in the open pit during market hours, these members

4. Quinn, pp. 597–98.

would either match the orders of customers against each other or take the other side of an order themselves, thereby assuming the "responsibility for the difference between the price of the initial transaction and the price at which the trade would be ordered closed."[5] The similarity between using a bucket shop and bucketing an order lay in the fact that in both instances the transaction was not made on the open market, in the pit where prices were set in response to supply and demand.

The Board opposed the bucket shops for several reasons. One obvious explanation was the economic competition the shops offered. Money misspent in these "dens of inequity" could otherwise be channeled into the market served by the legitimate exchanges. More important was the fact that the bucketing of orders either in the shops or in the offices of legitimate traders and commission men lessened the effectiveness with which the major exchanges were able to register the accurate shifts in commodity prices. Commodity orders were supposed to be executed only on the floor and only during market hours, to concentrate all relevant information concerning supply and demand. Out of this confluence of factors emerged the market price of the commodity. The exchanges could not serve as accurate barometers of market change if numerous grain transactions were carried on after hours or off the floor. But the major objection to the bucket shops went deeper than just competition or abuse of economic function; ultimately it was a matter of self-perception.

The Board of Trade saw itself as an impartial referee, maintaining an open market responsive to the competitive laws of supply and demand. In its view, it preserved and nurtured that free competition so loudly demanded by the critics of "big business." The Board did not consider itself to be a trading firm but rather an association of traders; not a corporation for profit but rather an autonomous group devoted to the administration and perpetuation of an open market profitable to buyer and seller alike; not a gang of bucket shop swindlers and wind-wheat speculators but rather a selective organization demanding and enforcing rigorous standards of market conduct upon its members. Yet the virtual identity of procedures within both the legitimate ex-

5. *Report on the Grain Trade*, 5:330.

change and the bucket shop caused many (especially those who lost money, and they were the vast majority) to equate the shops with the Board of Trade. Public condemnation of the former necessarily included criticism of the latter. Since the similarities between the two institutions were far more obvious than the differences, the carry-over was understandable.

Action against the bucket shops became for the Chicago Board of Trade during the late nineteenth century the ultimate test of the exchange's standing as a private administrative agency clothed with power and public responsibility, because the shops challenged the Board on the one point so vital to sustaining this image. How could the Board of Trade enforce its discipline upon the members and thus indirectly regulate the national market, when many of its regulations and restrictions could be violated with impunity through the bucket shops? Furthermore, how could the exchange claim any legitimate difference between itself and the shops where numerous Board members bucketed orders and gambled on the fluctuation of commodities prices with no intent of delivery?

Thus the Board of Trade faced a dual challenge in seeking to vindicate its legitimacy—block the bucket shops and also effectively penalize Board members for these illicit procedures in their own commodities transactions. Were one separable from the other, the task of the Board might have been much easier. And, indeed, at first the Board behaved as if the two could be separated, dealing with the shops and trying to ignore the problems closer to home. But the two were, in fact, inseparable; and until the Board realized and accepted this conclusion, all its efforts against the shops accomplished very little.

II

The first official mention of the bucket shops in the Chicago Board of Trade records appears on August 3, 1880, when the secretary noted, the "subject of the telegraph companies furnishing information to the bucket shops . . . in regard to the state of the markets on 'Change was discussed but no action taken." A year later the directorate briefly took up the bucket shop prob-

lem again. One of the directors noted the "demoralizing influence" of the shops "throughout the country, and their injurious
effect on the business" of the Board. He observed that the bucket
shops depended upon the telegraph companies for market quotations and urged the Board to take steps to suppress this information. The directors accordingly set up a committee to confer with
the various telegraph companies. The Board apparently was not
too eager to deal with the bucket shops, and not until January
1882 did the newly formed committee report that nothing had
been done "owing to various causes." The directors decided to
postpone any further action until the new slate of directors took
office later that month.

After consulting with the various telegraph companies, the new
directorate decided that after March 10, 1882, telegraph agencies
holding space on the floor of the Board would not be allowed to
furnish the current quotations to any person who wished to post
them publicly in order to make transactions based upon the reports.[6] This resolution had little effect, however, for the bucket
shops not only remained open but expanded and continued to receive the market reports. In November, after again consulting
with officials of the telegraph companies, the directors' committee on bucket shops reported that, even though the companies
seemed willing to cooperate, it was their recommendation that the
directors pass a "peremptory order" that, if the furnishing of
quotations to the bucket shops had not stopped by January 1883,
the commercial reporters for the various telegraph companies
would "not be allowed on the floor of the exchange." The directors voted in favor of the recommended action, in the hope that
it would effectively suppress the bucket shops, which were then
"rapidly becoming an unmitigated evil of great magnitude."[7] The
Board had waited until almost four years after the bucket shops
became popular to do anything about them, and by the time the
Board did act, the shops were well established. If the bucket
shops were as detrimental to the general public as the directors

6. *D.R.*: August 3, 1880, p. 550; July 13, 1881, p. 76; January 10, 1882, p.
174; February 28, 1882, pp. 202–3.
7. Ibid., November 21, 1882, pp. 355–56. "Members of the Board were losing business because parties could do business through the bucket shops at one
eighth cent commission, while the regular Board rate to outsiders was one
quarter cent commission." Ibid., October 24, 1882, p. 313.

stated in their report for 1882, why had they delayed so long before attacking them?[8]

Two possible factors may explain this hesitation. In the first place, as previously mentioned, the similarities between a legitimate exchange and a bucket shop were far more obvious than any differences—in spite of vehement assertions by Board spokesmen to the contrary—and exchange officials were thus understandably reluctant to point out evils of the shops when the same abuses could frequently be attributed to their own institution. Further, it was extremely difficult to oppose the shops when members of the exchange themselves were involved in such practices. Although no accurate figures are available, one study notes that "many members actually engaged in bucketing customers' orders and derived a substantial share of their business volume from such operations."[9] The Federal Trade Commission's exhaustive *Report on the Grain Trade* (1920) stated of this period that "the Board of Trade could not fight the bucket shop to good advantage when its own members were handling part of their trades in the same way."[10]

Late in 1882 the bucket shops responded to the directors' action. Over the next five years, they sought out numerous injunctions against the telegraph companies and the Board of Trade. The relief requested by the plaintiffs in virtually all cases was the same: that the defendants be restrained from "cutting off or detaching the wires from lines of wires or circuits over which general market information from the Chicago Board of Trade has been and is now being transmitted . . . from removing the ticker in said place of business . . . and from cutting off, diverting, withholding or in any way interfering with the supply of market information as it has been heretofore supplied, furnished and transmitted."[11] Counsel for the telegraph companies and the

8. "To say nothing of the injury to legitimate business which these places are inflicting upon the country, the so-called 'bucket-shops' which are numbered by hundreds, have become a stench in the nostrils of all good citizens, who have observed the demoralization wrought among the young and the unfortunate, who are tempted by the allurements of a chance gain to invest their scanty means in this most vicious system of trading." *Report of the Directors, 1882*, p. xxiii.

9. Kendall, p. 59.

10. *Report on the Grain Trade*, 5:330.

11. Copy of a writ of injunction served on November 25, 1885, against the Chicago Board of Trade by the New York and Chicago Grain and Stock Exchange.

Board sought to have the injunctions dissolved, and the cases were heard in both the Circuit Court of Cook County and the Federal District Court between 1883 and 1885.

Counsel for the bucket shops, including such distinguished Illinois lawyers as Lyman Trumbull and Leonard Swett, denied that the shops were primarily gambling establishments.[12] They were merely smaller boards of trade. Admitting that illegal actions could take place in the shops, counsel emphasized that the same illegal actions could also occur on the floor of the Board. Why then should the smaller exchanges be singled out as wrongdoers and the Board of Trade be permitted to monopolize the market reports? No existing law prevented the shops from dealing in grain, and settling by differences did not interfere with legitimate trading in the shops any more than it did on the big Board. Noting correctly that the law presumed contracts made on the exchanges were valid, counsel claimed that such time as the bucket shops were used for illegal purposes would be time enough for the Board to set up that fact at law and prove it.

The bucket shops argued further that the telegraph companies were "quasi-public" corporations with a corresponding public interest. The telegraph companies could not, therefore, discriminate as to whom they would or would not transmit messages. They had to send messages to all who paid for them. Counsel applied similar reasoning to the Board of Trade. The Board maintained a market, a market was a public place, the market price was the price paid at a public sale, and consequently such knowledge belonged to the public. The character of the Board, counsel asserted, was public. All trades had to be open, and Board rules forbade secret trading. Everybody, either as consumer or producer or distributor, had an interest in the transactions conducted on its floor. Yet the Board claimed the right to exclude semi-public corporations (the telegraph companies) from its floor, because the companies were willing, if not required, to circulate market information to all who agreed to pay for it.

The telegraph companies admitted that, in the regular business of transmitting messages, they had "to treat all persons offering to do business with [them] alike, and without discrimination." But, as counsel for Western Union maintained, the commercial news department, which collected and transmitted market

12. *Bench and Bar of Chicago* (Chicago, 1883), pp. 38–40, 546–47.

reports all over the country, had been built up as "an incidental branch of its regular telegraph business." This activity did not constitute the main purpose of the telegraph agency, but was rather a private concern of the company, coming under its sovereign powers as a corporation. Therefore, the telegraph companies had the option to furnish commerical news and receiving instruments or to withhold them from "any person it pleases."[13]

The Board of Trade presented a concise answer to the bucket shops' complaint: the Board of Trade was a private corporation; and, as such, the quotations were its private property. Also, the bucket shops were simply ill-disguised gambling houses and, thus, were contrary to public policy. Therefore, the Board should be encouraged and not restrained in its efforts to restrict the market reports.

The courts were thus placed in the position of having to decide whether to restrain the telegraph companies, the Board of Trade, or both. Not surprisingly, they sometimes came to opposite conclusions. In 1883 Judge Murray Tuley of the Cook County Circuit Court heard arguments seeking the dissolution of an injunction granted the Public Grain and Stock Exchange; and, to the surprise and disappointment of the Board, he refused to dissolve the order.

In his opinion Tuley rejected the Board's contention that the Public Grain and Stock Exchange was a gambling concern: "There is not proof that the complainant is engaged in any other than a legitimate business." He noted that, whereas it was true that bucket shops always "take the deal" or trade, the complainant did this also, but that this is "neither more nor less than every member of the Board does in every case where as a broker he buys or sells on the floor." Moreover, Tuley was unimpressed by the Board's emphasis on the immorality of bucket shop gambling: "The Board of Trade does not profess to be engaged in a moral reform movement. . . . It is competition—not immorality which the Board of Trade is seeking to put down."[14]

Counsel for the Board had argued that the vast number of commercial transactions carried on each day upon the floor made it necessary that gambling outfits like the Public Grain Exchange

13. Public Grain and Stock Exchange v. Western Union and Board of Trade, 1 Ill. Cir. Ct. 548, 550–51 (1883).
14. Ibid., p. 553.

be prevented from misusing the quotations. Tuley agreed that the scope of Board activity was indeed immense: "Millions upon millions of property, consisting principally of . . . the common necessaries of life are affected in value daily and hourly by the transactions had upon the floor of this Board of Trade." Such facts convinced him that the business of the Board was affected with a public interest to such an extent that the legislature—and "the courts in the absence of legislation"—could prevent the Board from discriminating as to who could receive the market reports. It might decide which telegraph companies would be permitted on the floor of the Board to collect and disseminate the reports; but neither the directors nor the telegraph companies could discriminate as to whom the reports were to be sent.[15]

Although Tuley's decision was generally followed by other circuit judges, it was not binding on the federal district court. Indeed, Federal Judge Henry Blodgett, in another bucket shop case, came to very different conclusions. Blodgett dissolved an injunction against the Board that had been obtained by the "Metropolitan Grain and Stock Exchange." He held that the Board of Trade was "a private corporation" which, unlike the telegraph companies, exercised "no franchise which clothes it with any of the duties of a public corporation." The Board represented only "an association of merchants . . . who, solely for their own convenience, provide a room where they meet to transact business." The claim of "public interest" had little relevance for this case. "It is absurd," Blodgett wrote, "to say that information thus obtained for private use becomes public property merely because it is collected and paid for through the agency of a private corporation." Nor were the quotations in themselves public. Members of the Board had every right to go upon the floor and deal with each other privately, under no compulsion to inform the public of the prices at which they bought and sold. "The mere fact that they have been in the habit of informing the public of prices is no evidence that they are obliged to do so if they do not see fit to do it."[16] By basing his decision entirely upon the

15. Ibid., pp. 554–56; Public Grain and Stock Exchange v. Baltimore and Ohio Telegraph Co., 1 Ill. Cir. Ct. 558, 560–61 (1883). See also *New York Times*, May 26, 1883, p. 5.

16. Metropolitan Grain and Stock Exchange v. Board of Trade, 15 Fed. 848, 850–51 (1883).

rights which the Board claimed as a private voluntary organization, Blodgett avoided any discussion of the claim that the bucket
shops were gambling establishments rather than legitimate exchanges. On the other hand, the fact that the Board emphasized
its rights, rather than the major differences between an exchange
and a bucket shop, may indicate that it was not yet able to dissociate its members from bucket shop practices.

The resulting discrepancy between the local and federal opinions left the Board of Trade somewhat confused as to what further action it should undertake. The Board decided to collect the
quotations itself, and it sought to carry a test case concerning its
right to control the quotations to the Illinois Supreme Court. The
case did not come up until 1888, and in the meantime the legal
picture remained uncertain. With one exception the federal courts
seemed unwilling to condemn the bucket shops as illegal.[17] The
Board seemed to have control of its quotations as long as it did
not release them to the telegraph companies for distribution.

Meanwhile, the bucket shops flourished. Besides attacking the
Board through litigation, the shops sought legislation to insure
that they would receive the market quotations, whatever the
courts decided. They circulated large numbers of petitions for
submission to the Illinois legislature in 1883, asking passage of
a law to compel all organizations in the State of Illinois dealing
in grain and provisions to make public all price quotations as
they occurred. Early in April 1883, representatives of both the
Board and the bucket shops appeared before the House committee in charge of the bill. In addition, the House voted to send
a special committee to Chicago to investigate "the methods of
the Chicago Board of Trade, and like organizations, in relation
to the matter of option deals and grain gambling."

Spokesmen for the Board took a patronizing attitude toward
the legislative committee. A former president of the Board,
Charles Culver, testified that the proposed legislation "would interfere greatly with his business." Another former Board president, John Bensley, stated that the committee should not make
the mistake of equating transactions made in the bucket shops or
on the curb with contracts made on the Board; however, he offered little aid to the committee to assist them in avoiding the

17. Bryant v. Western Union Telegraph Co., 17 Fed. 825 (1883).

mistake. While he noted that every Board contract "embodied the obligation that a seller must deliver and a buyer receive the property," he failed to discuss why so few did actually deliver or receive.

Another member to appear before the committee was Abner Wright, soon to become president of the Board. Wright warned that any legislative interference with the trading practices that had evolved through trial and experience would "drive all the trade to New York." In discussing the bucket shops, Wright admitted that "there were excrescences in every branch of trade" and that the shops were "dangerous and demoralizing to a certain extent." But this, he said, was no reason to attack the system as a whole. "He was not there to condemn the bucket shops—had nothing to say about them."

Spokesmen for the Board also hedged on the subject of privileged trading. Culver admitted that it took place but said "it was not as extensive as formerly."[18] In February 1883 the president of the Board had been much more candid; he had then stated to the directors that "there was a statute against trading in puts and calls but it appeared to be a dead letter, and that he, as well as almost every other member of the Board, had done more or less trading in them as it was a matter of protection and convenience very often to do so."[19]

The legislators found the Board representatives inconsistent and confusing. Every Board contract had to be fulfilled, but members did not explain why delivery was the exception rather than the rule. Any legislative interference with the system would drive the commodities market out of the state, but legislation against other exchanges, such as the bucket shops, was all to the good. Finally, the future president of the Board could find "nothing to say" about the bucket shops. If members of the Board could not point to any clearly understandable difference between its purpose and that of the bucket shops, neither could the committee. Its report stated, "The manner of conducting business on the various boards of trade, and in the exchanges or bucket shops, does not materially differ." It followed logically, therefore, "that no line can be drawn between the Board of Trade and the

18. All quotations from the hearings are taken from the *Chicago Tribune*, May 1, 1883, p. 7.
19. *D.R.*, February 27, 1883, p. 432.

bucket shops, because their methods of doing business are substantially the same." The committee concluded that, between the bucket shops and the Board, "one is as legitimate as the other, and the business of one is as honorable as the other."

The report of the legislative committee recommended that all the exchanges be required to keep a record of each transaction and that its identity from inception to close be maintained and open to public inspection. Furthermore, quotations should be free to the public, and the withholding of them "at any time should be severely punished." Finally, all option trades, except where the property "has an actual existence, or is capable of being delivered by the vendor, should be prohibited."[20] The wording of this provision reflected the position taken by the Illinois courts; it did not appear to matter so much if one actually delivered, as long as one could do so and had the intent to deliver at the time of making the contract. The Illinois legislature did not adopt the suggestions made by its committee, but its proposals should be kept in mind as subsequent Board rules and federal legislation are discussed later.

III

The expansion of the bucket shops between 1883 and 1888 forced the Board, albeit unwillingly, into a more militant stand against them. The tendency to equate the Board of Trade with a bucket shop also remained prevalent. In 1883, for example, the *Western Rural* delivered one of many attacks against the bucket shops and then turned on members of the Chicago Board of Trade: "Their business is gambling, too, and they operate upon the same telegraphy reports that the bucket shops do. . . . The principle of gambling is the same in both places and demands the same condemnation and the same treatment by the authorities."[21] Even the *Chicago Tribune*, hardly a radical newspaper, concluded that in attacking the shops the Board simply attempted "to do away with its [economic] rivals."[22]

Before 1882 the Board had no rule to prevent its members

20. Ill., General Assembly, House, *Journal* 33 (1883):817–19.
21. *Western Rural*, February 7, 1883, p. 52.
22. Taylor, p. 661.

from dealing with bucket shops either for themselves or for their customers. The absence of such a rule may help to explain the frequency with which critics of the Board compared it to a bucket shop. The Board began to recognize the inconsistency of its attack on the shops as gambling dens without taking action against its own members who patronized them. Whatever doubts existed at this time about the association's power to restrict its quotations, there was no question of its power to discipline its members. Early in 1883, as the bucket-shop battle went before the courts, the directors drafted a new rule aimed against those Board members who bucket shopped. According to this rule, such conduct was termed "an unmercantile offense," and a member convicted of bucket shopping was "liable to suspension" from the Board "until he shall have given satisfactory evidence that his objectionable connection has been dissolved." For a second offense, "he may be expelled."[23]

If the directors were to go too far ahead of member sentiment, they risked isolation from their constituency, an intolerable condition for an effective regulatory body. Yet Board members did expect their officers to set policies and goals; and, indeed, the directors were the logical group to respond to public criticism levelled against the bucket shops and, increasingly, against the Board of Trade. The strains apparent in reconciling these two tensions are well reflected in the new rule. A member could be suspended for bucket shopping until he proved that he had stopped the "objectionable" practice. He might be expelled for a second offense. The rule, which was at best a tentative first step toward disciplining members who bucket shopped, barely passed with a vote of 281 for and 251 against adoption.[24]

A similar sense of reality may be seen in Board efforts to control privilege trading. Although the Illinois courts had branded dealing in puts and calls illegal, Board members continued to deal in them, largely as a means of insurance. By having an option on whether or not to take or make delivery, a trader gained some protection against the usual sudden speculative shifts of the market. Critics of puts and calls based their opposition partly on the grounds that the practice was illegal, that Board policy should not condone what the law condemned.

23. *D.R.*, January 13, 1883, p. 395.
24. Ibid., January 26, p. 228; January 29, p. 289.

Yet there were also important economic factors. Extensive dealing in puts and calls during the daily market sessions limited the fluctuations in grain prices. But it was the fluidity of the market, the ease with which prices could shift in response to supply and demand, that attracted a speculating public seeking to trade "wherever there is a chance to make large profits in a short space of time." Denied this possibility in a market stabilized through excessive use of privileged trading, these speculators tended to seek other sources of speculative gain, namely the bucket shops. In 1886 a commission merchant wrote in a circular distributed to members of the Board: "Was trade ever so dull in the past as at present? Was trade in puts and calls ever so large as at present? Connect the two in your mind, think it over, and don't complain of dull trade."[25]

The fact that privileged trading continued twelve years after it was made illegal indicated, again, the hesitation with which Board officials sought to regulate the private economic activity of the membership. If they were to push too hard against puts and calls, members would trade elsewhere, the Board would be weakened, and the practice would continue unabated. On the other hand, privileged trading was supposedly unlawful. The practice did have detrimental economic effects, and the directors could not just permit flagrant violations of the law to continue without taking some action. For the time being, their noncommittal attitude toward enforcement of both the law and their own rules insured that privileged trading would remain in a sort of limbo—neither permitted nor prohibited, of doubtful legitimacy and dubious legality. Indeed, the actions of the directors as they tried to deal with cases of privileged trading resembled a sort of discipline waltz: one step forward, one step backward, and sidestep, sidestep, sidestep.[26]

The problem was complicated by the ambiguity with which Board officials themselves regarded privileged trading. In 1888 George Stone, secretary to the Board, admitted that there was no specific rule against puts and calls "any more than there is a rule against theft or any other crime." He acknowledged the existence of the 1874 statute but claimed that "it is no more the duty

25. *Northwestern Miller*, March 12, 1886, p. 252.
26. This slightly altered description is taken from the *Progressive* 32 (1968): 26.

of the directors . . . to investigate rumored transactions of this nature than it is its duty to hunt up the committers of a burglary. But when the evil becomes extensive, it is usually investigated by our officers, and once in a while a transgressor is disciplined." Similar inconsistencies attended the battle against the bucket shops. Board president Abner Wright, although very outspoken in his opposition to the shops, stated in 1887 that his company had placed orders for a bucket shopper: "We never thought it necessary to refuse to fill his orders, and on which he put up margins, because he was said to be in the bucket shop business. We take orders from all parties who make their orders good."[27]

On April 17, 1888, the directors voted to set up a special committee to investigate puts and calls. Such transactions, noted in the resolution (as had so many similar statements during the last ten years), were "in violation of the law, and considered by this Directory derogatory to the good name of the Association."[28] One week later the directors were told that most of the violations were committed by people on the Open Board. By the middle of May the directorate learned that "trading in puts and calls [was] being carried on quite extensively, but the trading was conducted so secretly that, so far, the committee has been unable to obtain any evidence against anyone." Finally, the group voted to set up a secret committee of three to suppress the traffic in privileged trading.[29]

The results of the committee's efforts became known in July, when three Board members—including S. J. Crafts, who had previously been suspended for the same offense—were brought to trial by the directors and were charged with dealing in privileges. Following a pattern of increasingly harsher penalties, the directors suspended Crafts for one year and the other two members for six months each.[30] The severity of the punishment outraged many Board members. One individual threatened to name several directors who supposedly dealt regularly in puts and calls. John Cantner, one of the original three who were suspended, de-

27. *American Elevator and Grain Trade* 7 (1888):9; *D.R.*, October 18, 1887, p. 401; Jonathan Lurie, "The Chicago Board of Trade, the Merchants' Exchange of St. Louis, and the Great Bucket Shop War, 1882–1905," *Bulletin of the Missouri Historical Society* 19 (1973):243–59.

28. *D.R.*, April 17, 1888, pp. 138–39.

29. Ibid., April 24, p. 141; May 5, p. 162.

30. Ibid., July 24, pp. 211–18, 220–24.

manded that the directorate punish all other guilty members, especially big name traders like Old Hutch, or else revoke his suspension.[31]

Benjamin P. Hutchinson, better known as "Old Hutch" was probably the most notorious member of the Board of Trade in the late nineteenth century. He exemplified the ambivalence with which the public regarded speculative ventures, and represented the best example to emulate if one admired the daring risks taken in the market or to avoid if one viewed such activities as destructive gambling and manipulation.[32] Old Hutch manipulated the market with a virtuosity comparable to Paganini's upon the violin. "In a business enterprise he fears no foe, as he recognizes no friend, and his tall spare form looms up as a tower of granite in the midst of the turbulent waves of speculation which surge around him." In 1888, when Hutch suffered a serious injury that caused the wheat market to fall, a newspaper commented, "If wheat declines three cents when Old Hutch tumbled down stairs, what should it do if he fell from a balloon?"[33]

Hutchinson's skill in speculation was matched by his candor in conversation. When his son Charles, who was elected president of the Board in 1888, made a speech to the effect that the Board of Trade was of great benefit to the farmer and was in many ways a great philanthropic institution, Hutch was quick to respond. On the floor of the Board, in the midst of a circle of brokers, he stated, "Did you hear what Charlie said? Charlie said we were philanthropists! Why bless my buttons, we're gamblers! You're a gambler! You're a gambler! and I'm a gambler!"[34]

Throughout his long career, Hutch maintained that his market

31. *New York Times*, July 27, 1888, p. 1.

32. According to an article in the *Chicago Tribune* (September 27, 1891, p. 7), Old Hutch "is unique. He is wonderful." According to the *Western Rural* (October 13, 1888, p. 652), Old Hutch was "a man with whom no self respecting man would exchange places for twenty four hours for all the wealth he possesses. His time is divided pretty evenly between drinking rum and plotting on the Board of Trade. He is . . . pitiably alone in the midst of seven hundred thousand people."

33. A contemporary described Hutchinson as "all legs and nose, with the complexion of a liver sausage, and weighing only one hundred pounds." *American Elevator and Grain Trade* 2 (1883):102; Quinn, p. 606; Edward J. Dies, *The Plunger* (New York, 1929), p. 128.

34. Scrapbook, undated clipping, probably 1888, Charles H. Hutchinson Papers, Newberry Library, Chicago.

ventures were neither unusual nor unethical. "What I have done may likewise be tried by anyone who wishes to risk his fortune. The field is open to all. I have issued no spurious stock certificates, stolen no railroads, joined no gold conspiracy. For a study of such type of 'ethics' I would respectfully invite your attention to the gentlemen of Wall Street."[35] Even in his declining years, "his name still had the ring of magic—Old Hutch, first on the floor and last to leave it."

> In dealing on 'Change whether little or much.
> All wholesomely fear the insatiate Hutch:
> O'er eyes of the sharpest he pulleth the wool,
> 'Mid bulls as a bear, and 'mid bears as a bull.
> How plaintive the tone as crieth each mourner,
> He'll find—thank the Lord—in heaven no corner.[36]

Whether the directors were intimidated in any way by Cantner's demand is not clear. There is no doubt, however, that between July 24 and July 31, 1888, the committee launched an "in depth" investigation into the extent of privileged trading by members of the Board. On July 27 it summoned more than thirty members to testify under oath, and by the end of the day, according to the *New York Times*, the probe was "popularly supposed to have implicated half the members of the Board." As the investigation continued, Board members began to hold impromptu demonstrations. One noisy meeting convened in the lower corridor, the scene of so much illicit trading in the past, and resolved, "It is an insult to the members on the floor that the Board of Directors should hire detectives to follow the members around to ascertain if they have broken any of the rules. . . . We claim to be honorable gentlemen and consider such an action an absolute insult." A Board member who openly admitted his guilt

---

35. Dies, p. 50.

36. Pierce, *History of Chicago*, 3:86–87. Old Hutch had already been involved with Board discipline. In 1887 he was charged with trading outside hours. Typically, he refused to appear before the directors, sending instead a curt note, "I made the trades as stated in your communications." The directors found him guilty, and on the fifth ballot suspended him for ninety days by a 7 to 6 vote. About two weeks later and not at his request, the directors voted to remit the rest of his sentence. He had sought no favors "but had come out manfully and pleaded guilty." Moreover, all during his suspension, he had been busy trading on a rival exchange. *D.R.*, 1887: September 30, pp. 295–98, October 18, pp. 390–91; Taylor, p. 746.

noted that if the directors were to suspend all guilty parties, "there would be no Board left to transact business." The *Times* predicted that "the committee would probably soon haul in its horns, [and] rescind the decree of suspension" against the three members.[37]

The committee drafted its report on July 31 and on August 2 it recommended to the directorate certain changes in the report. Since the Board papers contain the original report and the minutes include the later alterations, the historian can easily see how the committee did indeed "haul in its horns." The committee examined over eighty members of the Board, an action unprecedented in its history. In its report the committee urged that the Board suspend for one week those who had acknowledged their guilt, and it suggested that Cantner's suspension be reduced to a week as well. The report proposed that "any member of the Board . . . who hereafter may be found guilty of trading in privileges, in violation of the law of the state and the rules of the Board, be expelled from this association." In conclusion, the committee promised to submit, at the next directory meeting, a report dealing with the directors who were involved in puts and calls.[38]

The directors met two days later, but no mention of the promised second report has been found. The committee asked the directors to substitute for suspension censure by the president. The committee vitiated its resolution by inserting in two places the word "should," so that for privileged trades a member "should be expelled" and for irregular trades "should be suspended for not less than sixty days." Finally the committee asked, and the directors so voted, that the suspension of the three members be lifted completely. About thirty members were duly censured by the president, but no mention of the censure appeared in the official minutes.[39] The *New York Times* described the members summoned before the directors "huddled in an outer room while the tribunal put the finishing touches on its mind. . . . Finally the door of the inner room opened and the herd of of goats was induced to go in. Quite a number of the sheep stood around enjoying the situation. . . . President Hutchinson occupied

37. *New York Times*, July 28, 1888, p. 1.
38. *D.P.*, July 31, 1888.
39. *D.R.*, August 2, 1888, pp. 231–32.

an exalted position and wore a very solemn look. The other directors sat around and were equally determined not to smile if they could help it."[40] The privilege probe had not exactly been impressive.

Thus the membership successfully forced the directors to back down; but such action represented the exception and not the rule. In the first place, Board members had dealt in privileges since the Civil War era. At no time had the directors specifically forbidden the practice. On the contrary, through the vague wording of its numerous resolutions, the directorate had tacitly tolerated, if not allowed, puts and calls. Moreover, privilege trading was a practice common to the trade and was permitted on other exchanges, such as the Milwaukee Chamber of Commerce and the New York Produce Exchange. Indeed, it was not completely clear that privilege trading was illegal in Illinois, as the 1874 statute had not yet been challenged in the courts.[41]

Given these facts, to single out a few members for heavy penalties while leaving other equally guilty members untouched seemed inconsistent and unwarranted. Many members, such as William Baker, who personally opposed dealing in puts and calls, found the directors' use of private detectives and their detailed "probe" objectionable. In achieving effective regulations against bucket shops, as well as privileged trading, it was obvious that both a clear-cut rule against the practices and a marked consistency in enforcing that rule over a period of several years were essential.[42] If this is kept in mind, one can better understand why the Board ultimately succeeded against the bucket shops but failed in its attempts to eliminate privileged trading.

IV

There were few developments in the battle between the bucket shops and the Board of Trade in the years 1884–87. Where pos-

40. *New York Times*, August 3, 1888, p. 1.
41. Indeed, it was not challenged until 1900, when the Illinois Supreme Court unanimously affirmed the statute. See Booth v. People, 186 Ill. 143 (1900), affirmed again in Booth v. Illinois, 184 U.S. 425 (1902).
42. The difficulty faced by the Board in deciding whether to adopt a formal rule rather than an informal standard is not untypical of modern administrative agencies. See W. Gellhorn and C. Byse, pp. 18–43; W. Gellhorn, pp. 121–33.

sible, the Board tried to prevent market quotations from reaching the shops; but with injunctions against the Board still pending, the directors could do little. By 1884, however, the Board had awakened to the threat posed by these establishments. The directors' annual report published early in 1885 emphasized the "imperative need" for the Board not to "permit these [market] messages to be used by any person solely for gambling purposes." In justice to itself, "this Board should not take one backward step in the contest forced upon it in this matter."[43] During the annual Board election campaign of 1885, the presidential ticket calling for rigorous action against the shops was unopposed, and the newly elected vice president introduced himself to the Board members as the "unswerving foe of the gigantic gambling evils, with the stench of whose moral corruption the air reeks."[44]

The Board's hostility toward the shops surfaced as several state legislatures enacted measures against them. In 1884 Iowa passed a strong anti-bucket-shop statute. Ohio adopted a similar law the next year, and in 1887 the Missouri legislature, as well as the Illinois General Assembly, passed an act to "prevent, punish and prohibit" the establishment of bucket shops and the practice of bucket shopping. Both the keeping and patronizing of an establishment wherein was conducted the pretended buying or selling of commodities without the intent of delivery or receipt were prohibited. The bill, which had the enthusiastic support of the Chicago Board of Trade, went through the Senate with no recorded debate or change; it passed unanimously on April 29, 1887. Early in June it cleared the House by a vote of 103 to 12, again, without amendments.[45]

Encouraged by the enactment of a supposedly stringent anti-bucket-shop statute and believing that the courts would vindicate their right to control the market quotations, the directors confidently prepared to cut off distribution of the reports except to "approved" correspondents or customers. In August 1887 they voted that the market quotations collected by the Board's department of market reports "shall be considered and treated as portions of the official records of the Association and . . . may be disseminated in such manner and under such conditions and re-

43. *Report of the Directors, 1884*, p. xxxiii.
44. Taylor, p. 709.
45. *Ill. Ann. Stat., Supplement, 1885–92*, pp. 360–62 (Smith-Hurd).

strictions as may be prescribed by the Board. . . ."[46] The resolution was based upon the Board's assumption that it could control the distribution of the prices. Indeed, early in 1887, the directors had noted that a bucket-shop test case was set for appeal. "On the issue of this case (and it does not seem to be involved in much doubt) will depend all other cases of a similar character. Hence the Board may reasonably expect ere long to be able to exercise wholesome supervision over the distribution of its own market reports."[47]

The long awaited test case, *New York and Chicago Grain and Stock Exchange v. Chicago Board of Trade*, was decided by the Illinois Appellate Court in July 1888. The opinion upheld a trial verdict favorable to the Board. It echoed in all essentials the earlier federal court decision handed down by Judge Blodgett in 1883. Mr. Justice Garnett held that the Board had been and remained a private corporation. True, he stated, the organization had grown in public importance since 1848; but such growth "does not change its character," and "its charter does not impose upon it any duty of a public nature, nor has it assumed any." Moreover, he did not believe that nonmembers of the Board had any automatic right to receive the market reports. Accessibility to the quotations was one of the privileges of membership; and if the directors chose to be selective in distributing the prices, such action was clearly within the power granted them under the charter.[48] As Judges Tuley and Blodgett had done previously, Justice Garnett avoided any finding of wrongdoing on the part of the exchange. Again, therefore, the Chicago Board of Trade avoided the difficult issue of establishing whether or not the smaller exchanges were in reality bucket shops. The primary concern of both parties to the suit was with getting the issue before the Illinois Supreme Court. The Exchange appealed immediately, briefs were submitted by October, and the court handed down its decision in January 1889.

In presenting the case for the New York and Chicago Grain and Stock Exchange, counsel emphasized that the Board quotations had become a matter of public interest. Even if they were

46. *D.R.*, August 16, 1887, pp. 277–78; Taylor, p. 744.
47. *Report of the Directors, 1886*, pp. xl–xli.
48. New York and Chicago Grain and Stock Exchange v. Chicago Board of Trade, 27 Ill. App. 93, 101–2 (1888).

not originally a source of public concern, counsel argued, the manner in which the Board used them and their great importance to the national markets made them so. That the Board claimed to be a private association was irrelevant; the use to which the alleged private property was put rendered it of a public nature. Had the Board so conducted its business over the years that by discriminating it could "enforce a monopoly to the injury of the public?" counsel asked, and then concluded, "No matter what the nature of their corporation may be; no matter what the nature of their business, it comes back to this question of public interest."

Somewhere in the arrangements made between the telegraph companies and the Board for distribution of the reports, counsel for the Exchange sensed collusion. "It was and is always a question of monopoly," he argued. "Monopolies have always been abhorred by the law. . . . Wherever a monopoly would be injurious to the public interest there is found a case where property or franchise has become affected with a public interest." Counsel also rejected the argument that the legitimate needs of the public were served in that producer and consumer were brought face to face through the person of a broker who had access to all important market information: "It is the very essence of monopoly and vicious discrimination to compel producers and consumers to seek a market through certain individuals."[49]

For the Board of Trade, the issue was very simple: Did this private mercantile association have the power to control its private dispatches relating to the private business of its members? There was no doubt that the Board had power to make rules for the management of its business. The Illinois court had repeatedly upheld such authority in broad terms. The rule under which the Board sought to control its quotations had the same basic legality as the other rules adopted by the organization. As to the "sly, devilishly sly" insinuations of monopoly and insidious agreement between the Board and the telegraph companies—such claim, according to Board attorney Sidney Smith, was "simply a new phase of agrarianism." Anarchy, he explained, "in its modern phase is agrarianism reinforced by violence." In this case, the appellants sought to substitute for violence the judgment of a

49. 127 Ill. 153 (1889); *Argument and Brief for Appellant*, Clerk's Office, Ill. S. Ct. (Springfield), pp. 1–44. See, in particular, pp. 22 and 34.

court of law. "There would be little difference to the Board of Trade and its members whether they be deprived of vested rights and property interests by the violence of the anarchist, or the stroke of the judicial pen."[50]

In arguing the Board's case before the court that had decided the original *Munn* case, Sidney Smith erred in glibly dismissing fears of monopoly as a "phase of agrarianism." Indeed, the lawyers for the bucket shops were shrewd in selecting monopoly as a key component in their case. Smith would have done better to ponder the words of a Chicago judge who in 1887 had enjoined the Board from cutting off quotations to an alleged bucket shop:

> It is no answer that a man has a right to use his own property as pleases him. . . . Never has there been a time when this claim of immunity to private enterprise has been so speciously and persistently urged; gas trusts, oil trusts, coal trusts and trusts of all kinds, large and small representing a mobilization of capital to control prices on the one hand, and labor unions, trade unions, and associations to fix the price of labor on the other. Yet these new and alarming products of the age . . . all claim to be private enterprises and for the benefit of their members, and hence above law and regulation. It is no true answer. The pulse of trade must be allowed to beat full and free, and it cannot be permitted that an aggregation of private enterprise . . . should stop the flow of the rich warm current that brings health and prosperity to the body of the people.[51]

Speaking for a unanimous court, Mr. Justice Baker rejected Smith's argument and held that the doctrine laid down in *Munn v. Illinois* controlled this case. It did not matter that the quotations were the property of the Board: "If they have been used by the Board, and by the telegraph companies with the knowledge and consent of the Board, as to become affected with a public interest, then they are subject to such public regulation by the legislature and the courts as is necessary to prevent injury to such public interest." Nor did the Board's standing as a private corporation make any difference. "If the interest is public, then it is necessarily, to all alike, common to all, and upon equal terms."

50. *Brief for Appellee*, Clerk's Office, Ill. S. Ct. (Springfield), pp. 1–18. See, in particular, pp. 17–18.
51. Murphy v. Board of Trade, 20 *Chi. Legal News* 7 (1887). For laudatory comment on the decision, see *Nation* 45 (1887):323.

Smith had claimed that the daily appearance of the market reports in the press was sufficient for the public interest and that, in fact, the quotations were of little value except to Board members. The Court summarily rejected this argument; if the reports were of so little importance, why was the Board so anxious to restrict their distribution? "The persistent efforts of the Board of Trade itself to control these market reports are an indication of their estimate of their value."[52]

The Board was shocked at the decision and immediately sought a rehearing. On March 20, 1889, the Illinois Supreme Court denied its request. At the same time, however, it added one long sentence to its opinion: "We do not wish to be understood as holding that the Board . . . is bound, by law, to continue . . . collecting and furnishing to the public, market quotations, or that it may not voluntarily abandon such business; but we hold that so long as it continues to carry it on, either directly or indirectly, it must do so without unjust discrimination as to persons, and must furnish market quotations to all who may desire to obtain them for lawful purposes, and upon the same terms."[53]

Faced with an apparently unmodified opinion, the Board's directors voted that after May 31, 1889, no quotations would be distributed at all except to Board members. In seeking judicial approval for this step, the association argued that such action was surely within its powers over the membership. However, the Circuit Court in Chicago declined to modify injunctions still in effect against the Board, preventing it from interfering in any way with the flow of quotations. The judges reasoned that as the Illinois Supreme Court had forbidden discrimination in distributing the reports, and as it was not an easy thing to become a member of the Board, to allow the Board to send out the reports only to members would "indirectly, if not directly, unjustly dis-

52. 127 Ill. 164–65 (1889).
53. In support of his petition for rehearing, Smith cited a New York case that had just been decided: Wilson v. Commercial Telegram Co., 3 N.Y. Supp. 633 (1889). The case raised very similar issues, and Smith urged two points in the opinion upon the Illinois court: (1) its analysis of the New York Stock Exchange, and (2) its interpretation of Munn v. Illinois. See pp. 636–40. For another decision on the same subject and one critical of the Illinois Supreme Court's holding in 1889, see Matter of Renville, 46 N.Y. App. 37 (1899). See, in particular, pp. 44–46.

criminate as to persons, which is just what the Supreme Court says shall not be done."[54] One of the judges called the Board's theory a "sophism" and emphasized "it is not membership in the exchange that the court interferes with, but in a monopoly which is sought to be created."[55] The *Tribune* applauded the decision and concluded that, when the Board attempted "to shut out the public from knowledge of the proceedings, as well as from participation in them," it sought "to establish a monopoly more dangerous than has yet been achieved by any of the so called trusts."[56]

The directors next sought to discontinue the immediate and continuous transmission of the reports, to send instead, every fifteen minutes, a summary of prices that would be available on equal terms to all who desired it for lawful purposes. But the Circuit Court denied this request as well. At this point, as Taylor put it, "the Board acknowledged itself completely beaten and the Directors said they could see no way except to furnish quotations to all." On July 16, 1889, the directorate voted to send the reports to all seekers, at the same time claiming the right to control the reports.[57] The Board's attorney, the *Daily Business* noted, "has been very unfortunate in his conduct of the bucket shop litigation up to the present time."[58]

Even as the Board wrestled with the 1889 holding, the Illinois Supreme Court dealt another blow. As part of its campaign against the bucket shops, the Board had enthusiastically supported an anti-bucket-shop statute. In 1890 the court unanimously affirmed the new law, but in a case that dealt not with the bucket shops but with the branch manager of a prominent Board member![59] The Chicago Board of Trade, as the *Tribune* put it, stood with "both its eyes blackened, or rather it may be said that

54. Owen v. Board of Trade, cited in *Bradstreet's* 17 (1889):44. As early as May 25, 1889, *Bradstreet's* noted that the Board's plan to distribute the quotations only to members "seems to be very questionable indeed." Ibid., May 25, 1889, p. 325.

55. *Chicago InterOcean*, July 6, 1889, p. 5.

56. *Chicago Tribune*, July 6, 1889, p. 4.

57. *D.R.*, 1889: May 7, p. 130, May 14, p. 135, July 9, pp. 173–74, July 5, pp. 169–72, July 12, p. 179, July 16, p. 183; *D.P.*, July 16, 1889; Taylor, p. 787.

58. Quoted in *Northwestern Miller*, May 31, 1889, p. 683. The year 1889 was Sidney Smith's last as counsel for the Chicago Board of Trade.

59. Soby v. People, 134 Ill. 66 (1890). See also Weare Commission Co. v. People, 111 Ill. App. 116 (1903), affirmed in 209 Ill. 528 (1904).

one is badly bruised in the fight with the bucket shops and the other is closed by order of the courts." Perhaps unaware of the irony in what it reported, the paper noted that as a result of the first court decision the bucket shops flourished.[60]

The largest bucket-shop operator, who obtained the quotations because of an injunction issued against the Board, promptly proceeded to dole them out to other shops, maintaining a virtual monopoly and receiving extensive profits as he did so.[61] Indeed, on June 18, 1889, this bucket-shop operator, James A. Murphy, wrote to the Merchants' Exchange of St. Louis and offered to provide it with the Chicago quotations! All the Exchange had to do, in addition to paying a monthly fee, was to "see to it that . . . we could do business with our St. Louis correspondents without the public being any the wiser for it." The writer assured the Exchange secretary, George Morgan, "we would be only too glad to accommodate your Board."[62]

Judges do not always explain why they decide a case one way and not another. In the *New York and Chicago Grain and Stock Exchange* case, where the court had an opportunity to amplify its findings, it merely added the sentence noted above, a clause that did not appear to alter the thrust of the decision. However, a look at the court's findings as a statement of policy within the context of the late nineteenth century makes clear why the court acted as it did. During this period the growth and magnitude of the Board's market were well known. The impressive statistics of grain exports and sales were available for all to see. Newspapers took note each time the Board's annual report appeared, complete with statistics and tables. By 1885, when the new Board building was dedicated, every speaker at the event could pay tribute to the influence exerted by the Chicago Board of Trade, as indeed spokesmen for the Board frequently did. Typical of the florid oratory at the dedication were the exhortations of John Bensley, a former president of the Board: Let the Board of Trade "guard with jealous care against every assault upon its integrity, whether it come from within or without. Let it scourge from these floors as with a whip of scorpions all fraud, all extortion,

60. *Chicago Tribune*, January 28, 1889, p. 4.
61. Ibid., September 7, p. 1.
62. James A. Murphy to George Morgan, June 18, 1889, Merchants' Exchange Collection, Missouri Historical Society, St. Louis.

and all that maketh a lie. Let this temple of commerce be a temple of justice."[63] (Bensley later went into bankrupty as a result of an unfortunate corner in grain.) Thus, when Mr. Justice Baker, in observing the power of the Board, stated that its business was "so vast in its proportions" that it "seriously affects, and to considerable extent controls, the values of the necessaries of life throughout the United States and the civilized world," he was merely taking judicial notice of what was probably a simple fact.[64]

By 1889 the problems of units of power and monopolies were much discussed; indeed, they formed the spawning grounds of the Progressive Era. The great debate on how to deal with them should not obscure the virtual agreement that they constituted a challenge that public policy had to confront.[65] Power to discipline the membership of a private association was one thing, but possession of the means to control market quotations that were quite literally the bread and butter of commodity transactions throughout the country was quite another. It was a serious matter, the *Chicago Tribune* noted, when a group of men "arrogate to themselves the right to determine the prices which the consuming world shall pay for its food and [what] the smaller world of producers shall receive for it, without permitting both to know what it is doing."[66] Clearly, the specter of monopoly hung over the decision.

During the past thirty years, the Illinois Supreme Court had upheld the Board of Trade in virtually every case to which it had been a direct party. The court was aware of this obvious trend, because Smith had cited the various cases in his brief. In reality the Board had sought from the court legitimation for a greater exercise of power. It desired legal sanction for a monopoly, albeit one that from the Board's point of view was in accord with its rights as a private association. By its refusal, the court indicated that perhaps the Board had not sufficiently justified its right to the power it claimed to possess. The *Chicago Tribune* argued

63. Chicago Board of Trade, *Dedication Ceremonies* (1885), p. 15.
64. 127 Ill. 157, 161 (1889).
65. Hans B. Thorelli, *Federal Antitrust Policy* (Baltimore, 1954), pp. 54–232. Within one year of the Illinois Supreme Court's decision against the Board. Congress enacted the Sherman Anti-Trust Act.
66. *Chicago Tribune*, May 30, 1889, p. 4.

The Chicago Board of Trade Building. A. T. Andreas, *History of Chicago*, vol. 2 (Chicago, 1884). Courtesy Historical Pictures Service, Inc., Chicago.

that the Board had "partly invited" the unfavorable decision, because it had "winked at gambling" within the organization.[67]

It should be noted that the court refused to say the Board could not control distribution of its quotations. Its opinion left two very important loopholes. The Board was required (1) to distribute the prices without "unjust" discrimination (2) to all who sought them for "lawful" purposes. True, the burden of proof would be upon the Board to demonstrate that bucket shops were using the market reports for unlawful ends; but, clearly, the judges left the door open for future change.

Indeed, the direction change would take in the future was fairly clear. The organization had not yet effectively dissociated itself from the bucket shops, and neither had its ventures in internal discipline been remarkably successful. With an arrogance that was unfortunate, the Board had argued that it could control the quotations solely because they were private property belonging to a private corporation. Certainly the right to restrict the reports was compatible with effective internal regulation. But control over price distribution indirectly regulated the external market as well. The court realized this, whereas the Board, it seems, did not. Had the Chicago Board of Trade presented itself to the court as a quasi-public administrative institution clothed with regulatory responsibilities that made it incumbent upon the organization to restrict the quotations, the judges might have been more sympathetic. But in 1889 the Board had not yet come to this conception of itself.

67. Ibid., January 28, p. 4.

CHAPTER FIVE

Commodities Exchanges, Agrarian Political Power, and the Battle for Federal Antioption Legislation, 1890–94

THE TOTALLY UNEXPECTED DECISION handed down in 1889 in the *New York Stock Exchange v. Chicago Board of Trade* case was not the only source of external pressure for change within the Board.[1] A more dangerous source, from the organization's point of view, was the threat of regulation of the commodities market posed by the federal government. Even as the Board's directors tried to solve the problem of quotations distribution in accordance with the above decision, such a possibility seemed disturbingly real.

By 1890 currents of discontent were noticeable in many segments of American society. Much of the discontent stemmed from economic hardships, especially among the laboring and agrarian sectors. As currency shrank, creditors expanded, thus furnishing grievances to "debtors in all walks of life." Industrial unrest was rampant, and the year 1890 saw more strikes than any previous year in the country's history.[2]

The early 1890s also represented, according to conventional American historiography, the period in which agrarianism reached its peak as an effective political force. Whether one

1. This chapter is based in part upon two articles by this author previously published in *Agricultural History*: "Speculation, Risk and Profits: The Ambivalent Agrarian in the Late Nineteenth Century," 46 (1972):169–78; and "Commodities Exchanges, Agrarian 'Political Power,' and the Anti Option Battle, 1890–1894," 48 (1974):115–25.

2. J. Rogers Hollingsworth, *The Whirligig of Politics* (Chicago, 1963), pp. 3–4.

claims, as does Norman Pollock, that "Populism was a progressive social force . . . , a glorious chapter in the eternal struggle for human rights," or concludes, as did Richard Hofstadter, that "the utopia of the Populists was in the past, not the future," historians have accepted the argument that farmer discontent was an important political factor on the American scene.[3] Thus Grant McConnell states, "Agrarianism spoke in the name of all. The enemy which it challenged was power."[4] Perhaps the most extreme assessment of agrarian influence is that of William A. Williams, who writes that the farmers' demand for a free marketplace, profit, and expansion "provided the dynamic causal force for a steady movement by the [agricultural] majority towards an imperial foreign policy."[5]

Agrarianism itself revealed two related themes that constantly appeared in both the national and agrarian press. One was the idea of farmer power. Time after time both the farmers and the nation as a whole were reminded that the agrarians inherently represented a political power to be respected. At the same time, however, and with no awareness of internal inconsistency, the agrarian press frequently asserted that the farmers were continually being victimized and manipulated by outside forces alien to their way of life.[6] Speculators, bankers, unscrupulous middlemen, and commission merchants who dealt in inflated stocks of nonexistent grains supposedly preyed upon innocent and trusting farmers. Furthermore, the agrarians found themselves unable to understand, let alone control, a vast marketing machinery—of warehouses, railroads, Wall Street and boards of trade—that made their yeoman independence an empty phrase. To them it appeared that the increasing costs and falling prices resulted from the government's increasingly conservative monetary policy. Eastern capitalists, who produced nothing of their own, supposedly milked the farmers of the benefits of their many hours of toil.

3. Norman Pollack, *The Populist Response to Industrial America* (New York, 1962), p. 143; Richard Hofstadter, *The Age of Reform* (New York, 1955), p. 62.
4. Grant McConnell, *The Decline of Agrarian Democracy* (New York, 1953), p. 1.
5. William A. Williams, *The Roots of the Modern American Empire* (New York, 1969), p. 450.
6. Earl W. Hayter, *The Troubled Farmer* (DeKalb, 1968), passim.

Yet, when the historian examines the 1890s for concrete results of agrarianism, especially on the national political level, one is confronted with a serious problem that challenges the traditional viewpoint of agrarian political power: which, precisely, of the measures sought by the agrarians between 1890 and 1896, the height of the farmer-protest movement, were enacted? The *Chicago Tribune,* in March 1890, stated candidly, "The farmers have the call in this Congress," and later listed the following "farmer demands" made upon the Fifty-second Congress: a subtreasury proposal, the free coinage of silver, an antioption statute, the regulation of futures trading, and the direct election of United States senators.[7]

Only the senatorial proposal ever became law, but not until about twenty-five years later; and the wide spectrum of support this proposal attracted reached far beyond the agrarian sector. Of the remaining "farmer demands," an antioption statute passed both the House and Senate by 1893. Its enactment represented a sentiment that was enthusiastically supported by the agrarian movement and that appeared to reflect the traditional antagonistic elements: producer against processor, farmer against speculator, and rural values against urban mercantile cunning.

An analysis of how the opposing sides in the antioption battle—the agrarians and the major commodities exchanges—saw both the issue and each other casts some light upon the agrarian perception of market realities. It also indicates that agrarian political power—for all the space and attention given to it in the contemporary press—may have been more a myth than a reality. Most important, such a discussion helps explain why the exchanges were able to maintain their functions as private administrative organizations, even when confronted with the threat of federal regulation.

I

As has been noted in earlier chapters, by the 1890s the various components of the grain trade had coalesced into a complex

7. Williams, pp. 333, 507 (n. 78); *Chicago Tribune,* November 13, 1890, p. 5.

market mechanism. Impressive in scope, American grain distribution procedures attracted much attention from foreign observers.[8] One scholar goes so far as to claim that "east of the Rockies the business of assembling, handling, financing, and transporting grain was vastly superior to that of any other nation."[9] Those who endorsed the system saw it as efficient, well integrated, and advantageous to all parties involved—producer, manufacturer, distributor, and purchaser.

That considerable benefits accrued to farmers from the grain marketing machinery cannot be doubted. Yet there were serious disadvantages as well. The methods for settling futures contracts lent themselves as well to speculative gambling as to legitimate trade, and the major exchanges had to contend with the bucket shops. The bucket shops, perhaps an inevitable result of a speculative age, attracted capital away from the legitimate exchanges, tended to lower prices, and were held by agrarians to be a prime cause of their economic dislocation.

Although the farmers objected loudly to bucket shopping, they appreciated the availability of futures markets.[10] Thus the farmers tended to plant more, thereby contributing to the already serious problem of surplus. Furthermore, although the marketing system was efficient, it was at the same time impersonal and distant. It deprived the agrarians of the economic independence that supposedly had been so much a part of their past. Unable to plant less, unwilling to diversify crops, the farmers found that their long-held values and beliefs had increasingly less basis in reality; but they clung to such old ideas as, for example, that the yeoman farmer was the backbone of the country. A song from a collection of *Grange Melodies* published in 1891 asserted:

> There are speculators all about, you know.
> Who are sure to help each other roll the ball,
> As the people they can fleece, and then take so much apiece,
> While the farmer is the man that feeds them all.[11]

8. Morton Rothstein, "America in the International Rivalry for the British Wheat Market, 1860–1914," *Mississippi Valley Historical Review* 47 (1960): 410–18.

9. Ibid., pp. 410–12.

10. See supra, ch. 2, n. 8.

11. James L. Orr, ed., *Grange Melodies* (Philadelphia, 1891), p. 193.

Even as they extolled what they had been in the past, the agrarians could not fail to be affected and infected by the atmosphere of commercial risk, profit, and expansion so typical of the late nineteenth century.[12] Indeed, the economic gains they saw all around them made the agrarians' lot seem all the more unfortunate. Agrarian distress, as Wayne Morgan has well noted, "rested on material self interest."[13] Farmers argued that the prevailing economic dislocation was caused by the "selfish policies of Wall Street bankers."[14] Furthermore, they claimed the commodities exchanges were in reality gambling dens, where clever speculators manipulated nonexistent supplies of grain and thereby distorted prices, causing greater agrarian hardship. By 1892 thousands of petitions calling for some sort of law prohibiting speculative gambling in grain had been presented to Congress.[15]

In seeking to regulate futures trading, the agrarians lacked a detailed knowledge of the operations of the market. It was easy to point out the results of speculative abuses, but it was not quite so easy to correct the problem without losing the acknowledged advantages of the system as a whole. Without a clear awareness of the difference between speculation and gambling, they chose to focus upon what they called "antioption." In so doing, they ignored a fundamental difference between futures and options long recognized both in the courts and on the exchanges. Futures trading as practiced on the legitimate exchanges meant an explicit agreement to buy or sell a stated amount of a commodity for delivery and/or payment at a definite time in the future. Option trading, on the other hand, implied a choice or option whether or not one would make or take delivery, depending upon the state of the market.

Option trading had been illegal in Illinois since 1874, and by the 1890s virtually all major exchanges had joined the Chicago Board of Trade in declaring the practice against exchange rules. Yet the numerous antioption measures introduced into Congress between 1890 and 1894 lumped futures and options to-

12. See infra, sec. 3.
13. H. Wayne Morgan, *From Hayes to McKinley* (Syracuse, 1969), p. 384.
14. Hollingsworth, pp. 4–5.
15. Margaret Mary Wilson, "The Attack on Options and Futures, 1888–1894" (Master's thesis, University of Kansas, 1932), pp. 32–33.

gether as one and the same, and placed heavy taxes on dealers therein, including persons, associations, and corporations. Thus the Butterworth bill of 1890 stipulated that a dealer was to pay $1,000 a year for the privilege of trading in futures and options, plus five cents per pound of cotton and twenty cents per bushel of grain for every pound and bushel bought or sold.[16] The Hatch bill of 1892 required every dealer in options and futures to pay the sum of $2,000 annually, plus twenty cents for each bushel of grain dealt in by the dealers.[17] Different fees were included for other agricultural products. In 1892 the Chicago Board of Trade had about 1,900 members, of whom at least three-fourths, and probably more, dealt in futures trading. At the barest minimum, just to trade at all, Hatch's bill would have cost these members close to $2.5 million.

To judge from a sampling of the contemporary press opinion about antioption legislation, the political influence of the organized agrarians was awesome. Senator John Carlisle stated, according to the *New York Herald*, that "no one outside of political life understood the pressure of the Farmers' Alliance, and that many senators could not withstand this pressure."[18] The *Philadelphia Ledger* claimed that an antioption law would probably be vetoed, but added "certainly that would be its fate in any other year than a presidential one."[19] The *Chicago Tribune* repeatedly noted the existence of agrarian political power. In April 1890 it predicted (wrong) that the Butterworth bill would pass the House because a majority would "vote for it in response to a demand by numerous 'alliances' of farmers . . . and kindred organizations [which] form a constituency too numerous to be ignored."[20] Two years later, the paper concluded that the Hatch antioption bill would go through "in response to the demands made by the farming element through the country at large."[21]

In their public statements about the proposed legislation, exchange spokesmen expressed similar opinions. The secretary of the Toledo Produce Exchange admitted: "The average member

16. U.S., Congress, House: 51st Cong., 1st sess., 1890, H.R. 1321, pp. 1–4.
17. Id.: 52d Cong., 1st sess., 1892, H.R. 2699, pp. 1–12.
18. *Bradstreet's*, June 25, 1892, p. 405.
19. Ibid., p. 404.
20. *Chicago Tribune*, April 24, 1890, p. 4.
21. Ibid., June 29, 1892, p. 9.

of Congress believed in the necessity of some such legislation. And why? Because the leaders of the Farmers' Alliances throughout this country have busied themselves for years in propagating the sentiment that the work of the exchanges was all against the farmers' interest."[22] Murry Nelson, who testified on behalf of the Chicago Board of Trade in opposition to the Butterworth bill, asserted, "The bill was framed because the Farmers' Alliance asked for it."[23]

Historians should always be aware of a possible gap between the rhetoric concerning a given issue and the reality they seek to explain, especially when, as in the examples just cited, the rhetoric comes from newspaper accounts. However, an examination of various manuscript sources that were not intended for publication indicates that Board of Trade members said the same things in private as they said in public about antioption legislation. Thus Henry Aldrich, who represented the Board during the legislative hearings in 1892, wrote privately to the president of the Board that some member ought to talk with those Congressmen on the House Agricultural Committee "as may not wear an Alliance collar."[24] The following day, Aldrich added, "There was and is, no earthly use in talking to the committee as a whole."[25] Two days later he reported that a spokesman for the New Orleans Cotton Exchange had made an able presentation against the bill and that "with any but a farmers committee, [it] would have much weight."[26] He predicted correctly "a unanimous report from the committee"; and even though there would be some strong opposition in the House "with so large a majority in favor of the bill . . . , it will only delay the matter a short time."[27]

Opponents of antioption saw the agrarians as not only large in numbers but politically organized as well. Senator William F. Vilas of Wisconsin, who opposed the measure, admitted during a secret strategy session at the Chicago Board of Trade: "There is quite a large majority of the Senate that are very timid about the thing, but their fears now are chiefly excited with reference

22. *Bradstreet's*, February 27, 1892, p. 130.
23. *Chicago Tribune*, April 16, 1890, p. 3.
24. Aldrich to Charles D. Hamill, February 5, 1892, *D.P.*
25. Ibid., February 6, 1892.
26. Ibid., February 8, 1892.
27. Ibid., February 9, 1892.

to their support at home. They are afraid, and there are a great
many men . . . who are scared to death when we talk about
farmers." But Vilas concluded that the troublemakers were not
farmers in general but, rather, what he called "political farmers,"
"presidents of Alliances, and all sorts of agricultural organizations, or some men who are continually making political head-
way for themselves."[28]

Although the agrarians pointed to their own strength, not surprisingly they placed great emphasis on the opposition to antioption. The *National Economist* warned that "very influential
opposition to this proposed legislation exists." The friends of the
bill should not be "resting upon the merits of the measure,"
while "its enemies are active."[29] The manager of the Milton
George Publishing House informed Senator Vilas, "The country
is practically a unit in favor of antioption legislation." But
opponents of the bill were hard at work, through capital "being
invested in national banks, daily papers and financial institutions
of various kinds. Compact in organization, sagacious and shrewd
to a rare degree, a comparatively few men in number," the pub-
lisher wrote Vilas, "they bring an immense influence to bear."[30]

The basic justification given for an antioption measure by its
proponents was just that—*antioption,* the desire to forbid the
buying and selling of grain that supposedly did not exist. Supporters of the bill alleged that this short selling manipulated the
market, distorted values, and drastically lowered prices. Indeed,
an extensive survey of the antioption petitions filed in the National Archives indicates that short selling was what disturbed
the petitioners most.[31] One printed form asked that heavy taxes
be levied upon "those who, by selling their promises to deliver
any manufactured or natural produce of American farms, seriously depress values. . . ." A different form asked Congress to
"prohibit boards of trade, bucket shops and other mercantile
bodies and individuals from fixing the value on raw or manufactured produce of American farms by sales or promises of
future deliveries of anything but the actual produce of manu-

28. Stenographic Record, January 2, 1893, Vilas Papers, State Historical Society of Wisconsin Archives, Madison.
29. *National Economist,* 1892: May 6, p. 113; May 14, p. 136.
30. D. Bacon to William Vilas, July 6, 1892, Vilas Papers.
31. Record Group 46, National Archives, Washington, D.C.

facture," and further stated, "We must respectfully ask that all less important business be put aside until this most important question is righted." A third version noted: "We are profoundly impressed with the conviction that the gigantic gambling device known as short selling, in which one party agrees to sell what never did and never will exist, and the other agrees to buy what he knows is never to be delivered to him, has been a potent cause in producing the ruinous agricultural depression from which the country has suffered." Another printed form demanded that farmers "shall no longer be crippled, traduced and robbed . . . by the dealing and gambling of millionaires, and impecunious and unprincipled operators as well, in options and visionary quantities of farm products and farm supplies . . . which quantities said operators could not possibly deliver, or receive and pay for, were it to cost them their lives."

Implicit in these statements is an awareness that more than dealing in futures and options bothered the agrarians; in reality, calls for this sort of legislation were symptoms of deeper market discontent. As the *National Economist* put it, "The option bill cannon was aimed by Hatch, of Missouri, and it has hit the tender spot in monopoly's carcass plus center, and the air thunders with their howl."[32] In support of the Butterworth bill (the 1890 version of antioption), the Hurricane Grange No. 359 claimed, "By the combined action of certain persons . . . organized into . . . Boards of Trade, the prices of all kinds of farm products are so manipulated and depressed that they cannot be produced except at a loss to the farmer."[33]

Perhaps the statement that best articulates the varying causes of agrarian discontent is to be found in the lengthy memorial to Tennessee senators Isham Harris and William Bate from the "farmers and citizens of Shelby County," which warrants extensive quotation:

> Out of the debths [sic] of our poverty—which we feel and know to be at present extreme—we appeal to you . . . to give us relief by legislation against these great combines, trusts and monopolies . . . who have arrogated to themselves a more than kingly power to congest and obstruct legitimate commerce by inextrica-

32. *National Economist*, December 3, 1892, p. 1; supra, n. 29.
33. Sen. 51 A-J9. 2, Record Group 46, National Archives, Washington, D.C.

bly blending and interweaving futures contracts . . . that they kill off the real article.

Senators! God never made a richer land than ours is, as dowered by his natural laws—a land of marvelous fertility and exhaustless resources . . . but the hands of men exerted and extended from afar in evil combination are robbing us of the fruits of our industry and plundering us by the capitalistic legerdemain of "futures." We have no money left to employ paid lobbyists to counteract the machinations of lobbyists on the other side who doubtless swarm around the Capitol, nor can we bribe as they the organs of public opinion. The exacting nature of our vocations prevent our ready combination and assemblage in "Exchanges" and "Boards of Trade" to dictate legislation to our Honorable Congress. . . .

The Constitution—which we revere—seems in recent years to have been appealed to principally by those who wish to avoid interference with their unjust practices. Through the subtle and devilish perversions of reasoning practiced by the brightest prostituted minds of the age, retained and employed as paid attorneys and lobbyists by evil capitalistic syndicates with sinister designs, the Constitution is now used as a cloak to hide rascality, a shield to protect fraud, a buckler to defend villainy. Restore the days of its pristine purity when it subserved its original purpose to protect the great masses of our people.[34]

Other antioption petitions were less eloquent, perhaps, but more blunt and bitter in tone. A memorial to Senator John Sherman of Ohio concluded with the hope that "you will have the nerve to promptly give us this prayed-for relief."[35] A handwritten petition to Senator George Vest warned, "Put your ear to the Teliphone [sic] and listen to the mutterings of the thousands that are in earnest to Night. (A Moses is being formed)."[36] An undated clipping in an envelope addressed to Representative Wiliam Hatch, a leading sponsor of antioption legislation, described enemies of the Alliance as a "gang of measly, lousy, low, base, ignoble, abject, beggarly, wretched, degraded, degenerate, vulgar, vile, servile, groveling, despicable, contemptible, poor, lying wretches of plutocracy."[37]

34. Sen. 52 A-K3, ibid.
35. Ibid.
36. Sen. 51 A-73, JL. 1, ibid.
37. H.R. 52A F2.5, ibid.

The agrarians were, of course, correct in the assumption that they suffered from far more than speculative gambling and market manipulation. However, they do not seem to have explored the logical question arising from this assumption: whether antioption legislation would effectively solve their several problems. The major exchanges readily admitted that abuses did occur in commodities trading, but they maintained that the complaints were exaggerated. Produce gambling, according to the Chicago Board of Trade, "bears about the same relation to legitimate commerce and speculation . . . that the froth and foam of Niagara do to the mighty volume of water underneath. It is the bubble and fuss and fury, the froth and foam upon the surface that offends, not commerce itself."[38] The solution was legislation against bucket shops and option trading, but the exchanges argued that such laws had to distinguish between futures trading and illegitimate gambling—a distinction not apparent in the antioption proposals, as the *Chicago Tribune* frequently noted.[39]

Futures were completely different from options, but the Hatch bill lumped the two together. The restrictive and penal sections of the legislation applied equally to both. An option was just that, a choice or option whether or not to make or take delivery. There was no such choice in futures trading; delivery, or something like it, was mandatory.[40] Henry Norton of the Chicago Board of Trade explained that futures meant "the buying and selling of property to be delivered at certain times in the future regardless of whether the seller is or is not the owner of the property at the time the contract is made." However, the proposed laws defined futures as a "sale, when at the time of making the contract to sell, the party is not the owner of the article so contracted to be sold."[41]

The vital issue was: Did one have to possess the property *before* he could sell it? This was what concerned the exchanges more than most other parts of the measure, and the text of Hatch's bill indicates a clear yes as the answer. Much more was

---

38. *D.P.*, April 29, 1890.

39. *Chicago Tribune*, 1892: January 16, p. 4; February 9, p. 9; February 11, p. 4; March 6, p. 6.

40. U.S., Congress, House, Committee on Agriculture, *Fictitious Dealings in Agricultural Products* (Washington, 1892), 52d Cong., 1st sess., pp. 118–26.

41. Id., Senate, Committee on the Judiciary, *Options and Futures*, ibid., p. 99.

involved here than a mere question of semantics. The successful
marriage of speculation and futures trading depended upon the
ability to buy or sell rapidly in response to market needs and
conditions. Further, the right to make contracts for future delivery and *then* obtain the goods to be delivered had been consistently upheld in both the state and federal courts.[42]

A farmer from Illinois, B. J. Gifford, informed Hatch and his
committee of the need for a careful distinction in the statute
between options and futures. Gifford strongly supported a measure to prevent the speculative abuses and gambling sometimes
prevalent on the exchanges. At the same time, however, he
appreciated the importance speculation played in the marketing
system. Gifford told the committee that the Hatch bill failed to
distinguish between the ownership of property and the ownership of contracts for property. He suggested that the definition
of futures be expanded so as to permit "not only the owner of
property to sell it, but also any man who had previously bought
property to be delivered at a future time to sell it again before
it was delivered." The witness warned the committee not to
abridge "the right to buy for future delivery and to sell it again
before or after delivery." This speculation, he noted, "should not
be confused with gambling."[43] Even journals that criticized the
exchanges and supported some sort of antioption statute emphasized the need for this distinction. The *Northwestern Miller*, a
magazine that called the *Tribune* "the organ of the tin-horn gamblers, confidence operators and bunko steerers," wrote of the
1892 antioption bill, "How in the world a farmer can be benefited by the passage of such a measure . . . is beyond us."[44]

Those opposed to antioption called attention to the very real
benefits that the grain marketing system offered the agrarians.
One memorial to Congress described futures trading as "the
highest development, after years of labor and experience, of the
best system of handling the enormous crops of this country to
the most profitable advantage of the producer."[45] Reflecting an

42. See ch. 3 above.
43. Supra, n. 40, pp. 205–6.
44. *Northwestern Miller*, 1892: January 22, p. 115; July 22, p. 111.
45. *D.P.*, February 9, 1892. Invariably the exchanges tried to distinguish between gambling and speculation by noting that the former created a risk, while
the latter simply transferred an already existing risk to another bearer. But thus

ethos that the agrarians accepted as readily as any other segment of American society, the Pittsburgh Grain and Flour Exchange asserted to Senator Matthew Quay, "This is an age in which the human mind has been in the highest degree active, and has produced innumerable improvements, and institutions, which tend to promote the conveniences of life. . . . The future seller is an offspring of the modern facilities for transacting business." The letter concluded that the proponents of antioption legislation "are utterly at enmity with the progressive spirit of the age."[46]

Was it feasible to regulate through an antioption measure a market as vast as the grain trade? Critics of the measure pointed to the harsh realities of the market world and the inexorable force behind the laws of supply and demand. These, they insisted, were far more powerful and effective than any congressional regulation. As the most notorious speculator on the Chicago Board of Trade, Benjamin Hutchinson (Old Hutch), wrote concerning the market price of grain, "No man or combination of men can stand up against it. They may take measures to influence it, but they cannot positively control it. It is too mighty, too immense."[47]

---

stated, the point does not go far enough in clarifying the difference between the two practices. A risk is obviously created by going on the market, and the best way to avoid risk is not to speculate, but rather keep out of the market altogether. However, the exchanges could have argued that the assumption of risks by many served to even out the market, to spread out the risks through the multiple transactions, thus insuring a market that would attract people toward growing the grain in the first place.

46. Supra, n. 34.

47. Benjamin P. Hutchinson, "Speculation in Wheat," *North American Review* 153 (1891):414–19. To explore this point in any great detail is beyond the scope of this volume; but Hutchinson was not the only observer to note the awesome force behind the wheat markets. Frank Norris, in *The Octopus* (New York, 1957), wrote: "The grain seemed impelled with a force of its own, a resistless, huge force, eager, vivid, impatient." Norris concludes the novel with a description of wheat as "untouched, unassailable, undefiled, that mighty world force, that nourisher of nations, wrapped in Nirvanic calm, indifferent to the human swarm, gigantic, resistless" (pp. 446, 454). In another Norris novel, *The Pit* (New York, 1903), the speculator Jadwin states, after the wheat market has destroyed him: "The wheat cornered itself. . . . The wheat cornered me, not I the wheat." In the conclusion of this novel, which is similar to that of *The Octopus*, Norris wrote: "The wheat that had killed Cressler, that had engulfed Jadwin's fortune and all but unseated reason itself . . . had passed on, resistless along its ordered and predetermined courses from West to East, like a vast titanic flood had passed" (pp. 419–20).

II

The House Committee on Agriculture concluded its hearings on February 18, 1892. Other business then occupied the group, and not until March 31 did the committee, apparently by a unanimous vote, approve the antioption proposal.[48] On April 4, Hatch submitted the bill to the House, together with an explanatory report.

The report specifically stated that the makers of futures as defined and taxed are "men who constantly contract to sell and deliver what they neither own nor have any right to the possession of at a future time, and in order to comply specifically with their contracts depend upon their ability to make a future purchase of the article which they have agreed to deliver." Thus Hatch and his committee completely ignored Gifford's suggestion that they distinguish between ownership of property and contracts for the ownership of property. Although no one could state with certainty the statute's reach until defined and delineated by litigation, the bill eliminated futures trading as it had long been conceived by both the organized exchanges and the courts. Here the legislative process flew in the face of both mercantile and judicial experience.

The report took several swipes at the commodity exchanges in general. The Chicago Board of Trade, for example, was described as " so powerless for good" that it could not control some members who continually violated the rules. Hatch noted that the exchanges voiced loud condemnations concerning privileged trades, but that a great majority of members openly dealt in these transactions upon the major exchanges. "Yet no successful effort has ever been made, and but rarely attempted, by any exchange to discipline its members for such trading, the exchanges contenting themselves with a refusal to enforce such contracts." If the exchanges were so impotent that they could not suppress methods of dealing and practices "that all admit to be evil," he asserted, it then became the duty of the federal government, "in levying taxes for revenue, to protect the greatest of the industrial classes from the wrong inflicted by this unnatural mode of determining prices."[49]

48. U.S., Congress, House, Committee on Agriculture, *Minutes*, 52d Cong., 1st sess., pp. 30–32.
49. Id., *House Report 969*, pp. 1–7.

"It is difficult to believe," *Bradstreet's* editorialized, "that such a demagogical measure as the foregoing stands any chance of becoming a law. . . ."[50] The Hatch bill, however, was now upon the House calendar. As a revenue measure it took priority over other pending bills. Aldrich predicted it would easily pass the House, which it in fact did on June 6, 1892.

For a measure with such far-reaching economic ramifications, the brevity of debate on the Hatch antioption bill was surprising. In contrast with the lengthy sessions devoted to the tariff and the currency bills, both fully discussed proposals, the half hour devoted to the Hatch bill—fifteen minutes to each side—is striking. The arguments in favor of the proposal were based on three contentions: (1) the agricultural interests of the country needed, desired, and demanded this legislation; (2) the act would destroy gambling in agricultural commodities; and (3) the true law of supply and demand to the market would be restored, thereby enhancing the value of farm crops. Opponents of the Hatch bill, in addition to recapitulating the arguments used during the hearings, claimed the proposal was unconstitutional because it violated rights of the states and freedom of contract, prostituted the taxing power, and offered an ill-disguised and odious example of class legislation.[51]

The Fifty-second Congress was split in terms of party control. Republicans controlled the Senate 47 to 39, with 2 Independents; while Democrats controlled the House by an almost three-to-one margin: 235 to 88, with 9 Independents. But the Democratic control in the House, especially over its own members, was tenuous at best. In 1892 the factionalism that would break into the open in 1893–94 was already in evidence. Amid growing friction between rival Bourbon, Alliance, and Populist branches, it took the Democrats thirty ballots to elect a speaker for the Congress.[52]

The Hatch bill split even further an already divided party. The House vote on the bill was 167 for, 46 against, with one-third not voting. The supporting majority included 129 Democrats, 31 Republicans, and 7 Independents; while the opposition included 38 Democrats and 8 Republicans. More than half of

50. *Bradstreet's*, April 9, 1892, pp. 230–31.
51. U.S., *Congressional Record*, 52d Cong., 1st sess., 1892, vol. 23, pt. 6, pp. 5071–78.
52. Hubert Fuller, *The Speakers of the House* (Boston, 1909), pp. 242–44.

the House Republicans did not vote at all, and 68 Democrats also abstained.

A breakdown of these figures reveals an alignment by region and section rather than by party. Representatives from urban areas consistently opposed the measure. The regional split is particularly clear in the New England vote. Representatives from southern New England (Massachusetts, Connecticut, and Rhode Island) tended to vote against the bill, reflecting their link with the eastern markets. Congressmen from the rural New England states (New Hampshire, Maine, and Vermont) voted almost unanimously in favor of the act.[53] The Illinois delegation split in a similar manner, on the basis of region rather than party. All four representatives from Chicago voted against the bill, while the majority of downstate representatives voted for it.

Many congressmen found it expedient not to vote at all. Too many House members, opponents of the bill felt, had taken the cowardly way out by refusing to vote against a measure that supposedly had strong agrarian support, and by their abstinence the bill was passed. "Seldom has ignorant, ill advised and demagogic clamor achieved a more notable triumph," *Bradstreet's* complained, "than in the vote of the House on the anti options bill."[54]

The Senate seemed in no hurry to dispose of the bill. After some debate it tabled the measure on July 30 and voted not to take it up again until the Senate reconvened in December, when it would become the first order of unfinished business.[55] Other matters, notably party conventions and the forthcoming presidential election, were more important. The senatorial debate in July and thereafter followed what Cedric Cowing has aptly called a typical nineteenth-century pattern of "moralistic platitudes, Jeffersonian cliches, and constitutional quibbling."[56] By this time virtually all arguments concerning the bill, both pro and con, had long since been put forward.[57]

---

53. Cedric Cowing, *Populists, Plungers, and Progressives* (Princeton, 1965), pp. 21–22.

54. *Bradstreet's*, June 11, 1892, p. 371. See also ibid., 1891: December 26, p. 819; 1892: January 2, p. 3, January 9, pp. 22–23, July 2, p. 417, July 16, p. 453, July 23, pp. 467–68, July 30, pp. 482–83, December 24, pp. 818–19.

55. Ibid., December 10, 1892, p. 786.

56. Cowing, pp. 18–19.

57. U.S., *Congressional Record* 23 (1892) pt. 6, pp. 5980–93, 6394–96, 6402–5, 6437–51, 6507–20, 6560–82, 6649–61, 6693–6711, 6838–40, 6881–93.

The pending legislation hung over the Chicago Board of Trade like an ungainly albatross; and Board Secretary George Stone, in his annual report for 1892, did not mince words. He termed the antioption proposals "pernicious bills, whose title pages bore an unblushing falsehood." They obviously were not intended to create revenue, he complained, adding that "never before was the intelligence of congress so grossly and systematically insulted as by the introduction of those infamous bills." Stone concluded by venturing a hope, rather than a prediction, that the proposals would "be relegated as they deserve to the rubbish of two sessions of Congress."[58]

On January 31, 1893, with barely one month remaining in the life of the Fifty-second Congress, the Senate voted to adopt the Hatch bill, subject to minor amendments. The vote was 40 to 29, with 19 senators not voting. Among the majority in favor were 27 Republicans, 11 Democrats, and 2 Independents (Peffer of Kansas and Kyle of South Dakota); in opposition were 20 Democrats and 9 Republicans; and the senators not voting included 8 Democrats and 11 Republicans.[59]

The Senate, too, tended to vote on the Hatch bill by region rather than by party, as the House had done; and its alignment in general consistently followed the House pattern, except in the South. The majority of southern congressmen heartily favored the Hatch bill, perhaps reflecting the agrarian orientation of their constituencies. However, other southern senators were against the measure in equally impressive numbers.[60] Indeed, the way the states split on the issue is no better demonstrated than by Missouri, where Hatch himself, a Democrat, led the fight for the bill in the House. The opposition to the bill in the Senate was led by several men; the most prominent of them seems to have been George Vest, also a Democrat from Missouri. While Vest deplored speculative abuses, he claimed that the bill intruded upon police powers of the states.

The Hatch bill was returned to the House on February 2, 1893, with some thirty-four Senate amendments. The *Chicago Post* predicted that the House would not accept some of these,

58. *Report of the Directors, 1892*, p. xv.
59. U.S., *Congressional Record* 24, pt. 2, p. 995; Wilson, p. 74.
60. Cowing, p. 23.

and that this would cause the measure to go back to the Senate. "It can hardly be extricated from the legislative jangle, therefore, before the session ends on March 4." The *Post* also indirectly announced the strategy that opponents of the bill in the House would follow. Their plan was to delay congressional action until after adjournment of the Fifty-second Congress and, in so doing, to defeat "the anti option monstrosity," "a most odious and abominable measure."[61]

The *Northwestern Miller* believed that Minnesota Senator William Washburn should be congratulated for seeing the bill through the Senate. It expressed the opinion that the tone of those who objected to it "has become one of the strongest arguments in its favor." The journal had "seen too much of the high moral character of the Chicago Board of Trade and kindred bodies to look towards them for guidance in questions of ethics." If the bill ultimately became law, as the *Miller* predicted it would, many would approve, "not on account of the bill being meritorious, but because the arrogant pretense of the Chicago Board of Trade and the discreditable opposition which it has inspired will have received a well merited rebuke."[62]

As soon as the measure was returned by the Senate to the House, Hatch asked for a conference committee to meet with Senate representatives to promptly bring the bill into conformity with the wishes of both chambers. Although Hatch was no stranger to legislative legerdemain, this was a shrewd move for him to make. A conference committee could report at any time and was not subject to a point of order. Moreover, such committees were customarily composed of members favorably inclined toward the bill under consideration. Once the committee's report went before the House, all that would remain would be a vote on its adoption. Given the favorable votes that had been cast before, Hatch was confident the bill would pass.

However, Hatch got no further than his request for a conference committee; another representative raised the point of order that, under House rules, Senate amendments had to be considered by the House committee of the whole. Among the amendments proposed by the Senate was one which added flour to the list of

61. *SB*, vol. 72, n.p.: *Chicago Post*, January 31, 1893; *Chicago Herald*, February 2, 1893.
62. *Northwestern Miller*, February 3, 1893, p. 152.

commodities to be regulated by the bill. Noting that this addition changed the scope of the measure, House Speaker Charles Crisp ruled that the bill could not go into conference, but must go before the committee of the whole, and that it could not reach that committee until it had first been referred back to the Committee on Agriculture for its recommendation. This occurred on February 3, 1892.

Hatch and his committee, who were well aware of the meaning of these developments, hastily reconsidered their bill; and on the next day they reported it back to the House, urging that that body concur in the Senate amendments. Undoubtedly Hatch would have preferred to make some changes in his measure; but, as the *Tribune* had noted, even while the Senate considered the proposal, "if it comes to taking the Senate bill or no bill at all the committee will take the Senate bill." Under House rules, however, the bill now resubmitted to the House was placed at the foot of the calendar.[63]

During the remaining days of February, the House failed to take up the antioption matter. Representative C. B. Kilgore of Texas, who opposed the measure, began to raise the cry of "no quorum" at regular intervals, thus requiring a tedious poll of the full House each time. On February 6, the *Chicago Post* noted that a filibuster against the bill had been started. The *Tribune* reported that the House refused to postpone discussion of appropriation bills in order to take up the antioption proposal. Hatch tried in vain to block consideration of these bills with the claim that as a revenue measure the antioption bill was privileged to be called up at any time. To make matters worse, the House decided to adjourn over Washington's birthday.[64]

On February 27 Hatch blasted opponents of the bill for their dilatory tactics, but time was running out and he knew it. It was clear that under the rules, *this* House would not get to the bill in time for action before March 4. Hatch had only one option left, and it was a gamble. On March 1, with three days left in the life of the Congress, he asked that the House suspend the rules and vote on whether or not to concur with the Senate amend-

63. SB: *Chicago Tribune*, January 14, 1893; *Chicago InterOcean*, February 4, 1893.

64. SB: *Chicago Post*, February 6, 1893; *Chicago Tribune* and *Chicago InterOcean*, both of February 23, 1893.

ments. This tactic represented a gamble, because such a vote required a two-thirds majority.

The roll call proceeded, as the Speaker tried—sometimes in vain—to keep order on the floor of the House. When the call was completed the antioption bill had disappeared. The vote was 172 to 124, with only 33 members not voting as compared with the 1892 tally of 167 to 46 and 116 not voting.[65] The result was 26 votes short of the required two-thirds majority.

Where did the opponents of the Hatch bill get their needed votes? Of the 167 who had voted for the bill in 1892, 127 voted yea again in 1893. Even greater consistency was demonstrated by the negative vote. Of the 46 who voted nay in 1892, 40 again voted against the bill in 1893. The important switch came from those who had not voted at all on the 1892 roll call. Of the 116 who had not voted, almost half—57, including 41 Democrats and 16 Republicans—cast their vote with the opposition in 1893. This group, together with 22 Democrats who switched from yea in 1892 to nay in 1893 defeated the measure.

Additional negative votes came mostly from the East and South, with a scattering from the Midwest. The figures seem to bear out Cowing's contention that some southern representatives, although in favor of antioption, nevertheless voted nay because of the "tax to destroy" method used in the Hatch bill. The figures also confirm the inability or unwillingness of the Democratic House leadership to swing party votes in line for the measure. In the crucial days after the bill came back from the Senate, the House leadership did not cooperate with Hatch; and it was largely Democratic votes that blocked suspension of the rules, thus killing the legislation.[66]

As Hatch went down to defeat, the *Chicago Post* recorded, he was "the picture of combined misery, dejection and rage." On the floor of the Chicago Board of Trade, the pits were deserted, as members clustered around telegraph instruments awaiting the results of the vote.[67] The *Post* was moved to poetry:

65. U.S., *Congressional Record* 24, pt. 3, pp. 2357–58.

66. C. Vann Woodward (*Origins of the New South*, Baton Rouge, 1951, p. 241) notes that House Speaker Charles Crisp was "a Georgia Conservative and an outspoken opponent of Alliance Principles," one of which was a demand for antioption legislation.

67. Taylor, p. 857.

> Not a sound was heard, not a funeral note,
> As its corpse to the bone yard was hurried;
> Not a congressman gave it a parting shot
> As poor anti-option was buried.[68]

The rest seemed anticlimactic. As quickly as they had poured in, the petitions calling for an antioption law dwindled to a mere dribble. The election of President Cleveland, the currency problem, and the depression of 1893 assumed far more importance. To be sure, the House did, in 1894, pass another antioption measure that was sponsored by Hatch, but it never reached the Senate floor. The two leaders of antioption legislation, Hatch of Missouri and Washburn of Minnesota, were both defeated for re-election and never again sat in Congress.

Perhaps the agrarians began to realize by the mid 1890s that they, as much as the other groups involved in the grain trade, had become an inextricable part of a system that "produced both speculation and solid economic building."[69] The problem, easy to state but extremely difficult to resolve, lay in correcting one without threatening the other. The farmers suffered less from speculative grain gambling than from the unsettling transition to an industrialized urban society. In reality, therefore, antioption legislation could not have solved the farmers' basic difficulties, and ultimately the agrarians seem to have realized this fact. Indeed, the wheat harvest of 1891—over 677 million bushels—was the largest thus far in American history, and the 1892 harvest was almost as great.[70] Yet, from 1892 on, the Populist platform failed to mention antioption.

The Populist platform, according to William A. Williams, was "a basic document setting forth the crystalized consensus of the agricultural majority as it had developed over a period of three decades."[71] A contemporary observer noted in 1896, "the trade in futures has been one of the chief elements of complaint among the farmers; but the party has abandoned it as an issue."[72] Three

68. *SB, Chicago Post*, March 1, 1893.
69. Morgan, pp. 389–90.
70. U.S. Department of Agriculture, *A Century of Agriculture in Charts and Tables* (Washington, D.C., 1966), p. 25.
71. Williams, p. 353.
72. Frank L. McVey, "The Populist Movement," *Economic Studies* 1 (1896): 141–42.

years earlier, J. W. Gleed had stated of the Populists, "They do not ask for a new heaven or a new earth. All they want is more money. They are fast getting it, and the faster they get it the more reluctant they become to ride forty miles in a lumber wagon through the rain to hear Mrs. Lease and General Weaver make speeches."[73] Thus the much vaunted demand for federal intervention and antioption legislation turned out to be a dud. But congressional delay and party faction, although important, represent only part of the reason. An equally valid explanation for the legislative failure to act on antioption lies in the ambiguity with which Americans regard risk, speculation, and commercial success.

III

In 1885 Carter Harrison, the mayor of Chicago, spoke at a banquet held to celebrate the inauguration of the new Board of Trade building. "Yonder majestic temple," he declaimed, had been "erected in the name of Americans' worship—commerce" and was "dedicated to the Americans' genius—trade."[74] In his recognition of this attitude toward commerce and trade, Harrison echoed a theme reminiscent of that expressed many years earlier by a European traveler in America.

Fifty years before Harrison spoke, the visiting French aristocrat Tocqueville had remarked that he was "even more struck by the innumerable multitude of little undertakings than by the extraordinary size of some of [the Americans'] industrial enterprises." He observed that "the frequent reversals of fortune, and the unexpected shifts in public and private wealth all unite to keep the mind in a sort of feverish agitation." Indeed, he noted, for an American "the whole of life is treated like a game of chance." This element of risk, he concluded, is always present "in the minds of those who live in the unstable conditions of democ-

73. J. W. Gleed, "The True Significance of Western Unrest," *Forum* 16 (1893):257. See also Karel Bicha, "The Conservative Populists," *Agricultural History* 47 (1973):9–24.

74. Chicago Board of Trade, *Opening Ceremonies of the New Board of Trade Building* (Chicago, 1885), p. 144.

racy, and in the end they come to love enterprises in which chance plays a part."[75]

Tocqueville had stressed two themes: (1) the existence of large numbers of small entrepreneurs; and (2) the atmosphere of risk and chance that attracts Americans to trade "not only for the sake of promised gain, but also because they love the emotions it provides."[76] The American agrarian well reflected Tocqueville's generalizations. As William Parker wrote, "both in its Westward extension and in the transformations back east, American agriculture may be looked on as high risk enterprise with strong elements of speculation."[77] In this it did not differ from the usually favorable attitude toward risk and commercial gain so characteristic of nineteenth-century American society. But the farmer of the 1880s confronted a mercantile system far different from that described by Tocqueville.

By the 1880s and thereafter, the forces that had spawned "innumerable multitudes of small undertakings" had shifted. Now a complex national market existed, serviced largely by middlemen, agents, and branch offices. The communications revolution, the railroads, and the economic and technological innovations all made it increasingly difficult to sustain these innumerable small ventures. Yet, for the group most affected by this change, "the mythically self sufficient independent husbandmen," the ethos of chance and worship of trade that nurtured what Tocqueville had noted remained.[78] There seemed, however, to be fewer and fewer opportunities to use it.

When complaining about this condition, agrarian spokesmen were quick to reaffirm their love of profit and free enterprise in general. When they attacked the railroads, monopolies, boards of trade, and high finance, these critics were not rejecting the system that had produced them. At no point, as Lee Benson has stated, "was the enterprise system itself a focus of attack."[79]

75. Alexis de Tocqueville, *Democracy in America*, ed. Max Lerner and J. P. Mayer (New York, 1966), pp. 370, 526–27.

76. Ibid., p. 526.

77. William N. Parker, "Productivity Growth in American Grain Farming," in *The Reinterpretation of American Economic History*, ed. Robert W. Fogel and Stanley L. Engerman (New York, 1971), pp. 177–78.

78. Lee Benson, *Merchants, Farmers and Railroads* (Cambridge, Mass., 1955), p. 114.

79. Ibid., p. viii.

Free competition had simply become excessively free and now, paradoxically, appeared to repress and restrain those small farmers and businessmen who once had so much to gain from it. Free competition had to be tamed, but private enterprise remained sacred. "Too many men pictured themselves as tomorrow's kings to proscribe royalty."[80] A possible solution to this imbalance between private enterprise and free competition lay in governmental intervention. In proposing this, the yeoman farmers—heirs to the Jeffersonian ideal of freedom from government—turned their patron saint's philosophy upside down. They now deemed that government regulation was necessary to halt the increasing polarization toward extreme wealth and poverty. The economy could no longer assure the "good society" unaided.[81] Regulation was needed, as well as agrarian organization.

Writers who were sympathetic to the problems of farmers were generally quick to point out that they as a group had inherently more power than did any railroad or board of trade. What they needed to do was to use that power. In 1874 the "historian of the farmers' movement" claimed that "aggregated, the agriculturalists represent a power which all others may not equal." Let the methods of corporate enterprise be applied against those who have heretofore used them so well. Should the farmers "withhold for a single season the product of their labors, manufacturers, trade, commerce, and every other industry would languish and lie prone in the dust." Indeed, a "wail would go up such as has not been heard since the seven lean seasons in Egypt."[82]

The agrarian press made no secret of the commercial orientation of farmers. A "farmer" newspaper observed, "What we farm for are profits, and whether they are large or small they are important."[83] A Grange songbook published in 1877 candidly versified just that:

> We're a happy, social band
> Scattered o'er our native land.

---

80. Robert Wiebe, *The Search for Order* (New York, 1967), p. 9 and passim.
81. Benson, p. 151.
82. Jonathan Periam, *The Groundswell* (Cincinnati, 1874), p. 90.
83. *Farmer and Fruit Grower*, May 13, 1885, p. 1.

Toiling honestly each day
For the products that will pay.[84]

In 1880, at the Grange national convention, a report commented that the group could speak as eloquently as it might about social culture and moral elevation, but that "after all has been said and its truth acknowledged, still the great fact remains that to open the way for progress . . . the pecuniary circumstances must be made comfortable." Twenty-two years later, the Illinois Grange believed that "though we should not worship the dollar, we should respect it."[85]

Neither, contrary to some observers, did the farmers object to speculation. The Milton George Publishing House (publishers of the *Western Rural*) denied that opposition to futures trading implied hostility toward speculation. "This is entirely untrue. Speculation is recognized as a necessary factor in the economy of all business."[86] Joseph Brigham, former national master of the Grange, asserted, "We do not want to stop actual speculation in grain—that is, we want the capitalists to buy the grain, all we have to sell, and carry it for us, and realize a reasonable profit."[87] The *Farmer and Fruit Grower* noted in 1879 that "by a proper study and anticipation of the wants of the market, speculators amass fortunes. The farmer should do his own speculation."[88]

Even the *Western Rural* endorsed speculation, calling it "the principal motive power in the march of progress."[89] But where did speculation end and gambling begin? The question raised a very difficult problem to resolve both in law and in commercial transactions. The *Western Rural* claimed, "These two practices are as diametrically opposed to each other as are disease and

84. *Patron's Song Book: A Choice Collection of Original and Selected Gems* (Cincinnati, 1877), p. 27.

85. National Grange, *Journal of Proceedings*, 14th sess., 1880, p. 68; Illinois State Grange, *Journal of Proceedings*, 32d sess., 1903, p. 42. In 1887 the National Grange received a report from its committee on agriculture emphasizing that "we deplore the influence and sad effects of anarchy, agrarianism and communism, and rejoice that our Executive and State departments are determined to stamp it out." *Journal of Proceedings*, 21st sess., 1887, p. 159.

86. D. Bacon to William Vilas, July 6, 1892, Vilas Papers.

87. U.S., Congress, House, *Report of the Industrial Commission on Agriculture and Agricultural Labor*, 57th Cong., 1st sess., 1902, Document 179, p. 24.

88. *Farmer and Fruit Grower*, October 8, 1879, p. 4.

89. *Western Rural*, January 14, 1893, p. 24.

health," but the difference proved easier to claim than to clarify.[90] In 1885 the journal concluded that the difficulty lay in the inability "first to see any difference between speculation and downright gambling, and second to see anything in speculation but legitimate business enterprise." One who buys a farm and holds it for future sale, hoping to enhance its value, "robs nobody either when he buys or sells at an increased price." Yet, with no awareness of internal inconsistency, the editorial emphasized that "speculation has been the curse of the country."[91]

If the agrarians were unable to distinguish clearly between legitimate speculation and illegal gambling, they had no doubt of what the latter produced. They saw its results all around them in the forms of falling prices, erratic market conditions, and declining farmer income. When a man gambles, the *Western Rural* noted in 1885, "whether it be in the name of a lottery, board of trade speculation or through the gaming table, he sinks to the low level of the polite cut throat."[92] According to one critic, gambling in grain represented "a conspiracy against life, and is a system by which a board of lousy useless loafers charge the expense of their useless lives upon the necessaries of life, which is an injury to the producer, consumer and the country."[93] The agrarian press frequently warned its readers to avoid schemes involving boards of trade and stock exchanges, which it claimed were "among the most dangerous agencies existing."[94] "Keep your money in your pocket and be assured you will be the gainer."[95]

Thus the agrarians complained about certain abuses within the marketing system which, they claimed, caused much if not all of their economic hardships. But they also realized that this same market methodology, including commodity exchanges and futures trading, was permanent. Hence they tried to distinguish specific abuses from the system as a whole. No agrarian journal was more critical of the Chicago Board of Trade than the *West-*

90. Ibid.
91. Ibid., October 17, 1885, p. 664.
92. Ibid., June 6, 1885, p. 360.
93. Charles Patridge to Henry Demarest Lloyd, May 8, 1883, Henry Demarest Lloyd Papers.
94. *Western Rural*, January 27, 1883, p. 28.
95. Ibid., May 24, 1879, p. 164; December 4, 1886, p. 793.

ern Rural. Yet it frequently sought to differentiate between the beneficial functions of legitimate commodity exchanges and the "corrupt" Chicago Board of Trade.[96] Similarly, Henry Demarest Lloyd, after publishing a vigorous condemnation of the Board, assured its president, "My attack was not against the Board, but against the abuses that were threatening its very life."[97]

Farmer spokesmen tended to place most of the blame for their difficulties upon outside influences. Journals such as the *Western Rural*, the *Farmers' Review*, and the *Prairie Farmer* found it difficult to evaluate the agrarian's own contribution to his economic state. The *Rural* did observe, as one reason why the farmer was being "easily swindled," that "he is truthful himself. . . . It is to his honor that his integrity is so perfect that he does not suspect the integrity of others."[98] There may have been some accuracy in the conclusions of the *Rural*, but the truth lay much closer to home.

The farmers were gamblers in their own way, as much as were the average board of trade operators. They kept waiting for that one good year, that great harvest that would cancel all their debts. Instead of diversifying their crops, they gambled, hoping against hope that a bull market would come at last.[99] They consistently called for a market controlled only by the laws of supply and demand, while at the same time threatening to hold back their crops and force the market up.[100] Brigham could state that

96. Ibid., 1879: October 4, p. 316, October 25, p. 340; 1883: February 10, p. 52, June 30, p. 210; 1885: October 4, p. 696, November 15, p. 732.

97. Henry Demarest Lloyd to C. L. Hutchinson, May 2, 1888, Charles H. Hutchinson Papers.

98. *Western Rural*, May 24, 1879, p. 164.

99. By 1892 the latest cotton crop "with its enormous proportions and low prices" had convinced many southern planters that they had no choice but to diversify their crops (*American Elevator and Grain Trade* 15 [1892]:335). But diagnosis proved easier than cure. As Uncle Remus put it:

> Oh, Dixie Land is the land of cotton,
> That's why Dixie's now forgotten;
> Plant corn, plant corn,
> Plant corn down South in Dixie.

100. *Farmers' Review*, March 14, 1892, p. 162; *Western Rural*, June 30, 1883, p. 210. In 1891 *Bradstreet's* (July 11, 1891, p. 439) noted this inconsistency. "The labor section of the Farmers' Alliance may be interested enough to explain whether the . . . project of the Alliance as to cotton in Georgia is anything in the nature of a conspiracy to enhance the cost of one of the necessaries of life? Economists among the farmers may be able to make a dis-

farmers objected to "the selling of stuff we do not have."[101] But, in reality, had the farmers sold only the stuff they had when they had it, the market would have been glutted during harvest seasons and depressed during off seasons, exactly as it had been in the decades prior to the Civil War.

The agrarian press itself reflected the ambivalence in the farmers' attitude toward risk and commercial gain. The periodicals noted above saw no inconsistency in regularly blasting boards of trade as gambling dens and just as regularly printing the current state of the markets, advising readers to buy, sell, or hold. The *Western Rural* stated that, while a journal should never assume responsibility for predicting what future prices would be, it could nevertheless give its opinion, leaving its readers to judge for themselves 'after carefully weighing the facts, which they should be able to learn from the columns of their farm paper." The same editorial declared, "We should not like to advise farmers . . . to hold their crops. . . . But we think that the future for wheat is a bright one [and] without venturing to name any price, we think that everything points to higher prices."[102] Similarly, the *Prairie Farmer* warned, "It is never wise for farmers to become speculators upon futures." Speculation was better left to professionals, who were "usually shrewd men, of much experience in the business. They study the conditions of the supply and demand at home and abroad. . . . Who so well know the probable range of future prices as they? Surely not farmers." The editorial then advised, "What is wanted now, is for farmers to hold back all the grain they possibly can, and hold on to it" until the current level of grain "is greatly decreased."[103]

Had the farmers been isolated in their ambivalence toward risk, chance, and commercial gain, their resistance might have been stronger. In fact, the speculative ethos sensed by Tocque-

tinction between the attitude of Alliance holders under the foregoing plan and the holding of a few million bushels of wheat by Hutchinson or Keene, so called speculators; if so, will they kindly elucidate? Was not one of the demands of the Farmers' Alliance for a rigid law prohibiting the dealing in futures?" This same argument was also used by the bucket shops in the 1880s, as they sought to prevent the Chicago Board of Trade from restricting its quotations.

101. Supra, n. 87, p. 25.
102. *Western Rural*, July 5, 1879, p. 209.
103. *Prairie Farmer*, December 27, 1884, p. 824.

ville was endemic in late nineteenth-century American society as a whole; and, if anything, its pervasiveness had increased since the 1830s. One observer wrote in 1895, "The feverish, restless spirit of our time is easily adapted to the sporting world, and its victims, once tasting the excitement of the game, are possessed with it as by a very mania." Now, however, it was no longer a sport, but had become "a passion that takes hold on the life with all absorbing intensity."[104]

The economic instability of American democratic society and the ease with which one might gain and lose wealth, Tocqueville had reasoned, caused many to turn from agriculture to commerce. "Agriculture," he claimed, "only suits the wealthy, who already have a great superfluity, or the poor, who only want to live." The vast majority will undertake some "risky, but lucrative profession."[105] The pattern was even more distinct in the 1890s. "The opportunities for money making are many and varied. . . . A large proportion of the population have spare money to use as they wish. . . ." Indeed, "the barriers between the different classes of society are so low that any one can step over them."[106]

There were always those who consistently condemned speculative gambling. In an editorial entitled "A National Crime," the *Farmers' Review* asserted, "The passion for gambling seems to have become a national vice." Racing after riches, the "whole nation seems to have turned gambler with all the dreadful consequences to the public morals that that statement involves." So far "had the gangrene permeated the social body, that the malversation of property and deeds more reprehensible than common thieving are condoned." The worst development, however, was that a man who "has lost all, including his neighbor's money" could easily restore himself to public favor. All he had to do was "to get another chance at the game and play it succesfully."[107]

The editorial revealed an important ambivalence in contem-

---

104. Rev. C. H. Hamlin and Harry C. Vrooman, "Gambling and Speculation: A Symposium," *Arena* 11 (1895):417–18. For a contemporary bibliography on gambling and speculation, see ibid., pp. 426–28.

105. Tocqueville, pp. 525–26.

106. W. B. Curtis, "The Increase of Gambling and Its Forms," *Forum* 12 (1891):284. "The poor boy of today may in a few years become a merchant, next a millionaire, and then a senator."

107. *Farmers' Review*, May 8, 1884, p. 338.

porary ethical standards. The American morality was quick to condemn speculative ventures (especially when they failed), but equally prompt to applaud the successful speculators as exemplars of the "American way." This tendency was not new in the 1880s. In 1853 Henry Boardman had complained that gambling in stocks was as much in vogue as gambling at cards or billiards. "But the public sentiment tolerates and shelters it." Even worse, "it lavishes its respect and its honors upon the men who win the most bets and carry off the largest stakes."[108]

After all, success was the key, and the able speculator did succeed. He could not have done so in his field nor in any other calling without, as one author put it, "a genius for trade the same as men have special talent in art, oratory, law, literature and statemanship [sic]." This article, which appeared in a journal that frequently criticized speculative gambling, lauded "truly great speculators" because they combined "the daring of the natural gambler, reinforced by the grasp and conservatism of the merchant and the thrift of the financier."[109] In 1891 another observer listed the qualities essential to the successful speculator as "self reliance, judgment, courage, prudence, pliability."[110] The words could have come right out of Horatio Alger, and they were as applicable to the agrarian image as to the urban adventurer seeking his fortune.

Furthermore, lessons learned from the experience of market ventures that turned out poorly were of value. The *American Elevator and Grain Trade* believed that such "experience certainly keeps a dear school, but the majority of businessmen learn in no other, and the knowledge thus imparted is usually found to be of incalculable worth in [later] life."[111] Such incidents often brought out the best in people. Robert Stewart, in describing what he called a "composite photograph" of a Wall Street broker, stated: "He is kind and generous with his family. If a friend is in distress, he opens his purse like a man, and in his

108. Henry A. Boardman, *The Bible in the Counting House* (Philadelphia, 1853), p. 166.

109. *Northwestern Miller*, May 7, 1886, p. 453, citing *Daily Business*.

110. D. G. Watts, "Speculation as a Fine Art," *Cosmopolitan* 10 (1891): 592.

111. *American Elevator and Grain Trade*, March 15, 1886, p. 197.

business relations he is singularly honest and truthful."[112] Again, the sentiments expressed were held by many agrarians as peculiarly their own.

The American agrarian, then, appears to have been caught in a fundamental contradiction. Like so much of the society around him, he tended to condemn speculation while at the same time applauding certain of its attributes and benefits; he opposed "outside" speculators while seeing nothing inconsistent in his own speculations. How did the agrarian in the late nineteenth century perceive himself: as an independent yeoman impatiently awaiting an upturn in prices and *the* chance to make his fortune, or as the innocent and helpless country victim of a conspiratorial, monopolistic system that reached out from such sinister centers as Chicago and New York to twist values and destroy an open market? To assume that one or the other of these self-perceptions was completely correct would be erroneous. Many farmers could not form a clear judgment for one or the other alternative.

This ambivalence had certain results that should be noted. In the first place it diluted, even if it did not destroy, agrarian political power as an inherently effective force.[113] Thus, it prevented a dominant agrarian political constituency from emerging to force fundamental changes in the grain marketing system. Furthermore, the absence of sustained political pressure insured to private associations, such as the mercantile and commodity exchanges, the opportunity to develop in virtual freedom from governmental regulation. In an era characterized by federal intervention in the areas of railroads, commerce, finance, banking, public health, and corporate investment, federal regulation of the grain market and commodity exchanges is conspicuous by its absence.[114] Ironically, it was the constant waiting for the long

112. Robert Stewart, "Metropolitan Types—The Stockbroker," *Munsey's Magazine* 21 (1889):279–80.

113. For this reason, I find it difficult to accept Williams' hypothesis of agrarian power. Certainly other groups supported tariff adjustments, reciprocity, and foreign trade. To interpret such political support primarily as a response to agrarian agitation seems, to this writer at least, unjustified by the existing evidence.

114. This fact renders dubiously valid, if not actually invalid, the collusion theory of the Progressive period as put forth by Gabriel Kolko in *The Triumph of Conservatism* (Glencoe, 1963). In this work Kolko argues that various business leaders and associations representing corporate enterprise joined

chance, for that bonanza harvest, that contributed so much to the weakening of agrarian demands for change. The reason most often cited for not interfering by law with the operations of the commodities markets was that "the ethical distinctions involved between legitimate and illegitimate speculation are not easily reducible to exact legal definition."[115] Yet, with the niceties of legal language stripped away, another reason emerges: too many farmers did not want to see the market regulated externally because they also hoped to gain the wealth and success they saw coming to so many others.

Finally, the antioption battle reflected the depths of the speculative ethos in American society. Because the Butterworth and Hatch bills were not based upon a clear perception of the problems they sought to solve, they failed to offer workable solutions. The measures were drawn to eliminate virtually every sort of speculative commodity trading, whether legitimate or illegitimate, that had evolved over the years. In fact, a policing mechanism was needed that could curtail speculative abuses without interfering in the overall speculative market framework. Whether this could better come from the exchanges themselves or from an outside federal regulatory agency was by no means clear as the nineteenth century ended.

In the meantime, there just was no sustained demand for antioption legislation. Underneath his prairie grime, the American agrarian appears to have been as bourgeois as the other segments of society all around him. As in so many other events in this period, Mr. Dooley saw the real truth and expressed it best: "As a people, Hinnissy, we're th' greatest crusaders that 'iver

with each other and the national government to bring about federal regulation. Although the book purports to be about finance capitalism, it contains no analysis of the role of stock and commodities exchanges. One explanation for this may be that the attitude of the major exchanges toward federal regulation disproves rather than supports Kolko's thesis. For further comments on Kolko's conclusions, see John Braeman, "The Square Deal in Action: A Case Study in the Growth of the National Police Power," *Change and Continuity in Twentieth Century America*, ed. John Braeman, Robert Bremner, and Everett Walters (Columbus, 1964), pp. 35–80. See, in particular, p. 74, n. 79a; Stanley Caines, "Why Railroads Supported Regulation: The Case of Wisconsin, 1905–1910," *Business History Review* 44 (1970):175–89.

115. Newman Smyth, "Suppression of the Lottery and Other Gambling," *Forum* 19 (1895):246–47.

was—f'r a short distance. . . . But th' trouble is th' crusade don't last afther th' first sprint. Th' crusaders drop out iv th' procission to take a dhrink or put a little money on th' ace, an' be th' time th' end iv the line iv march is reached th' boss crusader is alone in th' job, an' his former followers is hurlin' bricks at him fr'm th' windows iv policy shops."[116]

116. *Literary Digest* 21 (1900):760.

CHAPTER SIX

The Chicago Board of Trade 1890–1900

I

By 1889–90 THE BATTLE waged by the Chicago Board of Trade against the bucket shops appeared to have collapsed completely. In reality, however, the Board itself had yet to strike at the shops directly. Thus far the association had sought to have outside agencies—the telegraph companies, the courts and the legislature—fight the battle on its behalf. The Board had hoped the court would assist it in blocking distribution of the quotations, and the legislature would eradicate the shops by statute thus eliminating any need to confront the problem on its own. But the new statute, while effective on paper, had in the few years since its enactment proved extremely difficult to enforce, and the Illinois Supreme Court had rebuffed the Board. Indeed, it was the unfavorable decision in the *New York and Chicago Grain and Stock Exchange* case that first forced the directory to take action.

The Illinois Supreme Court decision in this 1889 case left the Board with two apparent choices: (1) to give the quotations to all or (2) to give them to none. Although the directors had made repeated efforts during 1889 to have the injunction against its restriction of the reports modified, these attempts were unsuccessful. In Janury 1890 the membership elected William Baker to the Board presidency largely upon a platform of an all-out fight against the bucket shops.[1] Baker felt the shops had to go; and if this result could be achieved only by eliminating the de-

---

1. For biographical data on Baker, see *American Elevator and Grain Trade*, February 15, 1895, pp. 281–82; Andreas, ch. 2, p. 312, n. 7; Charles H. Baker, *Life and Character of William Taylor Baker* (New York, 1908).

partment of market reports and cutting off all quotations, then he was in favor of this "only remedy left the Board, even though it might be heroic."[2]

A majority of the Board's members agreed to this proposed line of action; and at the annual meeting in January, they authorized the directors to stop the collection and distribution of the reports "at their discretion." After one final unsuccessful attempt to get the injunction modified, the directorate acted. On March 1 it voted that after March 31, 1890, "the collection and furnishing of market reports and quotations be entirely discontinued and that the Board on that day abandon entirely the business of collecting and furnishing such market reports and quotations."[3]

The directors' action may have been, as the *New York Times* maintained, "a desperate measure."[4] On April 1 President Baker ordered all telegraph instruments and telegraph employees removed from the trading area, making it impossible for members to send messages directly from the floor.[5] Traders who wanted quotations for their customers were thus compelled to gather the information themselves and to hand their lists to messenger boys, who thereupon rushed frantically down the stairs and left them in the various offices.[6] Six days later, at the request of the directors, the leading commission houses agreed to discontinue the practice of posting the quotations on office blackboards for the benefit of their customers. Originally the directors had decided to order these firms to remove their wires, but they later voted that they could remain connected to the floor, provided continuous quotations were not sent out. These actions, together with a rule forbidding any "club, pool or association of members . . . directly or indirectly to collect market quotations on the floor of the exchange," were intended to obviate any lingering chances for the bucket shops to obtain the reports.[7]

2. *Bradstreet's*, January 18, 1890, p. 37.
3. *D.R.*, March 1, 1890, pp. 47–48.
4. *New York Times*, March 3, 1890, p. 8.
5. Taylor, p. 799. Shortly thereafter, the telegraph companies increased their rates to Board members, based upon a claim that removal of the instruments from the floor had made the transmission of messages more expensive. Board officials promptly condemned the move as one of "retaliation" and made vague threats about establishing their own independent agency. *New York Times*, April 5, 1890, p. 5; *D.P.*, April 29, 1890.
6. *New York Times*, April 3, 1890, p. 1.
7. Ibid., April 8, p. 1.

On April 12 the Board, by a large vote, empowered the directors to order member firms with private wires to stop using them, "and if they fail to do so . . . to exercise the discipline that they believe proper." Apparently the enthusiasm for Baker's program was still high. As one of the four hundred members present at the meeting put it, "let us . . . rest not until every rat is singed and every hole stopped. . . . We have thrown off the tarantula which was poisoning us. Let us tear off the brazen parasite which is gnawing at our vitals."[8] Although the resolution was supported by most of the larger firms that had private telegraph wires, the fact that the directors had already agreed to let the wires remain, on the condition that they be used for periodic reports rather than continuous quotations, vitiated the point of the resolution. It also placed the vast majority of Board members at a disadvantage. Before the meeting the *Chicago Tribune* had noted: "Private grumblings are beginning to be heard. Certain houses which have private wires continue to send quotations to their customers . . . but this gives them an important advantage over members who have no wires, and the harmony among the crusaders is not perfect. The bucket shop men know this. . . ."[9]

It soon became clear that the bucket shops continued to exist. Some of the shops tried to obtain the quotations through the Open Board of Trade, where many of the Chicago Board's members now began to do much of their business in an attempt to circumvent the directors' policy. The Board made a valiant effort to prevent its members from running (often literally) between the two buildings, but with minimal success. Board officials at first tried to lock most of the doors to the exchange to prevent members from pasing to and fro so easily. However, after one member literally battered down the door to the east side of the building, the directors abandoned this policy as impractical if not destructive. Later they seriously considered adopting a rule forbidding members to have any dealings on the Open Board, but the attorney for the association advised that such a rule would be of "doubtful legality." For a time the directors extracted a pledge from new candidates for Board membership that they would not "run over to the Open Board to deliver quo-

8. *Chicago Tribune*, April 12, 1890, p. 1.
9. Ibid., April 10, p. 3.

"Trading on the Board." *Harper's Weekly*, August 1891. Courtesy
Historical Pictures Service, Inc., Chicago.

tations, or for any other purpose, during our business hours."[10]

Some bucket shops tried to obtain market reports through Board members trading on the floor. On April 15 the directorate voted to extend its jurisdiction to include, besides the exchange rooms, "the other rooms, offices, corridors, halls, entrances and other parts of the building of the Association."[11] In May the group ruled that "no member or combination of members . . . , whether directly or indirectly, shall be permitted to collect or disseminate continuous market quotations or to use the Exchange hall or the approaches thereto for that purpose."[12] In June the directors ordered that the windows in the exchange hall be soaped.[13] Despite these precautions, the bucket shops, although reduced in numbers, continued to obtain the quotations and often at a faster rate than Board members engaged in bona fide trading.

There was an important reason for the directors' unusual efforts to enforce their ban on the collection of market reports. The courts had agreed to let the Board stop distributing the reports on the condition that the Board "would not permit continuous quotations to be collected or disseminated in any way what so ever."[14] If quotations were leaked from the floor, the directors might be faced with a contempt citation. To emphasize the point, in July 1890 they summoned for trial two members accused of violating the May rule against collecting the reports.

The defendants, Orvis and Sheldon, had worked out a clever code of signals to record the market fluctuations on the floor of the Board. With one standing in the wheat pit and the other at the end of the corn pit near the window, they relayed the reports to a room across the alley, from which they were sent through another building to the Open Board of Trade. Their code included, for example, the following signals: stroking beard with left hand, market 90, $\frac{5}{8}$; left hand to lapel of coat, market 90, $\frac{3}{4}$; left hand to pants pocket, market 90, $\frac{7}{8}$; and both hands clasped behind back, market 91. Although this code may have worked

10. Ibid., *New York Times*, April 10, 1890, p. 2; *D.P.*, April 5, 1890; *D.R.*, 1890: September 9, p. 227, October 21, p. 262.

11. *D.R.*, April 15, 1890, p. 103.

12. Ibid., May 6, p. 125.

13. Taylor, p. 801.

14. *D.R.*, July 8, 1890, p. 187.

well enough during a relatively quiet market session, one cannot help but wonder how the two would have looked during an extremely active trading period.[15]

The two were found guilty and were suspended for thirty days. The directors believed the penalty would serve as a warning and would thus deter other members from using similar tactics.[16] Two weeks later, however, another member was tried for using virtually the same code for exactly the same offense. The accused, in admitting his guilt, stated: "I thought I could make a little money, and I did not think I was hurting the Board." The directors thought otherwise, however, and suspended him for one year. In January 1891 they refused to remit the remaining period of his sentence.[17]

A large majority of Board members initially endorsed Baker's policy. Yet many believed that, no matter how popular the move might be from a moral standpoint, ultimately it flew in the face of economic realities. "Primitive practices," observed the *New York Times,* "although they had the merit of honesty and were well enough when business was light, were hardly adequate to handle the great bulk of trade now."[18] A former Board president, R. W. Dunham, probably reflected the consensus when he stated that he was "very much inclined to doubt the advisability of the action," but since it had been undertaken, he was "willing [that] it should have a full and fair trial in order to settle the question definitely."[19]

Baker had argued that the directors had no choice in their actions concerning market quotations, given the unfavorable court decision. "We have been forced to use this final resource" under court compulsion if "we furnish quotations at all, to furnish them to all alike. We will simply furnish them to none. . . ." He emphasized that the bucket shops "annually divert millions of dollars from legitimate business to the worst sort of gambling." Indeed, they were worse than gambling dens, because a bucket shop "is more public and seemingly more respectable."[20] Thus

15. *D.P.,* July 8 and 22, 1890.
16. *D.R.,* July 8, 1890, p. 191.
17. Ibid., July 22, pp. 204–5; January 27, 1891, p. 20.
18. *New York Times,* March 3, 1890, p. 8.
19. Ibid., April 3, 1890, p. 1.
20. *Chicago Tribune,* March 4, 1890, p. 2.

the new official Board policy, called "Baker's blackout," sought simply to prevent Board quotations from getting to the shops. But the Board apparently envisaged action against neither the shops themselves nor any members who bucket shopped; although Baker and the directors were prepared to discipline members who leaked the market quotations.

Contemporaries saw the fatal weaknesses in Baker's approach even as he announced it. The same newspaper that quoted the president also reported a member of a large commission firm, Lamson Brothers, as stating bluntly that the new policy "won't close the bucket shops." Although the operators might not get the official quotations from the Board floor, they could still obtain them from correspondents on other exchanges. "Even if the Board could so discipline its members" that they refuse to cooperate with the bucket shops, the Board "will hurt itself as badly as its enemy." Later, another Board member was even more succinct: "So long as members of the Board take orders to buy and sell on 'Change for bucket shop men, so long will the latter get the quotations."[21]

In editorials that appeared within two weeks of the new policy on market reports, the *Chicago Tribune* clearly articulated the basic problem confronting the Board as one that quotation restriction alone could not resolve. Applauding the Board for its efforts, the editorial suggested that "if the battle were fought on a different basis, that organization would probably succeed better and would certainly deserve to do so." It was true that Board of Trade gambling is no better than bucket shop gambling, "but the evil is only incidental to the one, while it is all there is in the other." The solution lay in emphasizing the differences between the bucket shops and the Board. Such action "would involve the necessity of occupying a higher moral ground by the directors . . . than has hitherto been assumed by them. It might also render necessary a little interior purgation, causing discomfort or even exposure to a few members. . . ." But the results would be worth it. Purified from bucket shop methods, the Board could then "stand before the world in its true function as a useful and honorable part of the great commercial machine." Then it could legitimately denounce the bucket shops; and, in so do-

21. Ibid., April 12, p. 11.

ing, "it would receive the moral support of all the respectable portion of the community and probably find itself no worse in the matter of dollars and cents as a result of shaking off both the interior and external incubus."[22]

II

After almost one year under the new policy, the result was inconclusive at best. The Board's action undoubtedly hurt some bucket shops, but others thrived and continued to get correct quotations in spite of everything the Board did. President Baker, a man described as "one of those upright and downright sort . . . who cannot blow hot and cold" staunchly defended his blackout. "What is right in his eyes today is right tomorrow, next year, and forever. . . ."[23]

While Board members continued to applaud Baker's zeal, it seemed evident that "the experiment has not been productive of the desired results." In the first place, the seven or eight private-wire houses had a real advantage over the rest of the membership. If the bucket shops suffered, the results might have been worthwhile; but they continued to thrive, even as the smaller Board commission merchants lost business to the larger firms with private wires.[24] In addition to this internal competition, upon being ejected from the floor, Western Union had increased its rates for service, placing a further burden on many members.[25]

Nevertheless, Baker ran for re-election on a continuation of his policy. He won an overwhelming victory for a second term (1,042 votes of 1,090 cast). At the annual meeting in January

22. Ibid., April 1, p. 4; April 12, p. 4.
23. Ibid., December 11, p. 1.
24. *American Elevator and Grain Trade*, November 15, 1890, p. 121.
25. "The Board must pay for its temerity in cutting off the information which the . . . telegraph companies have for years sold to the bucket shops without any benefit to the party originating the news, which was so important that the claimed right to receive it has been vigorously fought for in the courts." *Chicago Tribune*, April 5, 1890, p. 4. It was clear, to the Chicago Board of Trade at least, that the telegraph companies appreciated the large revenue received from the bucket shops. See ibid., May 21, p. 4. In the previous issue, the *Tribune* reported that a "large" bucket shop had failed. It had employed 75 clerks and telegraph operators, had 120 branch offices, and paid about $250,000 to Western Union in telegraph tolls. Ibid., May 20, p. 2.

1891, the members defeated a resolution to restore the telegraph instruments. In their report for 1890, the directors asserted that the program had been a success. Besides causing an upturn in business, it had relieved the Board "from furnishing quotations to certain concerns which had enjoined the Board from withholding such quotations."[26]

Baker regarded his victory as an endorsement of the blackout. In his inaugural address to the members, he claimed, "What has been accomplished already is gratifying enough to encourage a continuance of your vigorous policy, but we may as well understand that we must make the fight alone." This was because other exchanges, as well as Western Union, "have sought to reap a passing advantage by hampering us in our efforts" against the shops. Indeed, Baker went so far as to state that Western Union "has always been the open or secret enemy of this Board." Finally, he turned to the complaints concerning the economic advantages of those firms with private wires. "No one," he claimed, "will deprive such houses of the advantage that ultimately accrues to them as a result of their enterprise . . . , yet the interest of the association is not to foster monopoly in any direction."

Here, perhaps unintentionally, Baker alluded to the extremely troublesome ambiguities confronting quasi-administrative agencies in relation to the interests over which they have regulatory responsibilities. Certainly large commission houses with their own wires could only welcome Baker's policy of exclusion. Yet this program placed the majority of members, who did not have private connections, at a serious economic disadvantage. The efforts of the Board leaders to resolve this difficulty typify those of regulatory agencies seeking to avoid the claim that they had been captured by the very groups they were supposed to monitor. Emphasizing that "everyone should reap a share . . . of the increase in the general business," Baker urged that the Board not order private telegraph lines removed but, rather, that the exchanges without them build their own lines.[27]

This proposal was financially impossible. Furthermore, there was no proof that the increase in business cited by Baker and the

26. *Report of the Directors, 1890*, p. lxvi.
27. *Chicago Tribune*, January 13, 1891, p. 3.

directors had been caused by cessation of the reports, and the so-called increase turned out to be more temporary than permanent. Indeed, another solution to the problem of private wires appeared to have more support than Baker's suggestion: simply restore the reports. While this step is indicative of Board impotence in maintaining effective internal control, it at least insured benefit to all segments of the membership.

By 1891, if there was little evidence of hostility toward Baker himself, as witnessed by his triumphant victory, there was increasing evidence of objections to the blackout policy. One such indication was the appearance, in the 1891 Board election, of an opposition ticket for the five directory seats, consisting of members who openly favored the old system. These members argued that speculative trade comprised the foundation of virtually all Board business and that it should be fostered and not fettered. While this claim was exaggerated, it remained true that under Baker's policy the bucket shops were left to get market information on their own, while Board members were forbidden to collect the market quotations. As a result, the shops continued to operate, while legitimate Board business suffered.[28] The opposition slate went down to defeat in the annual election, but its viewpoint ultimately prevailed.

Another indication of opposition was the publication, in August 1891, of a pamphlet entitled *The Chicago Board of Trade and Its Policy*. Written by W. S. Crosby, a former director of the Board, the pamphlet articulated a viewpoint that many members supported. Crosby distributed a copy to every member of the Board, and this lengthy printed critique of the directors' policies by a member is one of the very few tangible examples of real disagreement between large segments of the membership and its leaders. In it Crosby accused the directorate of asking the wrong question and thereby coming up with a wrong answer. The important consideration was not the moral wrongs of the bucket shops and whether or not the Board of Trade ought to use all its power to suppress them; rather, Crosby claimed, every Board member ought to ask, "To what extent did the bucket shops injure the business of the Board and how much would it cost to suppress them?" No one really knew or could know the extent

28. Taylor, p. 818.

of the bucket shops' competition. Why then did Board officials blame every unfavorable market development on them?

More important, Crosby believed that the Board's policy helped the bucket shops while at the same time hindering its own market interests. He noted the existence of a vast speculative market from which both the bucket shops and the Board sought business. But, he claimed, the directorate had antagonized "those from whom our business comes." By decreasing the efficiency of its services, the Board had decreased the value of its membership. It had made it harder for a customer to speculate on his money. By cutting off the quotations and removing the telegraph instruments, the directors were doing everything to prevent "the knowledge of the constantly changing price of our wares from becoming known." In short, Crosby concluded, the Board's policy seemed to be one of cutting off its nose to spite its face. "Is this not the most supreme folly of which we as a Board were ever guilty?"[29]

It is impossible to state to what extent Crosby's booklet influenced the directors. However, one month after it appeared, the directors voted, effective November 1, 1891, to restore the public telegraph wires to the floor and to order the private wires removed.[30] Again, the prime reason seems to have been unfair internal competition. While a few of the major commission houses with their own private wires had prospered during the year, many other Board members had suffered, "as private wires monopolized business which before had been generally distributed."[31]

The returning telegraph companies agreed not to send out continuous quotations or to use the ticker and to restore rates to the lower level in effect before March 31, 1890.[32] The Board insisted that restoration of the telegraph agencies did not mean a resump-

29. W. S. Crosby, *The Chicago Board of Trade and Its Policy* (Chicago, 1891), pp. 1–50.
30. *D.R.*, September 10, 1891, pp. 192–94; *New York Times*, September 11, 1891, p. 5.
31. *American Elevator and Grain Trade*, September 15, 1891, p. 83; *Chicago Tribune*, 1891: September 9, p. 1, October 11, p. 7, October 12, p. 1.
32. The "halfway" measure of the directors in restoring the telegraph instruments but not the ticker incensed Crosby; and in October 1891 he published a shorter and more strident pamphlet entitled *The Chicago Board of Trade and Its Quotations*, which was a reiteration of his earlier statements.

tion of open, continuous quotations. In fact, however, there was little point in having them on the floor if the reports were not to be sent out. Indeed, the directors began to abandon Baker's blackout even before his term expired. On November 11 the *Chicago Tribune* noted pointedly that "all opposition by the Board of Trade to the bucket shops seems to have died away. . . . These institutions are apparently in as flourishing a condition as ever."[33]

Early in 1892 the newly elected Board president, Charles Hamill, told the membership that the "quotations problem" called for "such regulating as will give all members equal rights, and at the same time interfere as little as possible with the right to furnish our clients such information as is legitimate and necessary." It had become obvious that "present regulations seem to interfere with this desired result" and that they had also "failed to bring about that end for which they were enacted."[34]

As if to make the point even clearer, on March 14 the *Chicago Tribune* devoted major space to the "flourishing condition of the bucket shop evil." Various articles described the more than twenty-five shops, where they were located, and how they operated. These articles included interviews with several bucket-shop dealers, among them O. M. Stone, who was supposedly "the principal dealer in quotations on the Chicago markets." Stone admitted having an employee stationed on the floor of the Board gathering quotations for him, although he refused to state whether or not the individual was a member of the Board![35] From one article, which detailed the lengths to which bucket-shop operators went to plant their wires, it becomes apparent that the bucket-shop proprietors of the late nineteenth century are among the paternal ancestors of modern wire tappers. The *Tribune* also printed an interview with President Hamill, who, perhaps unintentionally, sounded the knell for Baker's blackout. "The Board is tired," he said, "of fighting the evil alone, especially because we have not been able to accomplish our object. . . ."[36]

By April the directors had concluded that the Board had four options to choose from in continuing its quotations policy: (1)

33. *Chicago Tribune*, November 11, 1891, p. 7.
34. Ibid., January 12, 1892, p. 10.
35. Ibid., March 14, pp. 1, 6.
36. Ibid.. p. 6.

to make no change; (2) to let Western Union and/or other telegraph agencies, without restrictions, collect and distribute the reports; (3) to reactivate its own market reports department, as it had existed before 1890, as "a service owned and controlled by the Board"; and (4) to allow a private company onto the floor, not under Board supervision, but open at all times to suppression "if it should be found playing into the hands of the bucket shops."

The *Tribune* asserted that if the harsh measures under Baker had worked, there would have been support for continuing them; but, it reported, the bucket shops were "running wide open." One of them supposedly had a better system of private wires than any member firm of the Board, and had offered to obtain quotes for member firms at a very fair rate. Only pride, according to the *Tribune* writer, prevented the houses from accepting the offer. Members wished to abandon what they were now willing to admit was a mistake, "but they would like to make the change without producing the impression that it was a retreat." In other words, they wished to come up with "a gloriously victorious plan of backing out."[37]

A brief period of campaigning ensued, during which the proponents of open distribution compared the Board rules of 1892 with the Puritan blue laws of 1692:

> "Thou shalt not inform thy neighbor of the continuous price of cereals, lest thereby he may obtain sufficient knowledge to do business." Thou shalt not send out quotations via Western Union lest "people may become aware that there is such a place as Chicago and that it contains a Board of Trade. Thou shalt do everything to kill thy great enemy, the bucket shop man, even at the risk of killing thyself." Thou shalt "build a wall around thyself that the world may not know of thy doings, and that thou mayest enjoy happiness and felicity of being the only human who knows the price of cereals. . . . Thou shalt obey above instructions, though the heavens fall. Thou shalt stand still . . . though all the world progresses with giant strides. Thy motto shall be, down with the bucket shops, for virtue is its own reward. SELAH."[38]

Then, on April 23, the membership voted that the Board should

37. Ibid., April 21, p. 1.
38. Ibid., April 24, p. 7.

provide for "early and general" distribution of the quotations. Barely half of the total membership voted, and the proposition carried by 111 votes, 544 to 433.[39] The prevailing attitude seemed to be that bucket shops would somehow continue to get the quotations no matter what the directors did to prevent it. As one journal observed: "It will not make much difference to the trade at large what action the Board takes in the matter, except that all will have a greater confidence in the quotations. It would also prove a source of revenue to the Board."[40]

On May 31, after protracted negotiations over the amount of money to be paid by the telegraph agencies, the directors approved the agreement to restore ticker service and continuous quotations. The reports were to be collected and distributed by the telegraph companies at their own expense, subject to the rules laid down by the Board. The reports were not to be sent out as official quotations of the Board of Trade; neither did that body take any responsibility for their correctness or accuracy.[41] The actions of the directors were an admission that Baker's policy had been a failure. In refusing to lend Board recognition to the new system of market reports, they provided a fitting epilogue for what had become a futile exercise.

III

By October 1890 the Butterworth bill had come and gone. Realizing that dealing in privileges provided a convenient weapon with which to assault the commercial exchange as a whole, the directors tried another approach to this perennial problem. Privileged trading was intimately connected with transactions made outside the approved hours of trade. Thus if the directors could reduce the amount of irregular trading, they would also lessen the traffic in privileged trades. On October 7 the directors met with a number of members representing the major commission houses. The officials appealed to the integrity and commercial honor for which the Board was supposed to stand.

The result of this meeting was a unique agreement circulated among the membership. Those who signed it promised that they

39. Ibid., Taylor, p. 842.
40. *American Elevator and Grain Trade*, April 15, 1892, p. 335.
41. *D.R.*, May 31, 1892, pp. 140–41.

would "neither directly nor indirectly, for ourselves or for others, engage in buying or selling for future delivery grain or provisions in any place or places whatsoever, outside of the hours prescribed for trading." In addition, members agreed to "exert our influence individually and collectively to stop all trading as above described, except within the hours specified. . . ." To this agreement they pledged their "honor as businessmen."[42] By November 11 a committee appointed to canvass the members reported that it had secured between 170 and 175 signatures, "including most of the prominent houses engaged in business on the floor."[43]

However, in spite of this appeal to commercial integrity, trading in privileges continued. By February 1892, with the Hatch committee holding hearings in Washington, H. H. Aldrich wired President Hamill urging that the Chicago Board of Trade stop privileged trading "at once and forever." The Board responded by closing the room except for settlements on regular contracts and by appealing once again to the leading commission firms to refrain voluntarily from dealing in privileges. For a short time many of them did so, but by the end of February a return to the old ways seemed clear. On March 3 three of these firms wrote to the directors. They had been "refusing all orders in privileges, expecting that such a movement would become general among our numbers." However this had not been the case, and the firms wrote to "earnestly ask that if it is the intention of your body" to end all privileged trading "that you take official and vigorous action to eradicate the evil before it has again assumed large proportions."[44]

Meeting two days later, the directors were told that some members now used the alley in back of the Board's building to deal in privileges. Other members, particularly those who had agreed to stop such transactions, voiced the old complaint that it was unfair for them to stop while others did not. "Unless an effectual stop was put to the practice of trading in puts and calls they would not consider themselves bound to further refrain from dealing in them."[45] Whereupon the directors took up the burden all over again.

42. Ibid., October 7, 1890, pp. 251–52.
43. Ibid., November 11, p. 280.
44. *D.P.*, March 8, 1892.
45. *D.R.*, March 8, 1892, p. 69.

This time they ordered the secretary to inform the Board by announcement and written notice that "all trading of whatsoever nature, either directly or indirectly, in puts and calls . . . as well as all transactions growing out of . . . such trading are, and will be deemed . . . dishonorable conduct." Members convicted of such conduct were to be disciplined under the rules. Thus far the announcement was similar to the many that had preceded it. However, the last sentence went right to the point. "It being the intention of the . . . directors to completely put a stop to all trading in puts and calls, and relieve the Board from the stigma of such transactions."[46]

Early in October 1892 a committee of directors reported that it had employed detectives to obtain evidence against certain members for trading in privileges. The committee was now prepared to move against these members, and the directors voted to proceed with the trials "whenever said committee are satisfied that they have evidence enough to convict."[47] On October 16, however, Director T. A. Wright proposed that the prosecutions for dealing in puts and calls be postponed. Wright, who had represented the Board in Washington before the congressional committees, pointed out that a critical time for the Hatch bill was coming up. He believed that there would be much quarreling among the Board members and the directors because of the way in which the evidence to convict had been secured. The prosecution of the cases was certain to involve the Board in lawsuits, focusing attention on its internal problems, which would delight supporters of antioption measures.[48]

Although the directors ordered the cases for trial in November, one of the defendants applied for an injunction against the Board. While the injunction was ultimately vacated as premature, the resulting legal delays prevented the directors from reaching the cases until January 10, 1893.[49] This date was also the last meeting of the current directory.

The trial was marred by discord among the directors. Several

46. Ibid., pp. 69–70.
47. Ibid., October 11, p. 245.
48. Ibid., October 16, pp. 259–60.
49. Two of the three defendants were fairly well known. W. E. McHenry had been a Board member for almost twenty years and was a former director and vice-president. Edwin Pardrige had a reputation for market manipulation

felt that the entire matter, having been so long delayed, ought not to be held until the new members of the directory took office. The vote to proceed with the trial carried by three votes. Only one witness was called, and his testimony was so vague that it served little purpose. Another witness suddenly refused to testify, throwing the prosecution into confusion. Further, the Board member representing the defendants made strenuous objection to the fact that the directors' proceedings grew out of a secret committee. The possibility of court litigation was apparent to all concerned.[50]

Apparently fed up with the entire problem, one of the directors moved that, since the evidence obtained could not be produced, the cases against the three defendants be dismissed and the resolution of March 8, 1892, "be rescinded absolutely and wiped off altogether and the committee discharged."[51] The directory so voted, and their action "caused the greatest surprise among the traders." "I suppose," concluded President Hamill, "that the directors thought it was useless to have a rule on our books which could not be enforced."[52]

Thus, even as the Hatch bill awaited Senate action, the Chicago Board of Trade rescinded a rule forbidding what many congressional critics of the Board found so objectionable—trading in puts and calls. At a time when the Board was seriously threatened with undesirable federal regulation, its action seemed unusual, to say the least; however, the vote of the directorate was in fact consistent with both the philosophy and past history of the Board. Hamill was only being realistic and candid in his explanation. The president reflected a similar sense of realism in his attitude toward the Board's quotations policy. Board rules that could not be enforced weakened the organization's entire self-regulatory process.

Certainly the exchange's action in 1892 and 1893 concerning the bucket shops and privileged trading cannot be called impressive. The organization had failed to adopt effective administrative

that equaled, if possible, the notoriety of Old Hutch. See Taylor, pp. 840–44. See also *SB*, 1894: *Chicago Times*, August 8; *Chicago Post*, August 13, 14; *Chicago Herald*, August 16.

50. *D.R.*, January 10, 1893, pp. 306–10.

51. Ibid., pp. 311–12.

52. *SB*, *Chicago News*, January 11, 1893.

regulations. Unwilling to implement appropriate remedial measures to solve those market abuses, the Board was thus unable to exercise any consistent and rigorous administrative supervision. This not only meant an inability to police its own membership directly, but also necssarily implied an indirect failure to provide an ordered external market framework. The fiasco of the quotations policy revealed that the Board was still unable to reconcile the tension between private gain and public need. Faced with internal disagreement over its actions, the directors heeded the shifting currents and retreated. It must be emphasized once again that the leadership of the Chicago Board of Trade, unlike that of modern administrative agencies, had to accept managerial responsibility for its actions. This fact may render the Board's dramatic failure understandable, but it also makes even more outstanding the organization's future success both in imposing regulatory policies and in dealing with the bucket shops.

During the period 1894 to 1905, the Board slowly but perceptively moved toward effective regulation of its members. It again tackled the problem of puts and calls, turned with a new and ultimately potent strategy against the bucket shops, and adopted other rules dealing with internal discipline which demonstrated an awareness of public responsibility that was noticeably lacking in the 1880s. These developments did not occur simultaneously, however; nor were they all entirely successful. That they occurred at all may well be largely a result of the travails just discussed.[53]

It is tempting to see the possibility of federal intervention as a prime factor in causing tighter internal regulation. To some extent the threat probably was a contributing factor, and the warning of the *Northwestern Miller* in 1892 seems especially appropriate for the Chicago Board of Trade. According to this

53. In this context some remarks by President Hamill are of interest. Submitting his annual report early in 1893, the president stated that boards of trade have no private interests to promote: "Their welfare depends upon the value of the services which they render to the commercial public in the interests of fairness and justice. . . . The commercial exchange stands, therefore, for equity and fair dealing." *Report of the Directors, 1893*, p. liv. Here was a distinct shift in emphasis, away from the rights of a private organization dedicated primarily to the profits of its members. It may, of course, be true that expediency more than ethics played a large role in the Board's apparent shift in perception. The extent to which it shifted is revealed by the events between 1893 and 1903.

journal, the public had had enough of the "flabby rules of commercial bodies"; and if officials of associations wanted to avert the ruin of sweeping—even radical—legislation, "they themselves should improve the present while it is in their power, and drive out the rats from among them. If they can do this they can save themselves and the house they live in. . . . If they can not, which seems probable, they must expect that they will suffer."[54]

Had the threat of federal legislation remained prominent, this factor would have been entitled to great weight. But as was shown in the previous chapter, after 1893 antioption faded as a visible and viable political issue. If an organization seeks to reform itself, it must start with an accurate assessment of both the problems to be solved and the necessary solutions. Only after it had been confronted with dramatic evidence of its own impotence, as was true of the Chicago Board of Trade in its bucket-shop battles between 1890 and 1892, did the association receive the needed stimulus for internal change.

IV

In its previous attempts to block the bucket shops, the Board had supported legislation, litigation, and limitation—all apparently to no avail. The anti-bucket-shop law of 1887 appeared extremely difficult to enforce, the judges ruled against the Board, and the policy of limiting the quotations was disastrous. In 1894 the directors determined to move in the only direction left that had not been seriously explored: the disciplinary authority held by the Board over its own members who were involved in bucket-shop activity. To be sure, the membership had approved a rule eleven years earlier that prohibited dealing in differences "on the fluctuations in the market prices of any commodity without a bona fide purchase and sale of property for an actual delivery." Violators were "liable to suspension" and could be expelled. But the rule had been ineffectual largely because it was so easy to claim that one intended to make or take delivery.

One technique for correcting this glaring loophole was to insist that Board members give to each of their customers the names of all parties with whom trades were made. If a mem-

54. *Northwestern Miller,* January 22, 1892, p. 115.

ber was unable to do this, it meant that he had taken the other side of the trade himself, without executing the order on the open market. In other words, he had "bucket shopped" the transaction. On October 30, 1894, the directors adopted a rule that required every member who traded in futures on the floor to "notify the party for whom such purchases or sale was made, of the price at which and the party with whom . . . , such notice to be in writing and to be given upon the day of such purchase or sale." Noncompliance was punishable by suspension or expulsion."[55]

The Board approved the new rule by a very narrow margin, 312 to 310. An explanation of the extremely close vote may be that a large number of members had continued to "bucket" their market orders in spite of the old rule and did not welcome the additional restriction. Almost immediately, some members disregarded the regulation, claiming that their customers did not care to know with whom the commission men did business, so long as it was done promptly and, if possible, profitably. Seeking the advice of counsel, the directors were informed that there were, indeed, two ways to construe the rule: (1) if the directorate believed the rule had been passed for the security and information of the customers, it could waive the obligation to divulge the names if the customer "explicitly stated that he did not wish them"; (2) if, however, the rule had been enacted "as a matter of public policy" to secure "the execution of all orders on the open market," the directors had the power to declare the rule mandatory and "a matter that [lay] between the commission house and the Board of Trade, not between the commission house and the customer." Without hesitation the directors ordered the secretary to announce that there was no way in which a commission house and its customers could legally disregard the rule and that all transactions were to be carried out according to its spirit and letter.[56] As if to emphasize the point, on December 18 the directors found a member guilty of violating the rule and suspended him for ten years.[57]

The action of the directors in interpreting the new rule should be noted, because it reflected a subtle but different change in

55. *D.R.*, 1894: October 2, p. 204; October 30, pp. 227–28.
56. Ibid., December 4, p. 244.
57. *D.P.*, December 18, 1894; *D.R.*, December 18, 1894, pp. 257–65.

administrative emphasis. Traditionally the Board did not interfere in a mercantile relationship between a member and his customers, except to establish a basic set of ground rules. But in
accepting the notion that "public policy" required the new rule
to assure an open market, the organization moved directly into
this hitherto restricted area. The new rule can be seen as an
adjustment of that perennial market tension more toward the
public interest and away from private economic gain. However,
the fact that it took the Board eleven years to get this far, and
then only by a two-vote margin, indicates the distance the association had yet to travel. Even in 1894, fifteen years after the
bucket shops had become newsworthy, the Chicago Board of
Trade still was unable to enact, let alone enforce, a simple rule
forbidding its members to bucket shop in any form whatsoever
and providing expulsion as the penalty for violation.

Those members of the Board who favored tighter internal regulation scored another gain late in 1894, when they secured the
triumphant renomination of William Baker as president for a
third term. A man of outstanding integrity, Baker had pushed
the unsuccessful policy against the bucket shops in 1890–91.
No candidate came forward to challenge Baker and he was
re-elected, the first third-term president in the history of the Chicago Board of Trade. During his inaugural address in January
1895, Baker discussed the problems of bucket shops and privilege trading that confronted the organization. He declared that
bucket-shop dealing seemed irremediable but that the shops
thrived because they had access to the quotations, and the Board
had only itself to blame. If the association did not distribute
market reports, the bucket shops would not receive them. Even
though his blackout policy had been a failure in 1890–91, Baker
again asked that the directors "be authorized to discontinue the
present plan of supplying continuous quotations to our markets."
Turning to privileges, he stated that they had "become so common outside of exchange hours as to impair the good name of
the association." Besides being unlawful, the insurance factor of
such transactions tended to discourage speculative business "that
you would count on in a free and unrestricted market." He sin-
cerely urged that "means may be taken to put an end to the
practice at once"; and he concluded by reminding the members
of the compact they had all signed, that they would "be in all

respects governed by and respect the rules . . . as they now exist, or as they may be hereafter modified, altered or amended."[58]

Board members responded to Baker's speech by adopting several resolutions. One asked the directors to "propose such rules and make such regulations as will entirely suppress privileged trading." Another gave the directors authority to cut off the quotations, and a third noted that the recommendations of Baker in his inaugural address "are hereby concurred in, and that he receive the support of this association in carrying them out."[59] The *Chicago Tribune* reported that "If the successive rounds of applause unanimously accorded his vigorous denunciations of bucket shops . . . and other evils are to be taken literally, the new administration will be one of the most noteworthy in the history of the Board."[60]

The first opportunity for the membership to do more than applaud Baker's suggested changes came in the matter of puts and calls. Acting on one of the resolutions, the directors restored, for the first time in almost thirty years, a specific rule against privilege trading.[61] They expanded the list of offenses punishable by suspension or expulsion to include a member guilty "of trading in privileges, directly or indirectly, in his own behalf or for or through others." A member was further forbidden to become party to a contract arising out of a privilege. The directors adopted the new rule on January 22 and submitted it to the Board at large for a vote on February 4.[62]

During the two-week interim period, organized and open opposition to the rule developed. Those against the change observed that, contrary to Baker's stand, privileged trading represented good business insurance and that all previous efforts by the directors to prevent it had failed.[63] How could this latest attempt be any different? Baker's supporters emphasized that approval would mean "a higher estimation in public opinion for grain merchandising, and an emphatic reminder that this the Chicago Board of Trade can and will uphold and obey the laws

58. *Report of the Directors*, 1894, pp. lxv–lxx.
59. *D.P.*, January 15, 1895.
60. *SB, Chicago Tribune*, January 15, 1895.
61. Supra, ch. 2.
62. *D.R.*, January 22, 1895, p. 9.
63. Taylor, p. 895.

of the state." They claimed, with some justice, that the Board could not seek help from the state in suppressing bucket shops while at the same time openly flouting a law that carried a $1,000 fine and a year in jail as penalties for violation. "Are we law abiding citizens, or are we CRIMINALS, ANARCHISTS, or GAMBLERS?" was a question posed by a handout distributed shortly before the vote; and it warned, "The public will judge by our vote."[64]

By February 1 opponents of the rule were offering to bet that it would be defeated, and it was. The membership rejected the new amendment by a vote of 604 to 505. Baker's response was typical. He immediately resigned, as also did two of his supporters on the directory, Zina Carter (later to succeed Baker as president) and John Hill, Jr., an outspoken advocate of reform and probably the Board member most responsible for the ultimate victory against the bucket shops.[65] On February 6 more than seven hundred members gathered for a riotous meeting, at which the resignations were all rejected. The directors' real estate committee closed the room where members traded in puts and calls. These trades were strictly forbidden in the Board building, and the secretary announced that the hours of trade would be strictly enforced.[66] In addition, a number of firms announced that they would no longer handle privileges. The *Chicago Post* believed that the Board's action represented a practical, if not "manly," solution. At least now the public could not point to the inconsistency of the floor closed to puts and calls with the Board rooms right across the corridor open to those who dealt in privileges.[67]

A majority of the directors, who still supported Baker, one week later adopted another rule, which stated that all purchases or sales of grain made in the exchange room of the Board, "when such purchases or sales result either directly or indirectly from privileges," were to be considered cause for suspension or expul-

64. *D.P.*, February 5, 1895.
65. No trace of Hill's letter has turned up, perhaps because, as Taylor puts it, the language was so "fervent that it was thought best not to include it in the minutes."
66. *SB*, 1895: *Chicago Times, Chicago InterOcean,* and *Chicago Herald,* February 7; *Chicago Tribune,* February 8. All three Board officials withdrew their resignations.
67. *SB, Chicago Post,* February 8, 1895.

sion.[68] The aim of this rule, clearly, was to get around the vote of February 4, and a number of members took exception to the directors' action. More than 375 of them petitioned that the new rule be rescinded because it went against the expressed majority vote of the membership. The rule stood, however; but while the directors held firm in principle, they bent in practice.[69] Word was quickly circulated that the new regulation would not be enforced, and trading in privileges—although a little muted—resumed. The directors did, however, use a clever method to enforce the rule relating to hours of trade. As the hour for closing struck, an employee of the Board appeared with a huge Chinese gong and proceeded to drown out all noise in the pits, making it impossible to trade.[70] Furthermore, the directors voted to refuse admission to any member who had not yet signed the agreement mentioned by Baker in his address.[71]

The bucket shop campaign was reopened on two fronts. In a departure from past policy, the Board launched a program of public information against the shops. In August the secretary placed advertisements in the local press, stating that he would be glad to furnish tentative investors with information concerning whether or not the firms they proposed to deal with were members in good standing with the Board. In addition, Secretary Stone circulated lists of Board members, to inform the public which firms were members of the organization and thus under its supervision.[72] More than 1,500 inquiries were received before the year ended. Of course, in answering these requests for information, Stone was quick to point out the "exceptional opportunities" open to members of the Board for executing orders "in the most favorable manner" possible. But he also emphasized the obligations "which rest upon the members of this commercial body, chartered for commercial purposes, whose chief, if not controlling object, is the maintenance and promotion of the highest mercantile integrity."[73]

68. *D.R.*, February 13, 1895, p. 24.
69. *D.P.*, February 19, 1895; *D.R.*, February 19, 1895, p. 30.
70. Taylor, p. 897.
71. *D.R.*, 1895: February 5, p. 20; February 19, p. 30.
72. *SB, Chicago Tribune*, August 1, 2, 1895; *New York Produce Reporter*, September 21, 1895.
73. *Report of the Directors, 1895*, p. lxvii.

The second part of the bucket-shop fight continued the attack against members who had bucket-shop connections, as well as against the shops themselves. Baker appointed a special bucket-shop committee, which apparently consisted only of John Hill; and, from October to December 1895, the directors brought four members to trial for bucket shopping with evidence he supplied. They expelled one member and suspended the other three, one for five years, and two for three years.[74] According to the *Chicago InterOcean*, the trials came as a surprise "to the majority of the members, who did not think the directors meant business."[75]

In preparing prosecutions Hill used three techniques: (1) investigations of various wires and cables in and around the exchange building; (2) the hiring of detectives who visited suspected Board of Trade members in the guise of customers seeking to bucket shop their trades; and (3) obtaining information from employees of suspect firms, particularly those who were supposed to telegraph orders to buy and sell. Testimony in this last area could be very important. Thus, in the trial of J. F. Harris, a telegraph operator testified that, when she was employed by a so-called "commission firm," she never had any orders to send to the Board of Trade. The various requests to buy or sell were all settled within the office. As all orders were required to be executed in the open market on the floor of the Board and during specific hours, such evidence generally convinced the directors of wrongdoing.[76]

Hill's tenacity and persistence resulted in a string of expulsions from the Board. Even though disagreement with the directors over an unrelated Board policy concerning grain elevators led him to resign from the group before the expiration of his second term, Hill continued to attack the bucket shops.[77] Occasionally his zeal for conviction led him to overlook elementary principles of due process. In the trial of Harris, for example, Hill

74. *D.R.*, 1895: October 29, p. 201; December 10, pp. 232–80. Biographical data on John Hill may be found in Taylor, 3:154–55.

75. *SB, Chicago InterOcean*, December 11, 12, 13, 1895.

76. *D.R.*, December 12, 1895, p. 282.

77. Hill was elected a Board director in 1892. He was re-elected in 1895, and his term would have expired in 1898. See Taylor, pp. 918–21. See also *D.R.*, 1896: July 14, pp. 123–28; July 21, p. 134; August 4, p. 138.

submitted as evidence testimony given by a witness at an earlier bucket-shop trial. Harris objected, claiming that he would have no chance to cross-examine such evidence. Upon being found guilty and suspended for two years, Harris took the case to court. The Board's attorney advised settlement, and Harris promised to drop the suit if he was reinstated. The directory agreed.[78]

Hill did more than prosecute Board members. He made evidence available to the Cook County Grand Jury, and he sought the aid of the post office in classifying bucket-shop circulars as "fraudulent" material, thus nondeliverable. There is no doubt that between 1895 and 1899 the number of bucket shops was reduced; but many continued to operate. Nevertheless, the directors appeared impressed with Hill's labors. In June 1897 a directorate committee noted that his services "are invaluable, and that the work accomplished by his untiring efforts and unselfish attention to the interests of the members of the Board of Trade . . . is deserving of the highest praise." They voted to pay him $2,500 for his work thus far, and to raise the sum of $25,000 for the continued fight against the bucket shops.[79]

V

At last the Board had experienced some success in its battle against the bucket shops, most notably in the prosecution of its own members for bucket shopping. The campaign of public education against the shops had also been beneficial, if only because it made the public more aware of the Board's increasingly hostile attitude toward them.[80] However, despite internal prosecutions and penalties, external publicity against the shops, and the persistent efforts of John Hill, Jr., the bucket shops remained in business. In January 1899, Hill claimed that the directors were

78. *D.P.*, September 29, 1896; *D.R.*, September 29, 1896, p. 160.
79. *D.R.*, June 29, 1897, pp. 125–26.
80. "It is likely that future operations may be facilitated by a more general appreciation by the community of what bucket shops really are," Baker noted in January 1896. "It is beginning to dawn upon the comprehension of the public that every one connected with the bucket shops are thieves and swindlers, and the man who is guilty of bucket shop practices can no longer shield himself under the cloak of respectability." Supra, n. 73.

not really in sympathy with the fight against them.[81] He may have been correct, but a more valid reason for the bucket shops' continued operation may have been the fact that the system of quotations distribution was essentially the same as it had been in the 1880s. When, in 1892, the directors admitted the failure of Baker's blackout policy by returning to open quotations, the telegraph companies undertook to collect and distribute the reports, paying an annual fee to the Board for the privilege.

Although the telegraph agencies had promised to withhold the quotations from bucket shops, the reports continued to be widely distributed. It may be that the companies lacked the facilities, if not the inclination, to investigate the background of those who sought the market reports. From the Board's point of view, it was clear that the telegraph companies—especially Western Union—were at fault. In the final inaugural address delivered by Baker in January 1897, he blasted the unholy alliance between the bucket shops and Western Union. He accused Western Union of being the only major telegraph company "that leases wires for the use of the bucket shops in swindling their patrons"; and he asserted, "The spectacle of a corporation with a hundred million dollars capital paying dividends gleaned from the vice and crime of the country is one to make any American blush."[82]

The telegraph agencies were not totally at fault, however. Whenever they did attempt to cut off quotations to a particular individual or firm, as they did in March 1897, the courts enjoined them, on the basis of the 1889 *New York and Chicago Grain and Stock Exchange* case, from taking any such action.[83]

81. *SB, Chicago Times-Herald,* January 5, 1899.

82. *Report of the Directors, 1896,* p. lxxxvii. Baker's strong condemnation represented an excellent example of local progressive sentiment in Chicago. The relationship between progressive reform and the Board of Trade's internal reform drive is discussed in chapter 8.

83. In general, the decision of the Chicago Circuit Court followed the Illinois Supreme Court's holding in 1889. However, the judge emphasized that the Board and the telegraph companies were obliged to furnish the information for legitimate purposes only. The Board was not bound "to furnish or permit to be collected or furnished . . . quotations or market news for the use of any bucket shop, and . . . in fact no person in any way connected with a bucket shop is entitled to receive such news." *Bradstreet's,* March 27, 1897, p. 193. Although it is not clear whether Board officials appreciated the significance of this finding, in fact the judge's decision pointed to a new line of attack against the bucket shops. See chapter 7 following.

But their efforts to check on bucket-shop activities seem to have been very few. "The truth is," the *Chicago Times-Herald* claimed, "the Western Union is and has been the chief support and bulwark of the bucket shops."[84] Members of the Board came, increasingly, to realize that some agency had to establish, through investigation, whether the parties who sought the quotations were seeking them for legitimate or illegitimate purposes. If the telegraph companies could not do this, the Board would have to assume the responsibility.

In October 1898 the attorney for the Board, A. W. Green, resigned. He had served since 1890, when he had replaced Sidney Smith. Green had been successful in dealing with all major legal issues that confronted the organization, with the exception of the bucket-shop fight. He had "ever striven," he wrote, "to keep the Board out of litigation."[85] This may have been the correct solution in 1890 in view of the Illinois Supreme Court decision against the Board; but by 1899 the directors and their new attorney, a University of Wisconsin Law School graduate named Henry S. Robbins, believed the time had come for the Board to take the offensive in litigation against the bucket shops. This determination appears at several intervals during 1899.

The Board president elected in 1899 hinted at the new viewpoint when he stated that the membership and directors "must decide whether it is best and wise to continue the warfare against the bucket shops along the lines adopted in the past." President Lyon urged that the association "continue to emphasize . . . disapproval of bucket shop methods, and lend . . . aid to stamp out this great blot on the body politic."[86] One method was to strengthen the Board rules against bucket shops.

In November 1899 the directors warned that any member "who shall have any such forbidden relation, by telephone, telegraph or otherwise, directly or indirectly, with any person or concern operating a bucket shop" would be liable to suspension or expulsion.[87] One week later the directorate ordered all mem-

84. *SB, Chicago Times-Herald*, March 23, 1897.
85. *D.R.*, October 25, 1898, pp. 168–69.
86. *Report of the Directors, 1898*, p. lxx. The Board was extremely fortunate that public and private interest could blend together so smoothly in battle against the bucket shops.
87. *D.R.*, November 21, 1899, p. 222.

bers "operating private wires or telephones to furnish a list of their correspondents communicated with over such private wires or telephones."[88] However, it was not until December 5 that a directorate committee struck at the real problem. It called for the Board to adopt "some plan for controlling its quotations, securing an adequate revenue therefrom, and holding in their hands their complete control." The committee believed that the execution of such a plan would "root up and out the bucket shop evil in Chicago—an evil which the Board has expended a large amount of money in its efforts to suppress."[89]

These indications of new steps to be taken against both the bucket shops and the Board members connected with them were accompanied by increased demands within the association for internal Board reforms. In November 1899 the *Chicago Post* quoted a former officer of the Board, probably John Hill, Jr., who claimed that "the regular bucket shop committee has not been able to remove the vicious influences which are appearing more and more on the Board."[90] Even the *Chicago InterOcean*, a bitter critic of John Hill and his efforts at Board housecleaning, had to admit that there was a spirit of reform among the members.[91] By November 1899, according to Taylor, "the atmosphere of the Board of Trade was surcharged with reform movements."[92]

With the annual elections at hand, the Board faction led by Baker and Hill fielded an "opposition" ticket headed by William S. Warren as the candidate for president.[93] Warren, a prosperous commission merchant, was closely associated with Baker and Hill in their calls for Board reform. With only two days given to campaigning in an election that saw more than seventy-three percent

88. Ibid., November 28, p. 226.

89. Ibid., December 5, pp. 233–34. Between 1896 and 1899 inclusive, the Board spent more than $55,000 against the bucket shops. *Report of the Directors, 1899*, p. lxxvii.

90. *SB, Chicago Post*, November 16, 1899.

91. *SB, Chicago InterOcean*, December 5, 1899. In an earlier issue, the paper had described Hill as an "erstwhile reformer . . . the former head of the notorious gang of blackmailers named Hill's detective agency."

92. Taylor, pp. 980–82.

93. *SB, Chicago InterOcean*, January 5, 1900. See also *SB*, 1900: *Chicago Chronicle*, January 5; *Chicago InterOcean*, January 6.

of the total membership voting, the Warren ticket won by a two-to-one margin.[94] Perhaps the Chicago Board of Trade was ready for reform at last.

94. The Board of Trade listed 1,803 members in 1900. At the annual election, 1,324 members cast their ballots. In the entire thirty-year period covered by this study, only once did more members vote in an annual election. In 1896, with a total membership of 1,840, 1,354 or 73.58% voted, in contrast with 73.43% in 1900.

CHAPTER SEVEN

Change and Reform, 1900–1905

I

When William Warren first addressed the members of the Chicago Board of Trade as their president on January 15, 1900, he admitted there was no "denying the fact that we are retrograding, and have been for some years." By that time the basic objectives of the organization had apparently been increased by two: "to grind out quotations for bucket shops and to provide a medium for collection of put and call money." In his condemnation of privileges, Warren echoed Baker, stating that the practice, besides being illegal, was also "a great detriment to the market, inasmuch as it hampers fluctuations and thus helps smother speculation." He was aware that members differed widely on the merits and values of privileges, but he stated that no one should "object to the propriety of suspending the practice until legal objections are removed either through legislation or the courts." Meanwhile, he said, the position of many firms surreptitiously trading in privileges "would discredit a lot of school boys," and the Board's attitude of "suppressing this traffic in the lower corridor, but tolerating it on the exchange floor, is ridiculous and reprehensible."

Warren noted that "the bucket shop question is the same old score as of old." One solution would be "a less generous distribution of our quotations. But here, up to this time, unfortunately, the Courts seem to have headed us completely off." More important was the elimination of bucket shopping within the Board, an insidious evil which "must be fought to the bitter end." Here Warren indirectly alluded to the reason why the courts "headed us off." Unlike his predecessors, including William Baker, the new president recognized a possible relationship between the courts' "heading us off," and the continued existence of bucket shopping by Board members. After "we have purged ourselves of contempt at the bar of public opinion we can more consistently combat evils outside."

The new president made some specific proposals for changes in the rules. He urged that the penalty for bucket-shop affiliation be mandatory expulsion and that this most stringent penalty also be attached to evasion of the long-standing commission rule. Further, a reward of $1,000 should be offered for information leading to the conviction of any member for its violation. Warren believed that some Board members had been "woefully deficient" in past years and that "false ideas have taken root regarding the duties of members in reporting violations of rules, which have seriously interfered with proper discipline." He warned the Board that "when we witness irregularities without bringing the perpetrator to justice we become accessories to the act and are false to the organization and false to ourselves."[1]

In 1895, at the urging of William Baker, the directors made a move to end privilege trading, but they were blocked by an adverse vote of the membership. Five years later the Board again tried to eliminate puts and calls. On January 17, 1900, the directors voted that all trading in privileges "and all transactions pertaining thereto, as well as all payments made in connection therewith, are prohibited in the exchange room." Violators were liable to censure, suspension, or expulsion.[2] Two days later a number of leading commission firms circulated an agreement "that we will not, directly or indirectly, either for ourselves or for others," trade in privileges.[3] These actions were but preliminaries to the big step that came on January 24, when the directors took the plunge again. They approved and ordered for vote by the members an extension of the "offenses" rule very similar to the ill-fated measure pushed by Baker five years earlier. The penalties of suspension or expulsion under the new rule now applied to a member, either in the exchange building or elsewhere, who dealt in privileges "in violation of any criminal

1. *Report of the Directors, 1899*, pp. lxxx–lxxxiv.
2. *D.R.*, January 17, 1900, p. 115.
3. *D.P.*, January 17, 1900.

statute of this state." Two weeks later, on February 5, the membership approved the amendment 623 to 373.[4]

Making privilege trading an offense punishable by suspension or expulsion marked only the beginning of the Board reform drive. In March 1900 the members approved two more important rule changes. By a vote of 712 to 326, they added a specific penalty clause to the old rule regulating hours of trade. Previously offenders had been subject to discipline "under the rules." The new section provided that any member found guilty of irregular trade "shall be suspended for not less than one month nor more than one year, and for a second violation he shall be expelled.[5] At the same time, the Board imposed the penalty of expulsion from the organization for any member violating the long-standing commission rule and offered a $2,500 reward for information leading to the conviction of any member for disregarding its provisions.

The Board had had a great deal of difficulty in enforcing a commission rule in the past. So many members had ignored the rule with impunity that in 1885 the penalties for violation had been repealed.[6] In the summer of 1887, the Board adopted a new commission rule, complete with enforcement and penalty clauses.[7] By 1890, however, the penalty clause had been quietly deleted, and until 1900 it appears that little effort had been made to enforce the rule.

Late in December 1900 the directors summoned John Dickinson to trial for illicit reduction of a commission fee to one of his customers. The case was postponed until February 5, 1901, on which date the directorate expelled him by a vote of 14 to 1.[8] When his efforts at reinstatement proved fruitless, Dickinson sought relief in the circuit court. Failing there, he turned to the Illinois Appellate Court and asked that the order of expulsion be set aside for three reasons: (1) because the commission rule was not authorized by the Board charter and thus was not "germane to the purposes and objects of said corporation"; (2) because the

---

4. *Association Records 1895–1939*, February 5, 1900, p. 117, Chicago Board of Trade Papers, University of Illinois, Chicago.
5. Id., March 12, 1900, p. 121.
6. *D.P.*, 1885: October 20, November 2.
7. *Northwestern Miller*, July 22, 1887, p. 95; *D.P.*, July 26, 1887.
8. *D.R.*, February 5, 1901, pp. 37–38.

regulation "unlawfully restrains the action of individual members . . . in the transaction of their business"; and (3) because the rule destroyed healthy competition in trade, interfering in the just rights of members to compete with each other, especially if they "are willing to conduct [business] for a less price, thereby reducing the price of such commodities to the consumer and the charges to the producer."[9]

Dickinson's points were not new. Indeed, they echoed an earlier opinion offered to the Board in 1886 by its lawyer, in which he advised against the legality of a commission rule. Attorney Sidney Smith had argued that any rule setting a rate of commission below which no member could transact business either for other members or for outside customers would be illegal. The public, he wrote, had an interest "in the free and unrestrained conduct of trade and commerce." Therefore, prices of merchandise, labor, and services ought to be "regulated only by the laws of demand and supply and by free competition." Any device or contrivance, whether it be an agreement, combination, or rule, that forced the price of commodities, wages, or services "above what [it] might be when left to free and unrestrained competition" was in restraint of trade and was thus illegal. This was especially true when trading in "the necessaries of life such as are dealt with upon the Chicago Board of Trade."

To Smith, a commission rule was an invasion of personal and private property rights. It interfered with the members' "private rights to freely contract for such rate of compensation as they might choose." The Board of Trade, in setting a commission rule, entered into an area as improper to it as would be an attempt by the legislature to set prices. He argued that such action embodied a principle "subversive of the rights of private property." Furthermore, it enforced a sort of equality in a market where by natural law there ought to be competitive inequality. The rule prevented the market from responding freely to the laws of supply and demand. It enabled to survive some traders who otherwise would not have survived, thereby placing an unnatural drag on the market. Worst of all, Smith saw the commission rule as an attempt by an artificial institution to interfere with natural economic forces.[10]

9. Dickinson v. Board of Trade, 114 Ill. App. 295, 299–300 (1904).
10. *D.P.*, March 17, 1886.

The similarity between Smith's view and a legal conservatism prevalent during the late nineteenth century is obvious. Yet in 1887 another lawyer, advising the Board on the same question, came to very different conclusions. Corydon Beckwith noted that there could be no question of the Board's power to "make such rules, regulations and by-laws as a voluntary association might make." Moreover, he claimed that it was "settled law of this country that persons not engaged in public or quasi-public employment may lawfully agree not to work for others, or for each other without being paid . . . such prices as they may demand." He held that Board members, in daily business dealings with each other, were not engaged in such employment. The purpose of the commission rule was to promote the welfare of the members. As such, it was an internal rule, and Beckwith saw no illegality in it.[11]

In earlier cases challenging the right of the Board to make certain rules that were binding upon the membership, counsel for the organization had emphasized that the Board was a private association and that the courts had consistently upheld its power to enact and enforce regulations of a nature similar to the one challenged by Dickinson. It was one sign of the new reform trend prevalent among the directors that, in defending the Board, Henry Robbins chose to focus not so much on this old viewpoint as on additional justifications for the Board's action. He called attention to the agreement that Dickinson, as well as all other members, had signed upon joining the Board of Trade. Far more important than the mention of this written promise to abide by the rules was Robbins's articulation of the factors that led the Board to adopt the commission rule and its stringent penalty in the first place.

One factor was "to strengthen and render effective the disciplinary power" of the organization. Robbins noted that the only way for the Board to secure compliance with its rules and regulations—"many of which are enacted for the purpose of maintaining among respondent's members a degree of business integrity and commercial honor"—was through its power of suspension and expulsion. Unless it was permitted to use this power

11. *D.R.*, 1887: February 1, p. 28, February 2, p. 53; *D.P.*, February 1, 1887.

of sanction, the Board could not function properly; and the results, in addition to injuring Board members, could only be detrimental to the public interest. Here Robbins alluded to the quasi-public regulatory responsibilities of this private association.

The new attorney to the Board saw no antagonism or incompatibility between these responsibilities and private economic gain for the membership through market transactions. Thus Robbins did not ignore the basic economic facts of life concerning the Board; rather he chose to demonstrate their interdependence with the administrative argument just mentioned. He claimed that, in order to survive as an exchange, the Board of Trade, as a non-profit organization, had to levy upon its members a yearly assessment "to maintain said exchange and manage its affairs." Unless membership on the Board was a source of profit to a businessman, he would not remain in the organization "and thereby the revenue of respondent would be much reduced." In point of fact, without the penalty of expulsion for violating the commission rule, this had happened. Some members "violated said commission rule by soliciting and doing business at lower rates than are therein specified, and lower than were remunerative when business was honestly transacted." Thus the advantages of membership were reduced, other members who obeyed the commission rule lost business to those who deliberately violated its provisions, and the Board's attractiveness as a commercial association was weakened. Such were the conditions that had led the Board to enact a penalty of expulsion for disregarding the regulation.[12]

Upholding the Board against Dickinson, the Illinois Appellate Court endorsed essentially the same arguments Beckwith had offered in 1887. Dickinson had neither claimed that "the minimum rate of commission fixed in the by-law is unreasonable in itself" nor proved that the enforcement of the rule was not in the interests of the Board and of the members themselves. The rule did not interfere with the commercial freedom of nonmembers. Rather, it was "confined in its operations to those who have voluntarily agreed to be bound by it," as had Dickinson. The court held that enforcement of the regulation "infringes no rule of law or public policy, confined as it is to the members of the Board

12. Supra, n. 9, pp. 301–2.

upon whom alone it operates, and by whom it has been enacted for their own government."[13]

Coming at a time when the Board was engaged in strengthening its own rules and doing battle against the bucket shops, the decision was important. Implicit in Robbins's argument was the awareness that the Board had quasi-public responsibilities that could only be met through effective internal discipline. True, the court had held that the rule was for and by a *private* organization, affecting only its members; but neither the Board nor the court was prepared to state that the Board of Trade was a *public* organization. However, no great legal insight is required to understand that the public did business through Board members and at rates set forth by the commission rule. Affirming the right of this private organization to make rules for the membership, the court in reality at the same time also acknowledged the Board's indirect function as an administrative regulatory agency, even as the Board itself admitted the existence of such a function.

The strengthening of the commission rule and the victory of the Board in the Dickinson case must be seen within the context of the larger reform drive discussed earlier. On April 30, 1900, the members again amended the rules by which they were governed. The long-standing regulation against trading in differences was changed to carry an automatic penalty of expulsion upon conviction. Further, a new section of the rule required that all orders for future delivery received by any member of the Board "must be executed in the *open market* in the exchange hall during the hours of regular trading."[14] Conviction for violating this section brought automatic expulsion. In February 1900 the Board had made the practice of privilege trading an offense carrying with it penalties of censure, suspension, or expulsion. Only two months later the members made the punishment of expulsion mandatory for any member who, either in the Board building or elsewhere, traded in privileges "in violation of any criminal statute of this state."

Together with the intricate legal moves against the bucket shops discussed below, these reform measures of the Board become noteworthy; and they demonstrated the Board's renewed

13. Ibid., pp. 306–7.
14. *Association Records*, April 30, 1900, p. 128 (italics in original).

potency as an administrative institution. Within three months it had enacted sweeping regulations dealing with problems that had troubled the organization for the previous thirty years. Even the *Northwestern Miller*, no friend of the association in the past, was impressed. "In its heroic struggle to accomplish certain long needed reforms," it said, "the Chicago Board of Trade has risen above the mere level of the commonplace and has dignified itself as a home for legitimate business."[15] In 1903 the Board went even further and finally adopted an iron-clad bucket-shop rule. Enacted on January 26 by a vote of 422 to 247, the new rule was an amendment to the previously strengthened regulation against trading in differences.

II

Although impressive in itself, the Chicago Board of Trade's reform drive was ineffective against the bucket shops without the intervention of the courts. In spite of rigid rules and stringent penalties against Board members who violated them, to the outside observer (and this included most of the general public) there still appeared to be little difference between the bucket shops and the legitimate exchanges. As long as the shops received the all-important market quotations, they could remain in business, no matter how dramatically the Board reformed its rules.

Board officials well recalled how the courts had treated earlier efforts to restrict market reports. Indeed, from 1892 to 1899, the Board had made no changes in the manner of distributing the reports, which were collected and disseminated by the telegraph companies at their own discretion, expense, and ultimate profit. While the organization maintained the theoretical right to control its quotations, the directors during this period made no move to do so, fearing a revival of the old injunctions against the Board.

However, by 1900 the picture had changed. Even before Warren was elected Board president, vague rumors spread among the members that the directors were about to reassert control over

15. *Northwestern Miller*, August 8, 1900, pp. 260–61.

the quotations.[16] There is no evidence that the directors had a specific plan of attack. Perhaps they were waiting for the bucket shops to make the first move. If so, they were not disappointed. One of the major bucket shops took legal steps, even before the directors had undertaken any action whatsoever, to block the Board from restricting distribution of the quotations. Here was the opportunity to reopen the bucket-shop war. Although it took five years and thousands of dollars, by the time the conflict was over the bucket shops were nearly empty.

In February 1900 the Christie-Street Commission Company, with headquarters at Kansas City, Missouri, filed suit against the Chicago Board of Trade and Western Union, seeking to prevent any cessation in distribution of the market reports.[17] C. C. Christie, whom John Hill, Jr., called the "bucket shop king," had been distinguished during the 1880's for his *opposition* to bucket shopping. Indeed, his 1887 memorial to the Missouri legislature, which called for an anti-bucket-shop statute, was widely reprinted. In February 1887, he published an article in which he equated falling commodities prices with bucket-shop activities. It is not clear when or why Christie changed his mind; perhaps his switch from legitimate grain trading to illicit, speculative gambling illustrates the tension and ambivalence between these practices. At any rate, once convinced that the bucket shops offered greater financial rewards than the commodities exchanges, Christie expanded his "establishments" until, by 1900, he was known as "king of the bucket shop keepers in the West."[18]

The *Christie* case came before Judge Murray Tuley, the same jurist who almost twenty years earlier had found against the Board. The initiative in the earlier cases had been taken by the bucket shops, with the Board of Trade defending the suits. Now, however, the Board took the offensive. It promptly filed a cross bill against both Christie and Western Union, seeking to enjoin one from using the reports and the other from distributing them

16. *American Elevator and Grain Trade*, 1889: July 15, p. 207; August 15, pp. 264–65.

17. *SB, Chicago Tribune*, February 24, 1900.

18. John Hill, Jr., *Goldbricks of Speculation*, pp. 48, 68–70; *American Elevator and Grain Trade*, February 15, 1887, p. 175; Lurie, "The Chicago Board of Trade, the Merchants' Exchange of St. Louis, and the Great Bucket Shop War," pp. 243–59.

so that they could be used. A large number of witnesses were examined, and numerous depositions were taken. "This case is the first one," the *Chicago Tribune* noted, "in which the Board of Trade has taken the aggressive [sic] and maintained its right to refuse quotations to concerns not doing a legitimate business."[19] Here, of course, was the reason for all the evidence presented by the Board.

For the first time in its battle against the bucket shops, the Board actively sought to prove beyond any doubt that a particular firm, in this case the Christie company, was doing an illegitimate business. In the court cases of the early 1880s the Board had not deemed this necessary, relying upon its "rights" as a private association. Now the organization asserted less its rights and more its administrative responsibilities toward the maintenance of an open, legitimate market.

Judge Tuley did not announce a decision in the case until June. In the meantime the directors took another step against the bucket shops. On May 25 the Board officially notified Western Union that after June 1 (or as soon thereafter as feasible) the Board of Trade "would collect its own quotations and assume control of the wires and instruments on the floor of the exchange."[20] The apparent bitterness of the Board toward the company was understandable, if not completely justified. President Warren stated publicly that the bucket shops had "increased and multiplied, and are flourishing today as never before . . . aided and supported by . . . Western Union . . . which is interested in the perpetuation of the system, owing to the enormous returns from the distributions of the quotations . . . , without which the bucket shops could not exist a day."[21]

This accusation was not altogether fair. Officials of Western Union responded, correctly, that it was the Board which changed its mind in 1892 and ordered quotations distributed to all applicants without discrimination. Furthermore, they pointed to the 1889 decision of the Illinois Supreme Court affirming that the telegraph company could not discriminate in distribution of the market quotations. It was not feasible for Western Union to

19. *SB, Chicago Tribune*, May 19, 1900.
20. Taylor, p. 998.
21. *SB, Chicago Chronicle*, June 7, 1900.

"resolve itself into a grand jury to determine which of its sub-scribers are lawbreakers and which are not."[22]

Knowing that a decision in the *Christie* case was imminent, the directors waited before taking over distribution of the reports, and on June 19, 1900, Tuley announced his findings. He had no doubt, from the evidence presented, that Christie was doing an extremely large bucket-shop business. The firm "never purchased or sold a bushel of grain, although it made trades amounting to 157,000,000 of bushels in a year." Tuley stated that the Illinois Supreme Court required equitable distribution of the quotations to all who sought to use them for *lawful* purposes. Thus Christie could not ask a court of equity to compel the delivery of the re-ports for his unlawful business; neither could he prevent the Board of Trade and the telegraph companies from coming to "an arrangement or understanding by which he shall be deprived of the market quotations in question."[23]

This finding took care of Christie's plan for an injunction. Next Tuley turned to the Board's counterplea for a ban against the plaintiff and Western Union. In a notable departure from the earlier cases of 1882–84, Henry Robbins argued that the custo-mers doing business with Christie were deliberately led to "be-lieve that their trades or contracts are with members of the Board, and are, in fact, executed upon said exchange," and that persons employed by Christie "are members of said Board of Trade." Thus the customers who lost money, and most did, con-cluded "that the losses they suffer are through the dishonesty of members of said Board." Such fraudulent, misleading actions im-paired "the good name and business reputation of the Board of Trade" and deprived its members "of many customers and large sums of money in emoluments and commissions which would come to them." It also deprived a legitimate market of beneficial capital.[24]

Tuley agreed. This "false pretense" was "a fraud which must necessarily injuriously affect not only the reputation of the busi-ness done upon the exchanges of the Board, but also the amount of business done thereon and . . . the value of this 'species of

22. *SB, Chicago Times-Herald,* June 11, 1900.

23. Christie-Street Commission Co. v. Board of Trade and Western Union Telegraph Co., No. 204543, Cir. Ct. Cook County (1900), 12–13.

24. Ibid., p. 14.

property,' the market quotations." Here Tuley used the argument of quotations as private property to support the Board. "The fact that private property or private business becomes affected with a public interest, does not destroy its character as private property or private business." The judge granted injunctions against both Christie and Western Union, as the Board had requested, and he observed with good foresight that "it would seem possible for the Board of Trade and [the] telegraph company, by a friendly cooperation, not only to protect the complainant's rights in these quotations, but also to prevent their use for unlawful or gambling purposes."[25]

The financial stakes in the fight between the bucket shops and the Board were great, and none knew this better than the bucket shops themselves. Barely one month after Tuley's decision in the *Christie* case, another firm sought to enjoin both the Board and the Cleveland Telegraph Company from cutting off the quotations. The Central Stock and Grain Exchange tried to show that its case differed from that of Christie in that it *did* make delivery on certain of its contracts. This difference apparently impressed the trial court, and in November 1900 Judge Edward Vail found against the Board of Trade. True, the contracts delivered were "a very small percent"; but it is true also that, as to future deliveries upon the Board of Trade itself, "a very small percent of deliveries are ever actually made."[26]

Moreover, Judge Vail believed that it was not within the legal province of the Board to determine who was running a bucket shop and who was not. As a private organization, the Chicago Board of Trade had no administrative right, let alone obligation, to impose its criteria of "legitimacy" on others. If a company did an illicit business, "then the criminal law of the land will take hold of it." Furthermore, he said, "I think it is of more interest to the people at large . . . that the quotations . . . should be made public generally than that the members of the Board . . . should

25. Ibid., pp. 21–22. Early in March 1900, the Illinois Appellate Court affirmed Tuley's decision. The Board quotations were indeed impressed with a public interest, "but it does not therefrom follow that a court of equity will lend its aid to a criminal enterprise by compelling the Board of Trade to furnish the quotations for such a use." Christie-Street Commission Co. v. Board of Trade, 94 Ill. App. 229, 236–37 (1901). See also 92 Ill. App. 604.

26. Central Stock and Grain Exchange v. Board of Trade, Cir. Ct. Cook County (1900), p. 6. Included in briefs to 196 Ill. 396.

have the exclusive business, or that what you call bucket shops should flourish or go down." Indeed, he implied that, by taking upon itself the power to restrict quotations indirectly when requiring agencies such as Cleveland Telegraph to sign stipulated agreements, the Board contravened the Illinois Supreme Court's doctrine of quotations to all without discrimination.[27]

While Vail's findings went contrary to the thrust of recent Board history, his opinion was neither the first nor the last of several judicial findings indicating real doubt that the methods of the Board were very different from the bucket shops. In appealing the judgment, the Board chose not to focus on this point, although it was clear that sooner or later Robbins would have to confront and rebut this belief.

Late in 1901 the Illinois Appellate Court reversed Judge Vail's decision, and shortly thereafter its findings were affirmed by the Illinois Supreme Court.[28] In his arguments before both tribunals, Henry Robbins emphasized the real nature of business transacted on the Central Stock and Grain Exchange, seeking to prove that their claim of actual delivery was fallacious.

Robbins pointed to testimony, given by Central Stock and Grain's own employees, that when a customer wanted the property, the telegraphic orders were marked "for delivery." "It is somewhat singular," he observed, "that legitimate transactions have to be so branded in order to distinguish them from the others." Another clerk for Central Stock admitted that he did not remember seeing the words *for delivery* on any of the telegrams coming to him and that he received "from fifty to one hundred telegrams opening trades every day."[29] In short, counsel for the Board contended, the bucket shops had "trumped up" a few transactions "after this suit was commenced . . . to make some show of legitimate trading upon the hearing of this case."[30]

For its part, Central Stock and Grain tried to build upon the conclusions of Judge Vail. Most of its brief was an effort to prove that "the Board of Trade is a gigantic bucket shop—the most

27. Ibid., pp. 2, 7.
28. 98 Ill. App. 212 (1901); Board of Trade v. Central Stock and Grain Exchange, 196 Ill. 396 (1902).
29. *Brief for Appellee*, p. 25, Central Stock and Grain Exchange v. Board of Trade, 196 Ill. 396 (1902).
30. Ibid., p. 27.

gigantic in existence."[31] Indeed, if the methods of the Board were declared legal, then of necessity its own procedures were equally valid.

The Illinois Appellate Court rejected these arguments. The evidence shows clearly, Mr. Justice Adams stated, that Central Stock kept a bucket shop and used the market quotations for that business. He admitted that perhaps some contracts were delivered but found that "such were exceptional and insignificant in comparison with the bulk of appellee's business." The claim that the Board's methods were no different from those of a bucket shop Adams dismissed as irrelevant. It was not the Board but rather Central Stock that sought relief. An attack on the Board in no way rebutted the proof that appellee was using the quotations for an illegal purpose.[32]

The decisions of the Illinois Appellate and Supreme Courts in this case effectively ended the bucket-shop boom in Chicago and settled, as far as Illinois was concerned, the right of the Board to restrict its quotations. Late in 1901 not a bucket shop was left in the city, according to the *Chicago Post*. "All the rest have been forced out in the cold by the crusade and the Central Stock and Grain Exchange was practically the only one left which was making a stubborn fight."[33]

After protracted negotiations that continued into March 1901, the Board of Trade and the two major telegraph companies came to an agreement on a new contract. The companies promised not to deliver the quotations to any bucket shop, but the responsibility of investigating whether or not the recipients were bucket shops was to rest with the Board of Trade. Each applicant for the reports had to sign a separate agreement with the telegraph company, pledging "we are not keeping or causing to be kept, and will not keep or cause to be kept" any bucket shop. In addition, the quotations could not be used for this purpose, and the applicants could not give the reports to any other parties, except

31. *Brief for Appellants*, p. 33, ibid.
32. 98 Ill. App. 212 (1901).
33. "For the first time in a number of years, there was not a bucket shop in Chicago posting Board of Trade quotations." There is, of course, no way to check the accuracy of the *Post's* conclusions. In point of fact, the bucket-shop battle was far from over. SB, *Chicago Post*, November 21, 1901; Taylor, p. 1020.

to those who had signed a similar agreement. Any violation of these rules automatically gave the telegraph companies the right to cut off the price quotations without prior notice.

When an applicant had filled out this agreement, a copy of it was to be sent to the Board of Trade; and, after suitable investigation, the market reports committee would decide whether or not the application was to be approved. If it was rejected, the telegraph companies could not send the party the reports. The contract also included provisions for cutting off quotations once they had been started and required that the Board of Trade assume all costs for any legal proceedings arising from its provisions. The Board was to receive $30,000 a year from the two telegraph agencies for the market quotations.[34]

The *Christie* case, later affirmed in the *Central Stock and Grain Exchange* case, established that the Board (and, through the new contracts, the two telegraph companies as well) had a property right in the quotations. But where did such a right end? Once the news had been sent out over the ticker and had been printed on the various rolls of tape located all over the country, was it still the property of the telegraph company? No one disputed, for example, that the ticker machines on which the news appeared belonged to Western Union; but what of the letters and numbers spewing forth on the tape?

The new contract went into effect on April 15, 1901. Shortly thereafter the federal court in Chicago, at the request of Western Union, granted an injunction against National Telegraph News Company, restraining it from copying any item on a Western Union ticker tape until one hour after it had appeared.[35] National Telegraph News controlled within Chicago "a system of wires connecting their operating office with tickers of their own, in the offices and places of patrons of their own." The company regularly "appropriated" the news items, consisting of racing scores, stock and commodity prices, and similar information, and thereupon "with the loss of a few moments only redistributing such news over their own wires to their own patrons."

National Telegraph did not deny its use of the material but claimed that, once the news had appeared on the printed tape in

34. *D.P.*, March 23, 1901; *Bradstreet's*, March 30, 1901, p. 197.
35. Taylor, p. 1018.

the places where the tickers were located, it became public and Western Union no longer had any monopoly on its distribution therein. The defendant argued that the contents of a ticker tape, unless copyrighted in accordance with the statutes, was "unprotected against appropriation by the public."[36] The issue raised here was both intriguing and important. Certainly such news as the Chicago Board of Trade market reports was not worth $30,000 a year if other agencies could pirate the information. National Telegraph appealed the injunction, and the United States Circuit Court of Appeals decided the case in October 1902.

The opinion in the *National Telegraph News Co.* case well illustrates the creative role of legal change and the reshaping of law by the court to bring it into harmony with economic growth and technological innovation. In this opinion Mr. Justice Grosscup focused on two questions: (1) Did the ticker tape come within the provisions of the copyright law? And, if not, (2) Was there any remedy that would protect this feature of the appellee's business against the kind of piracy shown?[37]

Grosscup took note of the economic factors involved. It was obvious that Western Union went to great expense maintaining offices, wires, equipment, and employees to collect and disseminate the news. Furthermore, if agencies like the appellant could appropriate the reports, escaping any expense for collection, "but one result could follow—the gathering and distributing of news, as a business enterprise, would cease altogether." This would mean the end of National News as well as Western Union. "The parasite that killed would itself be killed, and the public would be left without any service at any price."

The court found, as appellant had argued, that a ticker tape could not be copyrighted under the law, although it was true that the constitutional protection of copyright had expanded dramat-

36. National Telegraph News cited § 4956 of the federal statute dealing with copyright, "which provides that no person shall be entitled to a copyright unless he shall, before publication, deliver at the office of the librarian of Congress, or deposit in the mail addressed to the librarian of Congress . . . a printed copy of the title of the book or other article . . . for which he desires copyright." Obviously it would be difficult for Western Union to forward a copy of a ticker tape to Washington for copyright purposes.

37. National Telegraph News Co. v. Western Union Telegraph Co., 119 Fed. 294 (1902).

ically over the years to include "books that the old guild of authors would have disdained." But, in considering exactly the extent of copyright protection. Grosscup drew the line "at the point where authorship proper ends, and mere annals begin." News items such as stock and commodity reports are not comparable to literature—the latter a "product of originality, the other the product of opportunity." Moreover, this type of news lacked the enduring value expected of a book or article. "It lasts literally for an hour, and is in the waste basket when the hour has passed." The value of the ticker tape lay in the speed with which the information contained therein was communicated or, as Grosscup put it, "the precommunicatedness of the information."

Technically, therefore, Western Union could not copyright its ticker tapes; but this did not mean that the agency had no possibility of legal relief. A property right was involved—one that brought the case within the purview of a court of equity. Standing alone symbols, letters, and numbers were not property; but, when used as a means through which a legitimate business had been built up, a property right emerged. "It is enough that the act complained of will result, even though somewhat remotely, in injury to property."

For the court the case involved much more than the symbols on a ticker tape. The economic growth reflected in what appeared on the tape, together with the technological advances that made its transmission and distribution possible, demonstrated "that modern enterprise . . . which, combining the genius and the accumulations of men, with the forces of electricity, combs the earth's surface . . . for what the day has brought forth, that whatever befalls the sons of men shall come, almost instantaneously, into the consciousness of mankind." In conclusion Grosscup referred to the choices facing the judges:

> Is the service like this to be outlawed? Is the enterprise of the great news agencies, or the independent enterprise of the great newspapers, or of the great telegraph and cable lines, to be denied appeal to the courts, against the inroads of the parasite, for no other reason than that the law, fashioned hitherto to fit the relations of authors and the public, cannot be made to fit the relations of the public and this dissimilar class of servants? Are we to fail our plain duty for mere lack of precedent? We choose,

rather, to make precedent—one from which is eliminated, as immaterial, the law grown up around authorship.[38]

On the same day that it decided this case, the Circuit Court of Appeals affirmed, through the same reasoning, the right of the Cleveland Telegraph Company to withhold the Board quotations from the "Illinois Commission Company."[39] Thus, by 1902, both the state courts of Illinois and the federal courts had recognized a property right inherent in the Board's market reports.[40] The directors believed that this in itself was enough to win the bucket-shop war. However, the sword of equity cut two ways, as the Board was soon to find out.

III

The new phase of the conflict between the Chicago Board of Trade and the bucket shops began in 1900 with the *Christie-Street* case, and it was to last longer than the Board anticipated. The battleground was transferred largely to the federal courts; and by August 1903 the line of litigation, including forty-six cases, extended through eleven states and fifteen cities.[41] In virtually all of these cases, the Board sought, first, to establish a property right inherent in the quotation, and, even more important, to convince the judges that this right should be protected by a court of equity. If the Board had semipublic administrative responsibilities toward the maintenance of an open market, it had to have the right to protect the lifeblood of the market—its quotations—from illegitimate use. In the absence of other external restraints, the Board in effect, asked protection through the court equity power so that it might better meet these responsibilities—albeit as a private organization. Henry Robbins had little difficulty with the first point, but several jurists declined to invoke the power of equity to protect the property right recognized. As

38. Ibid., pp. 296–301.

39. Illinois Commission Co. v. Cleveland Telegraph Co., 119 Fed. 301 (1902).

40. In 1900 a federal district court had found that the Board possessed a property right in its quotations. See Cleveland Telegraph Co. v. Stone, 105 Fed. 794; *Chicago Tribune*, October 11, 1900.

41. *D.P.*, November 10, 1903.

with Judge Vail in 1900, it was not clear to these judges that the Board's methods were substantially different from the bucket shops'.

In 1902 the Board petitioned the federal district court in Ohio for an injunction against the O'Dell Commission Company. There was no doubt, Judge Thompson ruled, that O'Dell was doing a bucket-shop business, that the firm illicitly received the Board quotations without permission from or payment to either the Board or the telegraph companies, and that such actions damaged the value of the reports to the plaintiff.[42] But the judge held that these facts did not constitute the real issue. For Thompson the important question was whether the Board of Trade itself kept an establishment wherein were permitted transactions contrary to the laws of Ohio and Illinois. He had no doubt on this point either. It did. The finding was bad enough in itself; but, even worse, Thompson based his ruling on the evidence of Board President William Warren, who had been summoned—somewhat unwillingly—as a witness for the defense.

Warren and other Board members explained how the organization operated. The president admitted that in 1901 alone, he purchased 75,440,000 bushels of grain, of which 3,145,000 bushels were delivered to him, "leaving undelivered 72,295,000." This last amount was settled "by the parties paying and receiving the difference between the contract prices and the market prices. . . ." Warren was questioned at some length about the procedures of settlement by ringing up, substitution, and off set, as well as hedging. He further admitted that his methods of doing business were the same as those of the other Board members. For Judge Thompson that was enough.

Warren had testified that somewhere between 85 and 98 percent of the futures trading was settled by adjustment of prices. The amount of goods traded far exceeded "the entire production of such commodities in the United States." Up to this point what Thompson stated had been heard many times over. But the judge went further. Warren could not help knowing that it was "contrary to human experience that all or more than a small percent of such dealings could have been entered into with a bona fide intention to receive . . . or to deliver." The fact that delivery

42. Board of Trade v. O'Dell Commission Co., 115 Fed. 574 (1902).

might be required was not the same as the fact that it *was* required. Actual delivery was made by a transfer of warehouse receipts and not by "a mere notice of an intention to deliver, which is passed from hand to hand, through a 'ring' in which all deals except the last one are settled by the payment of the differences in prices."[43]

Thompson placed so much emphasis upon Warren's testimony because Warren was president of the Chicago Board of Trade and, thus, had the responsibility "of conducting its business and managing its affairs in accordance with the law of the land." The greater part of dealings on the Board, he said, were "bucket shop transactions" permitted by Board officials "in violation of the laws of Illinois." It was to the Board of Trade and "kindred organizations" that the bucket shops looked "for sustenance and life." Only after gambling had been suppressed on the exchanges would the bucket shops disappear "and not before." In the past, Thompson concluded, many bucket shops had asked that the Board be enjoined from cutting off quotations; their requests had been refused because "courts of equity will not lend their aid to carry on an illegal business." So, too, the court would not give its support to the Board in maintaining a place where bucket shopping was permitted.[44]

Thompson's decision expressed through law what many critics of the Board had long been saying. The similarity, for example, between his conclusions and some of the statements made by members of Congress during the hearings in 1892 is very clear. But if the opinion made good reading, it also reached some faulty conclusions. In June 1902 another federal district court decision, without citing Thompson directly, rejected his findings and the reasons for them.

The case involved none other than C. C. Christie, who was seeking to regain his throne as "king of the bucket shops." Following his defeat in the Illinois courts, Christie set up another commission company called Christie Grain and Stock. By the fall of 1902, thanks to the detective efforts of John Hill, Jr., the Board had proof that Christie, through illicit wiretapping, was receiving and posting the quotations.[45] He had not signed the re-

43. Ibid., pp. 576–87.
44. Ibid., p. 588.
45. Hill, pp. 64–68; *D.P.*, July 2, 1902.

quired agreements; neither did he deny that he was receiving the reports, which were not being sent through the telegraph companies. Again the Board sought to enjoin the distribution of the quotations, while Christie maintained that neither the Board nor the telegraph companies had any right to restrict circulation of the reports, which were clothed with a "public interest." In addition, he, like all other bucket shops, accused the Board of being itself a large-scale gambling den.

In the *Christie Grain and Stock* opinion, Judge Hook noted that, while the evidence presented "gives rise to the suspicion that in very many of such transactions a delivery of the property . . . was not contemplated by any of the parties thereto, it is not sufficient to justify a general decree of outlawry against the Board of Trade." The rules of the Board explicitly forbid dealing in differences "and impose upon the seller the obligation to deliver the property sold, and upon the purchaser the obligation to receive it."[46] Moreover, the United States Supreme Court had stated in a very recent case (which Judge Thompson had inexplicably ignored) that "of course we do not say that these rules actually prevent gambling on the exchange. It is possible, if not probable, that gambling may be and is in fact carried on there, but it must be in violation of, and not pursuant to, the rules."[47]

All parties admitted that "a vast volume of legitimate business is . . . transacted on the exchange." Indeed, the Board had come to play so important a part in the internal commerce of the country that people like Christie now claimed that it had become "a quasi-public corporation," its property "affected with a public interest." If this were true, Hook reasoned, how then could Christie assert that the Board was in fact a bucket shop? "A public interest can not be predicated upon the results of violations of

46. Board of Trade v. Christie Grain and Stock Co., 116 Fed. 944 (1902). It should be noted that, in mentioning the Board rule against trading in differences, Judge Hook took judicial notice of the fact that the penalty for violation was expulsion. As we have seen, the imposition of expulsion for violating this rule was one of the reform measures enacted in 1900.

47. Clews v. Jamieson, 89 Fed. 63 (1898); 96 Fed. 648 (1899); 182 U.S. 461 (1901). The case dealt with some disputed transactions executed on the Chicago Stock Exchange. The district and appellate courts held them to be gambling transactions and thus illegal under Illinois law. The Supreme Court reversed, noting that the view taken by the Circuit Court of Appeals "is a very far-reaching decision, and if followed would invalidate most transactions of every stock exchange in the country 'for the account,'" pp. 488–89.

the law." In conclusion, Hook—unlike Thompson—refrained from calling the Board's business methods contrary to Illinois law. To do so was the responsibility of the Illinois courts, tribunals that "have refrained . . . from declaring the Chicago Board of Trade a bucket shop."[48] The decision elated Board officials, who now believed, according to the *Chicago Tribune*, that the end of the war was in sight and "the bucket shop business entirely suppressed."[49]

Christie appealed the decision as he had done in the Illinois courts, but the Circuit Court of Appeals did not decide the case until October 1903.[50] Then it decided unanimously in favor of Christie. In its opinion the court ignored the question of a property right in the Board quotations and relied almost entirely on the Illinois Supreme Court's doctrine in the *New York & Chicago Grain and Stock* case and on Thompson's verdict in the *O'Dell* case. The Board had sought the protection of a court of equity in securing the pecuniary benefit derived from the communication and sale of quotations based upon "transactions conducted by it in open violation of the statutes of the state in which it maintains its place of business, and to which state it owes its corporate existence." To grant this request would be to distort the purpose of equity. "It will not lend its aid to the furtherance of transactions expressly forbidden by the statute, and thus declared to be contrary to the public policy. . . ." Because the Board "does not come with clean hands, not for a lawful purpose . . . its prayer for aid must be denied."[51]

At this point, late in 1903, the outcome of the bucket-shop fight did not look promising for the Board of Trade. The directors themselves were split, some urging an end to the litigation, while others wanted to see the issue through. On November

48. Supra, n. 46, p. 947.
49. *SB, Chicago Tribune*, July 8, 1902. The victory statement was premature, to say the least.
50. Christie Grain and Stock Co. v. Board of Trade, 125 Fed. 161 (1903).
51. Ibid., p. 169. *The Chicago Tribune* criticized the decision. If the transactions on the Board were illegal in character, what did the bucket-shop people want with the quotations? "Surely, if they are the virtuous people they pretend to be, they would disdain to touch these quotations with a long pole, instead of moving heaven and earth in the effort to obtain them." *SB, Chicago Tribune*, October 10, 1903. This, of course, was precisely what Judge Hook had noted in his findings as cited above: ns. 46, 48.

10 the directorate voted on the motion that relevant officials of the Board "be authorized to prosecute all bucket shop cases that they think necessary for the good of the Board of Trade." The motion passed by one vote, 8 to 7.[52] By so narrow a margin did the directors decide to persist in the cases still pending. In May 1904 the directors actually formed a committee to look into the possibilities of hiring a new attorney.[53] In their report the committee members noted that the cases "demanded unusual thought and time in their preparation and presentation," and they urged that the directors extend to Robbins "our hearty support and confidence."[54] Even as the directors voiced confidence in their attorney, however, the legal picture had already changed again.

IV

On April 12, 1904, the Circuit Court of Appeals for the Seventh Circuit handed down a decision in the case of *Board of Trade v. L. A. Kinsey Co.*[55] In the federal district court, Judge Anderson had denied injunctive relief for the Board and had focused on the question of the intent to deliver. "Ordinarily, men are presumed to intend to do what they in fact do." The evidence submitted shows that "the actors in these transactions, as their settled habit and practice, make contracts for future delivery, and immediately with a uniformity of practice almost complete, settle these contracts upon differences; and they do this continuously, day after day, month after month, and year after year. Under the ordinary rule of judging the intent by the act, there seems no room for doubt that these contracts are a mere cover for the settlement of differences; that no delivery is intended."

It was true that, when challenging a contract for future delivery as invalid, the burden of proof lay with the party making the assertion, in this case the Kinsey company. Judge Anderson found that the evidence proved the point. "If the rule was delivery, and settlement upon differences the exception, a different conclusion might be reached. But delivery is the rare exception,

---

52. *D.R.*, November 10, 1903, pp. 334–35.
53. Ibid., May 3, 1904, p. 114.
54. *D.P.*, May 17, 1904.
55. Board of Trade v. L. A. Kinsey Co., 130 Fed. 507 (1904).

and the intention to deliver is likewise rarely present. . . . I think that the proportion of these transactions which are illegal is so large as to characterize and taint them as a whole, and that whatever property right complainant may have in the continuous quotations in question is so infected with illegality as to preclude resort to a court of equity for its protection."[56]

On appeal the case came before the same three judges who had considered the *National Telegraph News v. Western Union* case, and there are definite hints of the latter decision in this latest bucket-shop case. The court stated that it had given "respectful consideration" to prior decisions against the Board and that it regretted "that we are unable to concur therein." Gambling, of course, did take place on the exchange, "but it was contrary to appellant's by-laws." The Board had been chartered for "a lawful and useful purpose, and the association adopted and promulgated suitable by-laws and rules." But this was a secondary point for the court.

The important basis for their finding was the property right "in the news, in the reports of prices." Even if it were true that ninety-five percent of the pit transactions were wagers, these price figures were the basis for legitimate business contracts made throughout the country. Thus "the news of the prices and the dissemination thereof are valuable to the community. News may be an object of lawful ownership though nine-tenths of the things reported be unlawful." The fact that the quotations could be used for illegal purposes did not make them in themselves unlawful. Gamblers could and did use them to advantage, just as legitimate dealers could and did use them "to make and settle their honest contracts." The court held that "news, as news, is not without the pale of protection, and that the moral quality is chargeable solely to the user."[57]

The direct conflict between decisions of the Seventh and Eighth Circuits was startling. Taken together the two rulings were irreconcilable, and the Board sought a writ of certiorari from the United States Supreme Court. In his petition Henry Robbins questioned the lower court's citation of the *Soby* case.[58]

56. Id., 125 Fed. 72, 75, 78 (1903).
57. Supra, n. 55, pp. 512–13.
58. Supra, ch. 4, n. 59.

The 1887 Illinois statute upheld therein prohibited the keeping of a bucket shop and the practice of bucket shopping, but the Board did none of these things. Neither a broker nor as a principal did the organization make any trades or transactions. It "only maintains an exchange hall, where others trade." Furthermore, no court in Illinois had ever concluded that the Board "was within the class of persons contemplated by such statute; nor has any indictment ever been rendered against petitioner under that statute."[59]

Robbins developed these points in a separate brief accompanying his petition for certiorari.[60] He denied that lack of delivery implied an intent to gamble or that such other Board practices as hedging constituted illicit bets. "The gambler upon exchanges is one who wishes to take the risk of the fluctuations of the market in order to thereby profit. The merchant who hedges resorts to the market not to take a risk, but to avoid all risk."[61] The Illinois statute forbade the keeping of a place wherein is permitted pretended buying or selling. In what then, did the misconduct of the Board consist? Of itself it transacted no business, but provided an exchange hall, admitted and expelled members, and adopted rules to govern them in relation to the Board and to each other upon its exchange. The rules prohibited dealing in differences and provided for a method of settling that had been upheld by the United States Supreme Court. Not surprisingly, Robbins cited the two rules of the Board that forbade dealing in differences and privilege trading—two of the rules that had been dramatically implemented during the "reform" year, 1900.

Finally Robbins turned to the difference between a speculative and gambling transaction. How could one be distinguished from the other? They "are alike in form, made in the same way, and to outward appearances are the same." What did differentiate the two was the *intention* of the parties involved. Since this is the

59. *Petitioner's Motion for Certiorari*, p. 7, Board of Trade v. Christie. Robbins argued that the 1887 statute did not apply to commercial exchanges. Soby v. People "had reference only to a broker's office. Its language should be confined to its facts. It does not decide that a commercial exchange is within this statute."

60. *Petitioner's Brief in Support of Motion for Certiorari*, pp. 20–23, Board of Trade v. Christie.

61. In commodities trading, "hedging" meant to offset a purchase of one commodity with a sale of another.

case, "how can petitioner ascertain what is in the minds of the traders or their customers?"[62] Robbins claimed that the speculative spirit "is innate" and will persist "so long as the desire for gain finds a place in the human breast." Speculators are always attracted toward "commodities susceptible to ready transfer." Exchanges "improve the facilities for transfer in aid of legitimate commerce." Indeed, the prominence of the Chicago Board of Trade indicated how well it performed this function. Because "it has done this, speculation resorts to it." Yet the Eighth Circuit "holds [the Board] a criminal and a discredited suitor in the Federal courts. For doing what? For furnishing facilities for legitimate commerce, which the speculative spirit also avails itself of."[63]

In two cases argued before the United States Supreme Court in April 1905, *Board of Trade v. Christie* and *Kinsey v. Board of Trade*, what started out as an attempt to prevent bucket shops from purloining the Board's quotations became, somewhere along the way, an effort to establish the legality and legitimacy of both the Board and its transactions. In a very real sense, the Chicago Board of Trade was as much on trial as was Christie. The crux of the position taken by the bucket shops was that the Board had no right to come before a court of equity, because its business was illicit, immoral, and illegal. The court, recognizing the importance of the issue at bar, dealt with it first and then turned to the secondary subject of a property right in the quotations. On May 5, 1905, the Court decided the cases, splitting 6 to 3, with Mr. Justice Holmes speaking for the majority.[64] Like so many of Holmes's opinions, his findings were stated briefly—covering, after the usual summary of facts, little more than seven pages— and reflected a distinct Holmesian outlook as well as the sentiments of his colleagues.

Holmes first noted that Christie and Kinsey were able to "get and publish these quotations in some way not disclosed." As they

62. In his finding against Christie, Judge Hook had made the same point. "Common experience justifies the observation that in the great majority of cases it is impossible to secure the requisite evidence of the gaming character of such transactions. And it is not competent to any finite being to search the minds of the participants, and discover their purposes and intentions." 116 Fed. 947.

63. *Brief for Respondent*, pp. 31–32, Kinsey v. Board of Trade.

64. Board of Trade v. Christie, 198 U.S. 236 (1905).

denied the right of the Board to restrict the reports, did not obtain them from the telegraph companies, and declined to sign the required contracts, he found that "it is a reasonable conclusion that they get, and intend to get, their knowledge in a way that is wrongful." On the other hand, he reasoned, if Christie's contention was correct, any property right in the quotations "is so infected with the plaintiff's own illegal conduct" that they "may be carried off by any one at will."

The jurist described the Board as "a great market, where through its eighteen hundred members, is transacted a large part of the grain and provision business of the world." Speculation, he noted, was "the self-adjustment of society to the probable." There could be no doubt that "success of the strong induces imitation by the weak" and that incompetent amateurs had brought themselves "to ruin" by ill-planned and unsuccessful speculative ventures. At this point Holmes revealed a strain of thought that permeates much of his judicial writings: "But legislatures and courts generally have recognized that the natural evolutions of a complex society are to be touched only with a very cautious hand, and that such coarse attempts at a remedy for the waste incident to every social function as a simple prohibition and laws to stop its being are harmful and vain."[65]

Holmes dismissed in one short sentence the contention that the Board's transactions were gambling: "Set off has all the effects of delivery." The ring settlement was "simply a more complex case of the same kind." The rules of the Board and the evidence, he stated, left no doubt "that the contracts made between the members are intended and supposed to be binding in manner and form as they are made. There is no doubt that a large part of those contracts is made for serious business. . . . The sales in the pits are not pretended, but . . . are meant and supposed to be binding. A set off is in legal effect a delivery."

Holmes echoed Judge Hook's opinion in the *Christie* case in rejecting the claim that futures contracts were primarily intended as mere wagers, without any intention of receiving or delivering. Without explaining why—a complaint levied against many of Holmes's opinions—he wrote, "It seems to us an extraordinary and unlikely proposition." The ease with which the Court in this

65. Ibid., pp. 247–48.

The Trading Room of the Chicago Board of Trade. *Century Magazine*, March 1903. Courtesy Historical Pictures Service, Inc., Chicago.

instance upheld Board transactions is all the more interesting when one notes that five of the seven federal courts that had heard bucket-shop cases preliminary to the Supreme Court's arguments accepted exactly what Holmes found to be so "extraordinary and unlikely."[66]

Having endorsed without reservation the market practices of the Board, Holmes next turned to the question of property rights. He noted that, even if the Board did keep a place where unlawful and false buying and selling were allowed, "which as yet the Supreme Court of Illinois, we believe, has been careful not to intimate," it was still entitled to the protection of the court. Here Holmes merely echoed the earlier opinions of the Seventh Circuit in the *National Telegraph News* and *Kinsey* cases. What if the quotations were the result of unlawful activity? "The statistics of crime are property to the same extent as any other statistics, even if collected by a criminal who furnishes some of the data."[67]

The Court agreed with the position taken by its Illinois counterpart that the Board's work was "clothed with a public use"; so, of course, did Christie, who claimed that this element of public interest entitled him to get and use the reports. Had Christie paid the Board for use of the quotations and submitted "to all reasonable requirements in relation to the same," and had the Board still refused to make the quotations available to the company, the issue would have been a very different one. These facts would have rendered the Board's position untenable. Holmes did not even consider the question, because, he noted, Christie's demand was "not qualified by submission to reasonable rules or an offer of payment. It is a claim of independent rights and a denial that the [Board] has any right at all. The Supreme Court of Illinois gave no sanction to such a claim as that."[68]

66. "Legislation Affecting Commodity and Stock Exchanges," *Harvard Law Review* 45 (1932):915.

67. On the importance of this point, see Harry D. Nims, *The Law of Unfair Competition and Trademarks*, 4th ed. (New York, 1947), p. 407.

68. Supra, n. 64, pp. 251–52. The three dissenting justices—Harlan, Brewer, and Day—gave no explanation for their actions. However, Harlan had dissented in the earlier case of Clews v. Jamieson on the grounds that the contracts upheld by the court were in reality gambling contracts. He would thus be perfectly consistent in believing that the contracts made on the Board of Trade were of the same kind and, hence, were illegal under Illinois law.

The opinion was notable because of the sweeping endorsement given the Board's mercantile methodology. Years later, one journal called it "a Magna Carta of free marketing."[69] This may be true, but the *Christie* case had a more important claim to distinction. It represents a classic example of the responsive legal process, the reconciliation of law with external economic custom and procedures. It is doubtful that, as the *Harvard Law Review* claimed, the decision was one of "revolutionary character."[70] Indeed, to describe the opinion as revolutionary is to fall into what Lawrence Friedman has well described as "one of the major traps of American legal history, mistaking formal ratification for innovation."[71] For the law did not initiate such practices as ringing out, set off, and substitution that were common on the exchanges. Rather, the innovation of such practices forced the law to harmonize with public policy the market growth that they symbolized.

There might have been and, indeed, there probably was some gambling on the Chicago Board of Trade, but the practice remained incidental to the legitimate purposes of the organization. It was not feasible, either in a legal or economic sense, to question the intentions of parties in thousands of contracts daily. Almost twenty-five years before the *Christie* decision, Holmes had written: "The life of the law has not been logic, it has been experience. The felt necessities of the time . . . have had a good deal more to do than the syllogism in determining the rules by which men should be governed."[72] The *Christie* case should be seen as an example not of legal revolution but of legal realism.

Further, the opinion indicated the importance placed by the courts upon the rules of the Board. Every federal decision favorable to the Board noted above made mention of the internal rules that governed its members. By denying Christie the right to take the quotations, the Supreme Court gave its support to the rules that the organization had adopted and strengthened over the years. Thus the Court also approved the Board's quasi-

69. *Chicago Journal of Commerce*, April 5, 1948, p. 2a.

70. Supra, n. 66. In a case decided one year after the *Christie* case, the Eighth Circuit explicitly endorsed settlement by "set off, and ringing off." See Cleage v. Laidley, 149 Fed. 346, 351–52 (1906).

71. Quoted in Herbert J. Bass, ed., *The State of American History* (Chicago, 1970), p. 12.

72. Oliver Wendell Holmes, Jr., *The Common Law* (Boston, 1881), p. 1.

public function as a private administrative regulatory body. In so doing, the justices did not establish any precedent but merely affirmed existing practice.

The link between the old law-merchant doctrine of the fifteenth century and the underlying issues in the *Christie* case is striking. Given the issues at bar, perhaps the decision was predictable. In fact, it had been predicted exactly twenty years earlier, when a noted Chicago lawyer addressed the distinguished guests gathered to celebrate the opening of the new Board of Trade Building. The words of the prediction made by Emery Storrs in 1885 were appropriate in the first chapter of this study, and they remain relevant even as it draws to a close: "This Board directly or indirectly has settled legal questions of the largest importance to the producing and financial interests of the country. It has demonstrated the fact that those customs which, for the convenience of business, merchants have established among themselves, are stronger than any mere legal technicalities, and that to those customs, when among merchants they become uniform, universal and well established, the law must bend, and if it does not it will break."[73]

73. Supra, ch. 1, n. 30.

CHAPTER EIGHT

The Ambiguous Legacy:
Internal Regulation, Public Policy, and the Chicago Board of Trade

I

THE BROAD MANDATE of the United States Supreme Court in upholding the Board's right to restrict distribution of the market reports was more than an extremely important legal victory for the association. It was also an affirmation recognizing the Chicago Board of Trade as an agency with private power of internal administrative regulation that was upheld in the name of public policy. Yet the Board's journey to this point had been both long and hazardous.

Between 1875 and 1882 the Board enacted stringent rules for self-discipline but failed to use them effectively. The organization seemed oriented to the ethos of a private business club, and this attitude carried over to the bucket shops. When the bucket shops first appeared, few members of the Board saw anything unethical about them, and even more members bucket shopped as a standard part of their commercial transactions. The shops were originally seen as economic rivals, and the Board opposed them in this light. When the directors moved against the shops, they did so as a private association striving to protect, for its own profit, what it claimed as its own property. Nor was the organization in any hurry to do battle with these establishments.

By the late 1880s the directors concluded that the bucket shops were, in reality, parasites leeching off the legitimate purposes of the regular exchanges. There is no way to gauge whether civic outrage or opposition to bothersome competition contributed more to the Board's change in attitude. It was probably a combination of both factors. Furthermore, the continued growth of the shops, together with attempts at federal regulation in the early 1890s, made clear that more than vocal opposition to these "gambling dens" was needed. Too many people were "mistaking" a bucket shop for a board of trade or, even worse, vice versa. Indeed, national agitation against commodity speculation contributed to a growing awareness that internal reform was needed within the Chicago Board of Trade. This awareness could only have been strengthened by the fiasco of the quotations restrictions policy between 1890 and 1897. During the late 1890s the association moved with increasing rigor against both the shops and those among its own members who violated its rules. By the turn of the century, the Board was in the midst of a reform drive unlike any in its previous history.

As the last two chapters have shown, there is no doubt of the extended reform drive successfully undertaken by the Board. The more difficult question is why the Board reformed itself during this period. Economic competition, of course, was a factor. Clearly the continuing operation of the bucket shops hurt the major exchanges by luring speculative capital away from legitimate markets. Moreover, the common bucket-shop practice of charging smaller commissions than members could charge under the rules ultimately lessened the value of a seat on the Board. By 1898 the "high" offer for a seat on the exchange was down to $800. When one notes that by 1902, with the effective enforcement of a commission rule, the high offer for a seat reached $4,350, the concern of the Board during these years becomes understandable.[1]

A more important explanation lies in the proliferation of progressive reform movements that swept Chicago at the same time. In his book *The Shame of the Cities,* Lincoln Steffens commented on the vigorous, if sometimes ineffectual, efforts of the Chicago Civic Federation in opposing all forms of gambling, whether it took place in the pool hall, at the race track, or in the bucket shop.[2] In 1898 the chairman of the Civic Federation Committee on Gambling was John Hill, Jr., a former Board of Trade direc-

---

1. Figures taken from membership file in treasurer's office, Chicago Board of Trade.
2. (New York, 1957), pp. 162–64.

tor and the Board member most active in exposing and prosecuting bucket-shop activities within the organization.

Some historians have discussed the excitement—almost a moral passion—that often characterized urban reform movements.[3] The Board itself, with its urban-oriented outlook, could not be immune to its effect. One speaker claimed, in 1897, that

> bucket shops and pool rooms are twin outlaws in nearly every state in the Union. Their united corruption fund has enabled them to baffle justice by debauchery of the constituted authority for the investigation and prosecution of crime, but they could not continue in existence for a day but for their alliance with the Western Union Telegraph Company. That company furnishes all the machinery and all the news on which bets are laid.

How typical of the muckraking era! The speaker, who sounded like Henry Demarest Lloyd, Ida Tarbell, or some other crusading spirit of the time, was none other than William T. Baker, president of the Chicago Board of Trade, addressing its assembled membership.[4]

Here then is the context in which the Board's reform drive should be seen. Under the leadership of William Warren, elected president in 1900, the organization once again joined the battle against bucket shops and related abuses. "It must be understood," Warren wrote in 1900, that the Board "has entered upon this contest for the last time and for a fight to the finish." He claimed that "if the laws will sustain us, we will root out this monstrous and growing evil entirely."[5] The president's point was well taken. No matter how much success attended the Board's battle against the bucket shops, final defeat was impossible without the aid of the courts. The judges consistently upheld the authority of the directorate to enact and enforce rules and regulations; indeed, even when the courts had found against the Board in cases tried prior to the *Christie* case, their decisions implied that the organization simply was unable to follow its own rules.

3. Thus, e.g., Dewey W. Grantham, Jr., in his review of Kolko's *Triumph of Conservatism*, mentions the "democratic faith and moral fire of the representative middle class progressive." *South Atlantic Quarterly* 63 (1964):434.

4. *Report of the Directors, 1896*, p. lxxxvii.

5. *Northwestern Miller*, August 22, 1900, p. 357.

Yet in 1900 the Chicago Board of Trade asked of the courts essentially what it had sought in 1889. What had changed to bring about the favorable verdict? The methodology of the bucket shops was still the same, and the arguments they raised against restriction of the reports were virtually those offered in the 1880s. There appeared to be no remarkable increase in popular opposition to gambling, which remained, as it had for many years, little more than a subject for frequent editorial condemnation. Nor did the Illinois Supreme Court, which in the 1900 to 1902 round of bucket-shop litigation found for the Board, appear to have reversed itself. In 1889 that tribunal had left the Board two loopholes. The organization, if it distributed the market quotations at all, had to distribute them without *unjust* discrimination to all who sought them for *lawful* purposes. Important changes had come not from external factors but from within the Board itself. It employed a different legal strategy against the shops, and it undertook important internal reforms as well.

During the litigation of the 1880s, the Board had based its entire case upon its rights as a private association to distribute its property (the quotations) as it saw fit. The issue of rightness or wrongness of a bucket shop was not raised by either side, probably by mutual agreement. The Board may have been willing to accept this stipulation because, perhaps, it realized that the distinction between itself and the shops was not clear during this period. In 1900 and thereafter, even as the Board reformed itself, the organization sought to demonstrate, through extensive presentation of evidence, the basic differences between the bucket shops and the legitimate exchanges. It argued less as a private association and more as an organization with quasi-public responsibilities that required tight control over its reports in the public interest. Finally, the Board maintained a property right in the reports (as it had done before), but it argued that this right was damaged by illicit bucket-shop activities and could thus be protected under equity jurisdiction.

On the other hand, Board leaders emphasized that its reform efforts, especially after 1900, represented a new policy and not "one of those ephemeral spasms of reform which so often manifest themselves in communities and organizations, only to be again supplanted by old conditions when the exciting cause is temporarily allayed."[6] President Warren candidly admitted that "twenty years of acquiescence in, or at best, but spasmodic and feeble resistance to the use of our quotations in bucket shops had debased and degraded us in the eyes of the public, the bench, the bar, and the press, until by common consent we came to be regarded as all tarred with the same stick."[7] Thus the significance of the favorable court decisions culminating in the *Christie* case rests in part on the fact that the Board was able to make sufficient internal reform to receive judicial support.

In cleaning house and at the same time calling for an all-out battle against bucket-shop gambling, the Board enjoyed popular approval. By 1905 muckraking magazines had added the bucket shop to their already lengthy list of evils.[8] At the same time "monopoly" was an equally attractive target for the muckraking press, and bucket shops were quick to emphasize the monopoly over the necessaries of life" that would accrue to the Board if it controlled distribution of the market quotations.[9] Inherent in the tension between these two positions is an example of the ambiguity between private regulatory activity and private economic gain. Inevitably the question arises why a private association such as the Chicago Board of Trade succeeded in regulating and enforcing its procedures at a time when big business, seemingly unable to police itself, came under federal supervision.

The answer lies in the nature and functions of the commodities exchanges. They provided the market and its participants with the same type of policing activities asked of the federal government. By standards of grading, inspection, and weighing, and through the disciplinary control of members, the exchanges regularized and rationalized competition in the marketplace. Unlike a private profit-making corporation in competition with others of its kind, the Chicago Board of Trade sought, not profit for itself, but to facilitate an ordered, competitive market for the economic advantage of all concerned. Without the trading pits,

6. *Report of the Directors*, supra, n. 4; *1900*, pp. lxxii–lxxiii; *1901*, p. lxxx.
7. Supra, n. 5.
8. Cowing, pp. 26–30; Frank Norris, "A Deal in Wheat," *Everybody's Magazine* 7 (1902):173–80. A series of exposé articles on the bucket shops appeared in the June through September 1906 issues of this magazine. See also, in the September issue, the story by James H. Gannon, Jr., "Smith, Debtor: A Bucket Shop Idyll."
9. C. C. Christie, "Bucket Shop vs. Board of Trade," ibid., 15 (1906):707–13.

according to the *Chicago Tribune,* "the smaller men in the business would be hopelessly crowded out of the race by the big ones who would control the situation as against them if the market ceased to be an open one."[10] While some large corporations may have turned to the government primarily to lessen competition, the exchanges, through their rules, regulations, and discipline, may well have served to stimulate and promote a more competitive marketplace.

It may be that the exchanges, as exemplified by the Chicago Board of Trade, escaped progressive regulation because they reflected so much of the progressive ethos: an ordered, efficient market system, self-regulated to large extent through its own expertise and authority, able apparently to maintain and nurture a reasonable competition that seemed to many progressives a thing of the past. In 1889 the Illinois Supreme Court had blocked Board control of the market reports because it feared for competition. In 1918 the United States Supreme Court affirmed an internal market regulation that had been adopted by the Board. It may be appropriate here to cite the words of the justice who handed down the opinion, the most famous progressive lawyer of his day—Louis Brandeis:

> The legality of an agreement or regulation cannot be determined by so simple a test, as whether it restrains competition. Every agreement concerning trade, every regulation of trade, restrains. To bind, to restrain, is of their very essence. The true test of legality is whether the restraint imposed is such as merely regulates and perhaps thereby promotes competition or whether it . . . may suppress or even destroy competition.[11]

Brandeis's point helps to illuminate the relationship between the growth of federal regulatory supervision and private internal rule enforcement, both of which grew dramatically during the period covered by this study. Indeed, it may be accurate to view the years from 1870 to 1920 as a time when both private and public policy sought to insure continued meaningful competition within reasonable and equitable boundaries. Seen in this light, there is little difference between the statutes enacted during the

10. *Chicago Tribune,* July 23, 1889, p. 4.
11. Chicago Board of Trade v. United States, 246 U.S. 231, 238 (1918).

Granger era and the system of internal regulation developed by the Chicago Board of Trade.

The Granger laws sought, through the establishment of supervisory commissions and rate regulation, to prevent the new railroad-related corporate structures from undermining what George Miller calls "the prosperity of the established order."[12] He notes that the prime movers behind the Granger laws were businessmen and merchants. Enactment of the statutes represented "victory for traditional mercantile interests" rooted in the "mercantile order of the ante bellum period."[13] Similarly, thirty years later, the Chicago Board of Trade sought judicial approval of its regulatory powers with much the same goals in mind. Both desired to insure an economic system in which competing interests could pursue their own ends without destroying an open market.

Although the Board regarded Holmes's opinion as a complete vindication of its mercantile practices, in fact the Supreme Court's decision did not end opposition either to boards of trade or to commodities speculation. For example, J. A. Everitt, in speaking for the American Society of Equity in 1905, said of the grain pits of the exchange: They are "a curse to everybody that they touch. They are barnacles that have attached themselves on the produce of the earth. The speculators and gamblers in farm products are sap-sucking, unholy, Godless things that are holding up and gorging themselves on labor's portion as it is created on the farms."[14] Similarly, in 1912 Congressman H. Robert Fowler of Illinois described the Chicago Board of Trade as "the greatest Monte Carlo in the world, where more people are held up and annually robbed in open daylight than any other city in the world." How long, he demanded, "will the patient people tolerate these polluting, stiffling [sic] dens of stench?" Fowler urged enactment of a law "strong enough to break up these dens of sin and hell."[15]

Indeed, at regular intervals between 1905 and 1921, congressional committees investigated and reinvestigated the grain

12. Miller, p. 195.
13. Ibid., p. 197.
14. J. A. Everitt, *The Third Power* (Indianapolis, 1905), p. 14.
15. U.S., Congress, House, *Congressional Record*, 62d Cong., 2d sess., 1912, vol. 48, pt. 9, p. 9012.

trade. On each occasion a spokesman for the Board of Trade
appeared before them clutching a copy of Holmes's decision as
if it were a talisman that could neutralize all criticism levied
against the exchanges. In February 1910, when testifying before
a House committee, the vice president of the Board quoted lib-
erally from the *Christie* case and then said of the decision: "It
covers every point that can be raised. It gives us as clean a bill
of health as any exchange could have. That is from the Supreme
Court of the United States."[16] In 1921, during the hearings that
were to result in the Capper-Tincher Grain Futures Act, the
representative of the Chicago Board of Trade indignantly denied
that the typical transaction made on the floor of the Board was
gambling. "It is not gambling: the decision here said it is not
gambling."[17]

The outbreak of World War I in Europe dramatically affected
grain trading in the United States. Encouraged by the sharp
increase in foreign demands for grain, American farmers responded by increasing acreage—a move that yielded a record
harvest of more than a billion bushels of grain in 1915. By
1917, with the United States at war, the Food Administration
Grain Corporation had taken over most domestic grain marketing, and futures trading in wheat was suspended for the duration
of the conflict. Crops continued to be extremely large, and
government price supports insured good returns to the grain
producers for their efforts. However, the government price guar-
antees ended in May 1920, as did the operations of the Grain
Corporation. In July 1920 the exchanges resumed trading in
grain. Suddenly the agrarians, who had planted huge amounts
of seed "as if the war's demand would continue indefinitely,"
found the falling demand exceeded only by declining prices.[18]

Statistics, although impressive, really fail to convey the shock
of the drop in commodity prices in 1920–21. "The initial price
crisis was the most crushing that American agrictulture had yet
experienced."[19] Indeed, from July through December 1920, the
average price of leading crops "fell 57 per cent, and by May

16. Id., Committee on Agriculture, *Hearings on Bills for the Prevention of Dealing in Futures*, 61st Cong., 2d sess., 1910, p. 567.
17. Id., *Hearings on Futures Trading*, 66th Cong., 3d sess., 1921, p. 591.
18. Harry Fornari, *Bread Upon the Waters* (Nashville, 1973), pp. 73–78.
19. James Shideler, *Farm Crisis 1919–1923* (Berkeley, 1957), p. 46.

1921, prices were but one third of what they had been the preceding June."[20] These conditions were exacerbated by the transition, difficult in itself, from a wartime to a peacetime society. Together they accomplished what Butterworth, Hatch, Everitt, and Fowler had been unable to bring about: federal regulation of the commodities exchanges.

In political terms the "plight" of the farmers could only have been important to Warren Harding, a newly elected president with deep ties to rural America, and to his secretary of agriculture, Henry C. Wallace, widely regarded as progressive, conscientious, and totally committed to the agrarian community.[21] Between July and August 1921, a series of bills were enacted into law, all designed to relieve the agricultural crisis. Four of these bills "were relatively noncontroversial and were adopted without much difficulty."[22] One of them was the Grain Futures Act.[23]

The organized exchanges, particularly the Chicago Board of Trade, opposed federal intervention, one speaker going so far as to insist that such intervention would kill the exchanges. Sponsors of the measure, of course, claimed otherwise. Senator Arthur Capper of Kansas insisted that the legislation envisioned federal supervision, not regulation.[24] Congressman J. N. Tincher, also of Kansas, admitted in the hearings that "the Board can regulate its own members. . . . They would have to comply with the regulations of the Board in order to remain members."[25]

Perhaps unintentionally, the comments of both Capper and Tincher well illustrate the ambiguous legacy of private regulation and public policy concerning the commodities exchange. Had the exchanges developed from the middle of the nineteenth century as organizations under continuous governmental supervision, and had the legal order been in control of market developments as its operations grew more complex and its transactions multiplied, the entire thrust of external regulation might indeed

20. Ibid.
21. Robert K. Murray, *The Harding Era* (Minneapolis, 1969), pp. 199–202.
22. Ibid., p. 207.
23. Ch. 86, 42 Stat. 187.
24. Cowing, pp. 90–91; Arthur Capper, *The Agricultural Bloc* (New York, 1922), pp. 82–85.
25. U.S., Congress, House, Committee on Agriculture, *Hearings on the Grain Futures Act*, 67th Cong.. 2d sess., 1922, p. 31.

have been different. But, as this study has sought to demonstrate, with the exception of occasional court cases and infrequent legislative hearings, for the most part external legal supervision did not attend the growth or operation of the American commodities markets.

In the first place, the ambivalent nineteenth-century attitude toward speculation and commercial risk prevented any sustained interest in governmental regulation. Ironically this ambivalence was most noticeable in the groups apparently fighting hardest for federal legislation, the agrarians. If the farmers, the group claiming to be most affected by abuses perpetrated on the exchanges, could not make up their minds as to how the speculative impulse could be curbed, neither could Congress. Furthermore, even if public policy had mandated external regulation, the results probably would not have been satisfactory, simply because the nineteenth-century administrative framework was unable to effectively guide economic and industrial modernization—of which the commodities exchanges were but a symptom.

As with so much of nineteenth-century American legal and administrative history, the commodities exchanges developed largely on their own. Not until the exchanges had matured— along with the market system they evolved—and had become institutionalized did the legal order respond. But by 1921 this response could be made only in the light of past institutional experience, which, as these chapters have tried to demonstrate, heavily involved self-regulation. Thus the Capper-Tincher Bill, which was upheld by the United States Supreme Court in 1923 and is the basis of all federal commodities regulation from that day to this, had surprisingly few sections dealing with internal regulation.

The law forbade any dealings in futures trading unless "the seller is at the time of the making of such contract the owner of the actual physical property covered thereby, or is the grower thereof," *or* "where such contract is made by or through a member of a board of trade which has been designated by the secretary of agriculture as a 'contract market'."

For a board of trade to become a contract market, its officials had to provide for the keeping of a record, either by the organization or by the members, showing the details and terms of all cash and future transactions entered into by them, consummated at, on, or in a board of trade, such report to be in permanent form, showing the parties to all such transactions, including the persons for whom made, any assignments or transfers thereof, with the parties thereto, and the manner in which said transactions are fulfilled, discharged, or terminated. Such a record shall be required to be kept for a period of three years from the date thereof.

Furthermore, the governing board of the exchange had to provide "for the prevention of dissemination by the board or any member thereof, of false or misleading or knowingly inaccurate reports concerning crop or market information or conditions that affect or tend to affect the price of grain in interstate commerce." The same officials also had to provide against "manipulation of prices or the cornering of any grain by the dealers or operators upon such Board."[26]

Long before 1922 the Chicago Board of Trade enacted rules of the nature now required by the statute. Since the 1870s, for example, the Board had prescribed expulsion for any member "guilty of making or reporting any false or fictitious purchase or sale, or . . . guilty of an act of bad faith, or any attempt at extortion or of any dishonest conduct." As early as 1887 the Board had similarly banned trading in differences without a bona fide purchase; while since 1894 it had required all members making any futures transations to "notify the party for whom such purchase or sale was made, of the price at which and the party with whom such purchase or sale was made, such notice to be in writing and to be given upon the day of such purchase or sale."[27] It was true that the Board had not required that

26. The first Grain Futures Act passed in 1921, cited at n. 21 above, contained all these provisions, as well as a tax on privileged trades and an additional tax on futures contracts that were not executed upon a contract market. These sections of the law were declared unconstitutional by the United States Supreme Court in Hill v. Wallace, 259 U.S. 44 (1923), and Trusler v. Crooks, 269 U.S. 475 (1926).

27. In addition, the Board required its members "to keep a settlement book in which shall have been entered the names of parties with whom settlements have been made, and the dates and terms of the trades included in such settlements, and the terms of such settlements, and the prices at which the commodities were originally sold or purchased, and the amounts due to or from him or them on each separate settlement, also the net amount due to or from him or them on all settlements." This rule was in effect by 1890.

these records be kept for three years or more. But the important aspect of the rule was that a written record of all futures transactions be kept, and this the members of the Board had been obliged to do for almost thirty years before the Grain Futures Act became law.

Passage of the Grain Futures Act, including subsequent amendments, illustrates an important characteristic of American public policy and the nature of legislative behavior. This behavior can be described only as a series of jerks and halting progressions. Typically, once the legislature has intervened in an important market area, it will not do so again for a number of years. Furthermore, the initial intervention itself might not occur for many years. This tendency toward infrequent legislative action helps to explain the evolution of private organizations with strong regulatory powers. The needs of the market called for consistent day-to-day monitoring by an institution capable of rule enactment and enforcement. Conversely, with the increase of doubt about the ability of the exchanges to police the markets effectively, interest turned toward a federal supervisory agency that could provide the continuous attention deemed necessary.

The Grain Futures Act was one of the first to address itself to this problem. It did so, however, strictly within the context of the self-regulatory functions long undertaken by the exchanges. Not surprisingly, this same focus was also evident in the development of the Securities Exchange Commission. Indeed, as its chairman, William O. Douglas, noted in June 1939, "Legal mandate is an inferior method of getting the work of the world done."[28] A few weeks later, he made the point even more strongly: "Government regulation at its best should be residual. We should not have to be in a position of watching the details of operation. Those are for the exchanges themselves."[29]

As this study has sought to demonstrate, federal administration of the commodities markets arrived as the final step after a long series of internal regulatory actions. But this is not to claim, contrary to Kolko, that the exchanges sought federal interven-

---

28. Michael Parrish, *Securities Regulation and the New Deal* (New Haven, Conn., 1970), p. 182.
29. Ibid., p. 184.

tion as did other economic institutions.[30] There is a very real difference, after all, between calling for federal regulation and grudgingly accepting it as inevitable. The major exchanges never advocated federal regulation. Rather, they sought to work with federal authorities to insure a supervisory system within which the exchanges could function. It is this latter policy that has characterized the relationship between the commodities exchanges and the federal government during the last half century.

III

Since 1923 the commodities exchanges have been under national supervision. In subsequent years the scope of federal administrative regulation has grown dramatically. Yet the ambiguous legacy of nineteenth-century internal regulation and twentieth-century external administration continues to trouble public policy. The legitimate exchanges, as typified by the Chicago Board of Trade, remained the focal point for commodities trading. In fact, the amendments to the Commodities Exchange Act in 1936 restricted all commodities trading to boards of trade that had been designated as contract markets, with their participants subject to the exchanges' rules and regulations. Yet the continued growth of federal exchange regulation conceivably lent credence to the claim that organized exchanges have not successfully met the need for effective policing of either the market or the membership.

Indeed, the difficulties encountered by the Chicago Board of Trade in banning privileged trading, even as it moved against the bucket shops, may well illustrate the point. The Board's directors, in their report for 1900, claimed this type of trading had been suppressed, thus freeing the exchange from practices which "seriously impaired our influence . . . and reflected upon the good name and dignity of the Association." A year later the directors admitted that the continued trading in puts and calls "tends to thwart the efforts of this Board to uphold, without evasion and in absolute good faith, the statutes of the State."

30. Kolko, *Triumph of Conservatism*. The Kolko thesis appears attractive in part because the author has clothed it with copious citations, all presumably carefully chosen to support previously drawn conclusions.

By 1905, in spite of the opposition of a majority of the directors, the members voted to eliminate the penalty of expulsion for privileged trading. Members who so traded were to "forfeit the right to have said contract enforced under the rules of this Association." Thus the Board went back to the status quo of 1865. John Hill, Jr., leader of the anti-bucket-shop faction, bluntly criticized the Board's "backward step." "The lawless element of the Board is a constant menace to its welfare," he said; and he warned that the vote to end the penalty "is an index of what the exchange would be were it not for the herculean efforts that for five years have been exerted to lift it out of the mire."[31]

Amendments to the Grain Futures Act (now known as the Commodity Exchange Act) ultimately banned all privileged trading.[32] Furthermore, supervision of the exchanges has increased; and in 1974 an independent federal regulatory commission, the Commodity Futures Trading Commission, was established.[33] It is too soon to gauge effectively whether or not the new commission will be a success; but the serious difficulties confronting it since 1975 do not give ground for optimism. It is still unclear whether such supervision can best be implemented by the exchanges or by an external administrative agency. The answers to this perplexing problem remain a key element in the continuing debate over private versus public economic regulation.[34]

31. *D.R.*, 1901: April 16, p. 106, May 21, p. 139, May 28, p. 151; 1903: November 3, p. 323, November 10, pp. 328–29, November 19, p. 338; 1905: July 25, p. 193. *D.P.*, 1901: May 21, June 10; 1903: March 24, 31, May 5, October 20, 27; 1905: July 15, August 30. *SB*, *Chicago Tribune*, 1905: August 31, September 1; see also *SB*, *Chicago Post*, same dates.

32. 7 U.S.C.A. § 6c.

33. Pub. L. No. 93–463, 88 Stat. 1389; 7 U.S.C. § 4a.

34. The continuing interplay between internal regulatory power and the steadily increasing extent of federal supervisory authority over the exchanges since 1923 is the subject of two articles by this author forthcoming in the *Policy Studies Journal* and the National Archival Conference volume *Farmers, Bureaucrats and Middlemen*.

Appendix

PERCENTAGE OF MEMBERS VOTING IN ANNUAL ELECTION

	CHICAGO BOARD OF TRADE[1]			MILWAUKEE CHAMBER OF COMMERCE[2]		
	Total Membership	*No. of Voting Members*	*Percentage Voting*	*Total Membership*	*No. of Voting Members*	*Percentage Voting*
1880	1793	1050	58.72	561	208	37.07
1881	1936	970	50.10	561	261	46.52
1882	1936	1213	62.65	630	145	23.01
1883	1936	1171	60.48	629	321	51.03
1884	1933	1196	61.87	628	124	19.74
1885	1925	1002	52.05	624	125	20.03
1886	1933	1205	62.33	620	113	18.22
1887	1930	974	50.38	613	111	18.10
1888	1920	1289	67.13	609	286	46.96
1889	1923	658	49.81	608	268	44.07
1890	1913	1021	53.37	607	110	18.12
1891	1909	1090	57.09	607	204	33.60
1892	1903	1304	68.52	601	131	21.79
1893	1888	1115	59.05	600	Data Not Available	
1894	1880	1246	66.27	604	100	16.55
1895	1848	1051	56.87	600	247	41.16
1896	1840	1354	73.58	596	117	19.63
1897	1835	1130	61.58	588	197	33.50
1898	1833	1339	73.04	598	170	28.42
1899	1809	1267	70.03	590	260	44.06
1900	1803	1324	73.43	588	138	23.46
1901	1796	975	54.28	588	158	26.87
1902	1793	967	53.93	606	165	27.22
1903	1792	1024	57.14	605	126	20.82
1904	1785	1210	67.78	603	130	21.55
1905	1774	1006	56.70	602	112	18.60

[1]Source: Board of Trade, *Annual Directors' Reports, Directors' Minutes,* 1880–1905.

[2]Source: Milwaukee Chamber of Commerce, Yearbooks, 1880–1905.

Bibliography

THIS BRIEF ESSAY lists some of the important published work of probable value to readers who are interested in pursuing this subject further. Full citations are given in this essay only for works not directly cited in this study. Complete information on all other works mentioned herein has been included in the bibliography that follows.

I

The development of the Board of Trade during the late nineteenth century took place while important changes were occurring throughout American society. The best overview of the period is Robert Wiebe's *The Search for Order*. Wiebe's earlier book *Businessmen and Reform* (Cambridge, Mass., 1962), while not so gracefully written, contains insights into the ethos of reform during the Progressive Era from the corporate point of view. On the same subject but of dubious value is *The Triumph of Conservatism* by Gabriel Kolko. Kolko argues that segments of large-scale corporate enterprise connived both with each other and the federal government to bring about what he claims has wrongly been labeled "progressive regulation." His thesis is questionable, to say the least. Kolko appears to have selected with care "the evidence" assembled to prove his contention, even to the extent of taking quotations out of context. For one good example of this tendency, see John Braeman's critique of Kolko's work in "The Square Deal in Action: A Case Study in the Growth of the 'National Police Power'," found in *Change and Continuity in Twentieth Century America,* ed. J. Braeman, R. Bremner, and E. Walters. A further weakness of Kolko's work is his omission of material that does not support his thesis. Thus, in a study that supposedly deals with "finance capitalism," there is virtually no analysis of the role of stock and commodity exchanges. One explanation for this may be that the attitude of the major commercial exchanges toward federal regulation disproves rather than supports Kolko's thesis.

Although only indirectly related to my topic, Lee Benson's outstanding study of *Merchants, Farmers and Railroads: Railroad Regulation and New York Politics, 1850–1887*, has some very meaningful explanations of the specific forces behind the push for federal regulation. Cedric Cowing, in his *Populists, Plungers and Progressives*, has attempted "a social history of stock and commodity speculation." The book is helpful as a general survey of contemporary attitudes toward speculation, but it tells us nothing about the factors causing the establishment of exchanges and their internal administration. By neglecting this important dimension, Cowing fails to explain adequately why the regulation that ultimately occurred took the form it did. Indeed, only in recent years has the subject of regulation begun to receive the attention it deserves. Much of the work has emphasized the supposed ineffectiveness of governmental regulation in America. The best analysis of the current literature is in Thomas K. McCraw's summary "Regulation in America: A Review Article."

Again, a serious weakness of much of the otherwise valuable material discussed by McCraw is the neglect of internal self-regulation, especially in the private sector. This tendency also detracts, for example, from Michael Parrish's able study *Securities Regulation and the New Deal*, which is probably the best work of its kind available. Vincent Carosso's *Investment Banking in America* (Cambridge, Mass., 1970) is an outstanding analysis. Published at the same time, although it deals with an earlier regulatory era, George Miller's *Railroads and the Granger Laws* is strongly recommended. Miller delineates the era in which institutions such as the Chicago Board of Trade matured, and shows the compatibility between internal regulatory institutions and the aims of those seeking "Granger Laws." Although not directly related to this study, the works of Alfred Chandler, Jr., and Louis Galambos are vital to an understanding of American economic growth and regulation. See, for example, Chandler, *Strategy and Structure: Chapters in the History of Industrial Enterprise* (Cambridge, Mass., 1962), and Galambos, *The Public Image of Big Business in America, 1880–1940: A Quantitative Study in Social Change* (Baltimore, 1975). See Ari and Olive Hoogenboom, *A History of the ICC: From Panacea to Palliative* (New York, 1976), for a new and balanced account of the Interstate Commerce Commission.

II

The interplay between law, economic growth, and public policy —three factors that spawned organizations such as the Chicago Board of Trade—has been set forth in several studies that have become standard works. See Oscar and Mary Handlin, *Commonwealth: A Study of the Role of Government in the American Economy: Massachusetts, 1774–1861*; Louis Hartz, *Economic Policy and Democratic Thought: Pennsylvania 1776–1860* (Cambridge, Mass., 1948); Harry Scheiber, *The Ohio Canal Era: A Case Study of Government and the Economy, 1820–1861*; Willard Hurst, *Law and the Conditions of Freedom in the Nineteenth-Century United States*. See also *A History of American Law* by Lawrence M. Friedman.

There is a surprising paucity of historical studies dealing with the organized commodity exchanges. One reason may be the difficulty of access to records and papers of these private organizations, assuming such records have been preserved. Occasionally historians have written about the stock and commodity exchanges in spite of this drawback, and the result does not tell us much about the internal development and nature of the exchanges. See, for example, *The Big Board* by Robert Sobel (New York, 1965).

The only "historical" study of the Chicago Board of Trade is a three-volume opus by Charles H. Taylor, *History of the Board of Trade of the City of Chicago*. A highly colored, laudatory work that extols the successes of the Board while ignoring its failures, Taylor's work has been used extensively by writers delving into the history of the association. The research that went into the writing of this book seems to have come mostly from newspaper accounts and a superficial survey of the directors' minutes, although the specific quotations or citations from this latter source are few. Within limitations, this book is useful. Taylor assembled a vast amount of material, much of it anecdotal in character, that amplifies the stark narrative of the official minutes. On the other hand, because of the numerous errors it contains, including typographical mistakes, it would not be wise to rely upon it for much more than corroborative detail. In that sense it has been used here.

There is a fairly comprehensive literature dealing with the technical function of commodity exchanges and speculative practices. One of the earliest, and still of considerable value, is a dissertation by Henry Emery, *Speculation on the Stock and Produce Exchanges of the United States*. George Hoffman's *Futures Trading on Organized Commodity Markets in the United States* is a thorough analysis. His previous study, *Hedging by Dealing in Grain Futures* (Philadelphia, 1925), offers a good bibliography. The legal problems of futures trading, as well as the technical aspects of commodity speculation, were comprehensively treated in a volume by Julius Baer and George Woodruff: *Commodity Exchanges*. An updated treatment of this material is found in Julius Baer and Olin Saxon, *Commodity Exchanges and Futures Trading*, and Edward Duddy and David Revzan, *Marketing: An Institutional Approach* (New York, 1953). See also Duddy and Revzan's *The Grain Supply Area of the Chicago Market* (Chicago, 1934); Henry H. Bakken, "Historical Evolution, Theory and Legal Status of Futures," in *Futures Trading Seminar, History and Development* (Madison, 1960); James Schonberg, *The Grain Trade: How It Works* (New York, 1956); Harold S. Irwin, *Evolution of Futures Trading* (Madison, 1954); Morton Rothstein, "The International Market for Agricultural Commodities," in *Economic Change in the Civil War Era*. An excellent discussion of litigation and legislation concerning modern agricultural marketing is the study by Benjamin F. Goldstein, *Marketing: A Farmer's Problem*. An extensive bibliography of material on commodities futures trading, regularly updated, is available from the library of the Chicago Board of Trade. Indeed, in the years since this author began his research at the Board, its library has expanded into an impressive collection of contemporary sources on commodities trading, exchange practices, option trading, and related topics. See also John G. Clark, *The Grain Trade in the Old Northwest* (Urbana, 1966). Although this study deals with the grain trade before commodity exchanges appeared, it is the best analysis of its kind available and is indispensable as background for understanding the needs which resulted in a modern grain marketing system.

Since the 1930s there has been a huge outpouring of federal reports on the grain trade, issued under the auspices of the Commodity Exchange Authority, the agency charged with administering the Commodity Exchange Act until 1974; but several earlier government reports should also be noted. The much neglected but very informative United States Industrial Commission's *Report on the Distribution of Farm Products* (U.S., Congress, House Document 494, 56th Cong., 2d sess., 1900–1) has a great deal of information. See also the Commission's final *Report*, No. 4349, and companion volumes 4340–41. Any exploration of the grain trade has to start with the monumental seven-volume series published by the Federal Trade Commission, *Report on the Grain Trade* (Washington, D.C., 1920–26). A product of the progressive emphasis on facts and figures, this study explores every facet of the grain trade: price trends, marketing conditions, transportation, and storage. Laced throughout the volumes are sections dealing with the historical development of the major exchanges. The *Report* was most valuable to this study for its explanations of how the grain markets work, whereas most of the historical information on the Chicago Board of Trade was taken from Taylor.

The standard accounts of agrarian agitation, such as John D. Hicks, *The Populist Revolt* (Minneapolis, 1931), Solon J. Buck, *The Granger Era*, and Buck's later survey, *The Agrarian Crusade* (New Haven, Conn., 1920), are helpful as background sources. Norman Pollock, in his controversial *The Populist Response to Industrial America* (Cambridge, Mass., 1962), fails to recognize the agrarian ambivalence concerning commercial success, risk, and speculation. The same criticism may be made of William A. Williams's sprawling study, *The Roots of the Modern American Empire* (New York, 1969). A useful antidote to much of the earlier work on populism is found in the text and notes of two articles by Karel Bicha: "The Conservative Populists: A Hypothesis," and "Western Populists: Marginal Reformers of the 1890s," *Agricultural History* 50 (1976):626–35. Illinois agricultural discontent is well analyzed in Roy V. Scott's study, *The Agrarian Movement in Illinois* (Urbana, 1962). Valuable insights are found in the following contemporary accounts: Stephen Smith, *Grains for the Grangers* (Chicago, 1873); Jonathan Periam, *The Groundswell: A History of the Origins of the Farmer's Movement*; N. B. Ashby, *The Riddle of the Sphinx* (Des Moines, 1890); N. A. Dunning, *The Farmer's Alliance History and Agricultural Digest* (Washington, D.C., 1891); Bud Reeve, *The Letter: An Epistle by a Granger to Brother Grangers* (Fargo, 1892); Thomas C. Atkeson, *Semi-Centennial History of the Patrons of Husbandry* (New York, 1916); *Patron's Song Book: A Choice Collection of Original and Selected Gems*; George F. Root, *The Trumpet of Reform* (Cincinnati, 1874); J. A. Everitt, *The Third Power*; James Wallace Darrow, *Origins and Early History of the Order of Patrons of Husbandry in the United States* (Chatham, N.Y., 1904); A. E. Paine, *Granger Movement in Illinois* (Urbana, 1904); Edward W. Martin, *History of the Granger Movement* (Chicago, 1874); M. W. Quick, *Modern Speculation* (Titusville, Pa., 1888). An intriguing updating of many of the themes emphasized in these sources is Arthur Capper's *The Agricultural Bloc*.

The most important source for newspaper accounts relating to the Chicago Board of Trade after 1890 is the huge collection of scrapbooks compiled for the Citizens' Association of Chicago, which are housed in the library of the Chicago Historical Society. The collection includes large numbers of excerpts from every major newspaper of the city. For the 1874–90 period, the *Chicago Tribune* and *Chicago InterOcean* are of special value. The bucket-shop fights and the Board's internal problems over privileged trading were reported regularly in the *New York Times*. The journal best articulating the commercial community's attitude toward the exchanges was *Bradstreet's*. Other important "interest" periodicals are the *Northwestern Miller* and the *American Elevator and Grain Trade*. It is impossible to classify a particular periodical as *the* farmer's journal, but several did claim to represent agrarian sentiment. The *Farmers' Review* and the *Prairie Farmer*, together with the more outspoken *Western Rural* and *National Economist*, well reveal the agrarian attitudes, often contradictory, toward the commodity exchanges. See also the fascinating collection of clippings from Alliance and Populist newspapers compiled by Richard T. Ely and deposited in the John Crerar Library in Chicago.

The intertwining themes of the grain trade, agrarian discontent, and federal legislation are treated in Charles R. Detrick, "The Effects of the Granger Acts," *Journal of Political Economy* 11 (1902):237–56; Louis Schmidt, "The Internal Grain Trade of the United States, 1860–1900," *Iowa Journal of History* 19 (1921):196–245, 415–55, and 20 (1922):70–131. Arthur G. Peterson, "Futures Trading with Particular Reference to Agricultural Commodities," *Agricultural History* 7 (1933):68–80, is an excellent background article. It should be read in conjunction with Thomas Odle, "Entrepreneurial Cooperation on the Great Lakes: The Origins of the Methods of American Grain Marketing." See also Morton Rothstein, "America in the International Rivalry for the British Wheat Market, 1860–1914"; George Cerny, "Cooperation in the Midwest in the Granger Era, 1869–1875," *Agricultural History* 37 (1963):187–205; Roy V. Scott, "Grangerism in Champaign County, Illinois, 1873–1877." An early study of the declining wheat prices was produced in 1892 by Thorstein B. Veblen, "The Price of Wheat since 1867," *Journal of American Politics* 1 (1892):68–103. The futile and little-known efforts by Senator John Ingalls of Kansas to attach an antioption clause to the Sherman Anti-Trust Act are discussed in a fascinating article by David F. McFarland, "The Ingalls Amendment to the Sherman Anti-Trust Bill," *Kansas Historical Quarterly* 11 (1942):173–98.

In the years since federal commodity regulation became a reality, numerous articles have appeared on the effect of such regulation upon the exchanges. See James C. McMath: "Speculation in Grain for Future Delivery," *Central Law Journal* 98 (1925):365–77, and "Investment, Speculation and Gambling on the Fluctuation of the Market Prices," ibid., 93 (1921):221–27. The latter article includes an excellent bibliographical footnote. See also Clay Judson, "Validity of Transactions on the Board of Trade," *Illinois Law Review* 19 (1925):644–58. The broad topic of gambling in Illinois is treated by George D. Smith in his "Gambling in Illinois," *Illinois Law Review* 16 (1921):23–45. See also G. Wright Hoffman, "Governmental Regulation of Exchanges," *Annals* 155 (1931):39–55; H. J. Loman, "Commodity Exchange Clearing Systems," ibid., 100–9; H. S. Irwin: "Legal Status of Trading Futures," *Illinois Law Review* 32 (1937): 155–70; and "Nature of Risk Assumption in the Trading on Organized Exchanges," *American Economic Review* 27 (1937): 267–78; Edwin W. Patterson, "Hedging and Wagering on Produce Exchanges," *Yale Law Journal* 40 (1931):843–84; "Commerce—Contracts—Illegality—Gaming—Dealings in Commodity Futures," *Minnesota Law Review* 18 (1934):544–64; Telford Taylor, "Trading in Commodity Futures: A New Standard of Legality," *Yale Law Journal* 43 (1933):63–106; "Legislation Affecting Commodity and Stock Exchanges," *Harvard Law Review* 45 (1932):912–25; Hugh B. Killough, "Effects of Governmental Regulation of Commodity Exchanges in the United States," *Harvard Business Review* 11 (1933):307–15; J. M. Mehl, "Federal Regulation of Futures Trading," *Federal Bar Association Journal* 4 (1941):195–98; "Federal Regulation of Commodity Futures Trading," *Yale Law Journal* 60 (1951): 822–50; Donald A. Campbell, "Trading in Futures under the Commodity Exchange Act," *George Washington Law Review* 26 (1958):215–54; J. M. Mehl, "Objectives of Federal Regulation of the Commodity Exchange," *Journal of Farm Economics* 19 (1937):313–18.

PRIMARY SOURCES

Chicago. Chicago Historical Society. *Charter: An Act for the Incorporation of Boards of Trade and Chambers of Commerce.* N.p., 1849.
———. *Scrapbooks.* Compiled for Citizens' Association of Chicago.
Chicago. Newberry Library. Charles H. Hutchinson Papers.
Chicago. University of Illinois. Chicago Board of Trade Papers. *Association Records 1895–1939.*
———. *Directors' Papers.* Various dates 1875–1905.
———. *Directors' Records.* Various dates 1873–1905.
———. *Rules.* Various dates 1865–1967.
Madison. State Historical Society of Wisconsin Archives. Henry Demarest Lloyd Papers.
———. Howard A. Merritt Papers.
———. Vilas Papers.
———. Milwaukee Chamber of Commerce. *Rules.* 1890.
St. Louis. Missouri Historical Society. Merchants' Exchange Collection.
Washington, D.C. National Archives. Record Group 46.

SECONDARY SOURCES

I. Books

Andreas, Altred T. *History of Chicago.* Vol. 3, 1871–85. Chicago, 1886.

Baer, Julius B., and Saxon, Olin G. *Commodities Exchanges and Futures Trading.* New York, 1949.

Baer, Julius B., and Woodruff, George. *Commodity Exchanges.* New York, 1935.

Baker, Charles H. *Life and Character of William Taylor Baker.* New York, 1908.

Bass, Herbert J., ed. *The State of American History.* Chicago, 1970.

Bench and Bar of Chicago. Chicago, 1883.

Benson, Lee. *Merchants, Farmers and Railroads: Railroad Regulation and New York Politics, 1850–1887.* Cambridge, Mass., 1955.

Bentley, Arthur F. *The Process of Government.* Cambridge, Mass., 1967.

———, and Ratner, Sidney, eds. *Makers, Users and Masters.* Syracuse, 1969.

Berman, Harold. *Western Legal Tradition.* Cambridge, Mass., 1972.

Boardman, Henry A. *The Bible in the Counting House.* Philadelphia, 1853.

Bruchey, Stuart. *The Colonial Merchant.* New York, 1966.

Buck, Solon J. *The Granger Era.* Cambridge, Mass., 1913.

Cambridge Economic History of Europe. Vol. 2. Cambridge, 1952.

Capper, Arthur. *The Agricultural Bloc.* New York, 1922.

Carey, Peter B. *The Rise of Exchange Trading.* Chicago, 1933.

Chitty, Joseph. *Treatise on Law of Contracts.* Vol. 1. 11th ed. New York, 1874.

Cowing, Cedric. *Populists, Plungers and Progressives.* Princeton, 1965.

Davis, Kenneth C. *Administrative Law Treatise.* 3rd ed. St. Paul, 1972.

Dies, Edward J. *The Plunger.* New York, 1929.

Emery, Henry C. *Speculation on the Stock and Produce Exchanges of the United States.* Studies in History, Economics, and Public Law, no. 18. New York, 1896.

Everitt, J. A. *The Third Power.* Indianapolis, 1905.

Federal Trade Commission. *Report on the Grain Trade.* Vols. 2, 5. 7 vols. Washington, D.C., 1920–26.

Fleming, Donald, and Bailyn, Bernard, eds. *Perspectives in American History.* Cambridge, Mass., 1971.

Fornari, Harry. *Bread Upon the Waters.* Nashville, 1973.

Friedman, Lawrence. *A History of American Law.* New York, 1973.

Fuller, Hubert. *The Speakers of the House.* Boston, 1909.

Gale, Edwin O. *Reminiscences of Early Chicago.* 1902.

Garceau, Oliver. *The Political Life of the American Medical Association.* Cambridge, Mass., 1941.

Gellhorn, Ernest. *Administrative Law and Process.* St. Paul, 1972.

Gellhorn, Walter. *Federal Administrative Proceedings.* Baltimore, 1941.

————, and Byse, Clark. *Administrative Law: Cases and Comments.* 5th ed. Brooklyn, 1970.

Goldstein, Benjamin F. *Marketing: A Farmer's Problem.* New York, 1928.

Handlin, Oscar and Mary. *Commonwealth: A Sudy of the Role of Government in the American Economy.* Cambridge, Mass., 1969.

Hart, Henry, Jr., and Sacks, Albert. *The Legal Process.* Cambridge, Mass., 1958.

Hays, Samuel. *The Response to Industrialism.* Chicago, 1957.

Hayter, Earl W. *The Troubled Farmer.* DeKalb, 1968.

Hicks, John D. *The Populist Revolt.* Minneapolis, 1931.

Hill, John, Jr. *Goldbricks of Speculation.* Chicago, 1903.

Hoffman, G. Wright. *Futures Trading on Organized Commodity Markets in the United States.* Philadelphia, 1932.

Hofstadter, Richard. *The Age of Reform.* New York, 1955.

Hollingsworth, J. Rogers. *The Whirligig of Politics.* Chicago, 1963.

Holmes, Oliver Wendell, Jr. *The Common Law.* Boston, 1881.

Horwitz, Morton J. *The Transformation of American Law.* Cambridge, Mass., 1977.

Hurst, Willard. *Law and Economic Growth.* Cambridge, Mass., 1964.

————. *Law and the Conditions of Freedom in the Nineteenth-Century United States.* Madison, 1956.

————. *Legitimacy of the Business Corporation in the Law of the United States.* Charlottesville, Va., 1970.

Jaffe, Louis L., and Nathanson, Nathaniel L. *Administrative Law: Cases and Materials.* 3d ed. Boston, 1968.

Kent, James. *Commentaries on American Law.* Vol. 3. 12th ed. Boston, 1874.

Kohlmeier, Louis. *The Regulators.* New York, 1969.

Kolko, Gabriel. *Railroads and Regulation.* Princeton, 1965.

————. *The Triumph of Conservatism.* Glencoe, 1963.

Levy, Leonard. *The Law of the Commonwealth and Chief Justice Shaw.* Cambridge, Mass., 1957.

Lipset, Seymour M. *Political Man.* New York, 1960.

————; Trow, Martin; and Coleman. James. *Union Democracy.* Glencoe, 1956.

McConnell, Grant. *The Decline of Agrarian Democracy.* New York, 1953.

————. *Private Power and American Democracy.* New York, 1966.

Michels, Robert. *Political Parties.* Intro. by Seymour M. Lipset. New York, 1962.

Miller, George. *Railroads and the Granger Laws.* Madison, 1971.

Morgan, H. Wayne. *From Hayes to McKinley.* Syracuse, 1969.

Murray, Robert K. *The Harding Era.* Minneapolis, 1969.

Nims, Harry D. *The Law of Unfair Competition and Trademarks.* 4th ed. New York, 1947.

Norris, Frank. *The Octopus.* New York, 1957.

————. *The Pit.* New York, 1903.

Orr, James L., ed. *Grange Melodies.* Philadelphia, 1891.

Parrish, Michael. *Securities Regulation and the New Deal.* New Haven, Conn., 1970.

Patron's Song Book: A Choice Collection of Original and Selected Gems. Cincinnati, 1877.

Pennock, J. Roland, and Chapman, John W., eds. *Voluntary Associations.* New York, 1969.

Periam, Jonathan. *The Groundswell: A History of the Origins of the Farmer's Movement.* Cincinnati, 1874.

Pierce, Bessie. *A History of Chicago.* Vol. 3, 1871–1893: *The Rise of a Modern City.* New York, 1937 –.

Pollack, Norman. *The Populist Response to Industrial America.* New York, 1962.

Quinn, John Philip. *Fools of Fortune.* Chicago, 1890.

Robinson, Glen O. ,and Gellhorn, Ernest. *The Administrative Process.* St. Paul, 1974.

Scheiber, Harry. *Ohio Canal Era: A Case Study of Government and the Economy, 1820–1861.* Athens, O., 1969.

Schonberg, James S. *The Grain Trade: How It Works.* New York, 1956.

Scott, Roy V. *The Agrarian Movement in Illinois.* Urbana, 1962.

Sharfman, I. L. *The Interstate Commerce Commission.* New York. 1931–37.

Shideler, James. *Farm Crisis 1919–1923.* Berkeley, 1957.

Smith, Constance, and Freedman, Ann. *Voluntary Associations: Perspectives on the Literature.* Cambridge, Mass., 1972.

Steffens, Lincoln. *The Shame of the Cities.* New York, 1957.

Taylor, Charles H. *History of the Board of Trade of the City of Chicago,* Chicago, 1917.

Thorelli, Hans B. *Federal Antitrust Policy.* Baltimore, 1954.

Tocqueville, Alexis de. *Democracy in America.* Edited by Max Lerner and J. P. Mayer. New York, 1966.

Watts, John. *Letter Book.* New York, 1928.

White, Leonard. *The Federalists.* New York, 1948.

————. *The Jeffersonians.* New York, 1951.

————. *The Republican Era.* New York, 1958.

Wiebe, Robert. *The Search for Order.* New York, 1967.

Williams, William A. *The Roots of the Modern American Empire.* New York, 1969.

Woodward, C. Vann. *Origins of the New South.* Baton Rouge, 1951.

II. Articles

Bicha, Karel. "The Conservative Populists: A Hypothesis," *Agricultural History* 47 (1973).

Braeman, John. "The Square Deal in Action: A Case Study in the Growth of the 'National Police Power'," in *Change and Continuity in Twentieth Century America,* edited by J. Braeman, R. Bremner, and E. Walters. Columbus, 1964.

Caines, Stanley. "Why Railroads Supported Regulation: The Case of Wisconsin, 1905–1910," *Business History Review* 44 (1970).

Christie, C. C. "Bucket Shop vs. Board of Trade," *Everybody's Magazine* 15 (1906).

Curtis, W. B. "The Increase of Gambling and Its Forms," *Forum* 12 (1891).

Galambos, Louis. "The Emerging Organizational Synthesis in Modern American History," *Business History Review* 44 (1970).

Gannon, James H., Jr. "Smith, Debtor: A Bucket Shop Idyll," *Everybody's Magazine* 15 (September 1906).

Gleed, J. W. "The True Significance of Western Unrest," *Forum* 16 (1893).

Grantham, Dewey W., Jr. Review of *The Triumph of Conservatism* by Gabriel Kolko, *South Atlantic Quarterly* 63 (1964).

Grob, Gerald N. "The Political System and Social Policy in the Nineteenth Century: Legacy of the Revolution," *Mid America* 58 (1976).

Hamlin, Rev. C. H., and Vrooman, Harry C. "Gambling and Speculation: A Symposium," *Arena* 11 (1895).

Hart, Henry, Jr. "The Relations Between State and Federal Law," *Columbia Law Review* 54 (1954).

Horwitz, Morton. "The Emergence of an Instrumental Conception of American Law, 1780–1820," *Perspectives in American History* 7 (1971).

————. "The Historical Foundations of Modern Contract Law," *Harvard Law Review* 87 (1974).

————. "The Transformation in the Conception of Property in American Law, 1780–1860," *University of Chicago Law Review* 40 (1973).

Hutchinson, Benjamin P. "Speculation in Wheat," *North American Review* 153 (1891).

Jaffe, Louis L. "The Effective Limits of the Administrative Process: A Reevaluation," *Harvard Law Review* 67 (1954).

————. "Law Making by Private Groups," *Harvard Law Review* 51 (1937).

Ladinsky, Jack, and Grossman, Joel. "Organizational Consequences of Professional Consensus: Lawyers and Selection of Judges," *Administrative Science Quarterly* 11 (1966).

Lee, Guy A. "The Historical Significance of the Chicago Grain Elevator," *Agricultural History* 11 (1937).

"Legislation Affecting Commodity and Stock Exchanges," *Harvard Law Review* 45 (1932).

Lloyd, Henry D. "Making Bread Dear," *North American Review* 137 (1883).

Lurie, Jonathan. "The Chicago Board of Trade, the Merchants' Exchange of St. Louis, and the Great Bucket Shop War, 1882–1905," *Bulletin of the Missouri Historical Society* 19 (1973)

————. "Commodities Exchanges, Agrarian 'Political Power,' and the Anti Option Battle, 1890–1894," *Agricultural History* 48 (1974).

————. "Commodities Exchanges as Self Regulating Organizations in the Late 19th Century: Some Perimeters in the History of American Administrative Law," *Rutgers Law Review* 28 (1975).

————. "Henry Demarest Lloyd: A Note," *Agricultural History* 47 (1973).

————. Review of *A History of American Law* by Lawrence Friedman, *Rutgers Law Review* 27 (Winter 1974).

————. "Speculation, Risk and Profits: The Ambivalent Agrarian in the Late Nineteenth Century," *Agricultural History* 46 (1972).

McConnell, Grant. "The Spirit of Private Government," *American Political Science Review* 52 (1958).

McCraw, Thomas K. "Regulation in America: A Review Article," *Business History Review* 49 (1975).

McVey, Frank L. "The Populist Movement," *Economic Studies* 1 (1896).

Norris, Frank. "A Deal in Wheat," *Everybody's Magazine* 7 (1902).

Odle, Thomas. "Entrepreneurial Cooperation on the Great Lakes: The Origins of the Methods of American Grain Marketing," *Business History Review* 38 (1964).

Parker, William N. "Productivity Growth in American Grain Farming." In *The Reinterpretation of American Economic History*, edited by Robert W. Fogel and Stanley L. Engerman. New York, 1971.

Rothstein, Morton. "America in the International Rivalry for the British Wheat Market, 1860–1914," *Mississippi Valley Historical Review* 47 (1960).

———. "The International Market for Agricultural Commodities, 1850–1873." In *Economic Change in the Civil War Era*. Wilmington, Del., 1965.

Scott, Roy V. "Grangerism in Champaign County, Illinois, 1873–1877," *Mid America* 43 (1961).

Smyth, Newman. "Suppression of the Lottery and Other Gambling," *Forum* 19 (1895).

Stevens, Albert C. "Futures in the Wheat Market," *Quarterly Journal of Economics* 2 (1887).

Stewart, Robert. "Metropolitan Types—The Stockbroker," *Munsey's Magazine* 21 (1889).

Treleven, Dale E. "Railroads, Elevators and Grain Dealers," *Wisconsin Magazine of History* 52 (1969).

Unger, Irwin. "The 'New Left' and American History," *American Historical Review* 72 (July 1967).

Watts, D. G. "Speculation as a Fine Art," *Cosmopolitan* 10 (1891).

Wilson, Woodrow. "The Study of Administration," *Political Science Quarterly* 2 (1887).

Woodman, Harold. "Chicago Businessmen and the 'Granger' Laws," *Agricultural History* 36 (1962).

III. Newspapers and Periodicals

American Elevator and Grain Trade. Various issues, 1883–95.

Bradstreet's. Various issues 1889–1901.

Chicago InterOcean, 1874: March 31, August 1, November 8, 9, 21, 24, 25.

Chicago Journal of Commerce, April 5, 1948.

Chicago Tribune. Various issues 1874–1900.

Farmer and Fruit Grower: October 8, 1879; May 13, 1885.

Farmer's Review: May 8, 1884; March 14, 1892.

Literary Digest 21 (1900).

The Nation 35 (1882); 45 (1887).
National Economist, 1892: May 6, 14, December 3.
New York Produce Reporter, September 21, 1895.
New York Times. Various issues 1883–91.
Northwestern Miller. Various issues 1886–1900.
Prairie Farmer, December 27, 1884.
Progressive 32 (1968).
Western Rural. Various issues 1883–93.

IV. Miscellaneous Publications

Chicago Board of Trade. *Board of Trade Report,* 1877. Appendix.
————. *Dedication Ceremonies.* Chicago, 1885.
————. *Opening Ceremonies of the Chicago Board of Trade Building.* Chicago, 1885.
————. *Report of the Directors.* Various 1874–1901. See *Yearbook* below.
————. *Yearbook.* Chicago, various volumes 1874–1905. Contains among its prefatory material the annual *Report of the Directors.*
Crosby, W. S. *The Chicago Board of Trade and Its Policy.* Chicago, 1891. In the holdings of the Newberry Library, Chicago.
————. *The Chicago Board of Trade and Its Quotations.* Chicago, 1891. In the holdings of the Newberry Library, Chicago.
Illinois, General Assembly, House. *Journal.* 1883.
Illinois State Grange. *Journal of Proceedings,* 32d session (1903).
Laws of Maryland. 1781 (November session), chapter 22.
National Grange. *Journal of Proceedings,* 14th session (1880); 21st session (1887).
Smith-Hurd. *Illinois Annotated Statutes, Supplement,* 1885–92.
United States. *Statutes at Large.* Public Law No. 93–463. Vol. 88.
————. Vol. 42, ch. 86.
United States, Congress, House. *Congressional Record.* 52d Congress, 1st session, 1892. Vol. 23, pt. 6.
————. 52d Congress, 2d session, 1893. Vol. 24, pt. 2.
————. 62d Congress, 2d session, 1912. Vol. 48, pt. 9.
United States, Congress, House. *House Report 1321.* 51st Congress, 1st session, 1890.
————. *House Report 969.* 52d Congress, 1st session, 1892.
————. *House Report 2699.* 52d Congress, 1st session, 1892.
United States, Congress, House, *Report of the Industrial Commission on Agriculture and Agricultural Labor.* 57th Congress, 1st session, 1902, document 179.
United States, Congress, House, Committee on Agriculture. *Fictitious*

Dealings in Agricultural Products. 52d Congress, 1st session, 1892.
———. *Hearings on Bills for the Prevention of Dealing in Futures.* 61st Congress, 2d session, 1910.
———. *Hearings on Futures Trading.* 66th Congress, 3rd session, 1921.
———. *Hearings on the Grain Futures Act.* 67th Congress, 2d session, 1922.
———. *Minutes,* 52d Congress, 1st session, 1892.
United States, Congress, Senate, Committee on the Judiciary. *Options and Futures.* 52d Congress, 1st session, 1892.
United States, Department of Agriculture. *A Century of Agriculture in Charts and Tables.* Washington, D.C., 1966.
United States Code. Vol. 7, sec. 4a.
United States Code Annotated. Vol. 7, sec. 6c.

V. Unpublished Works

Berman, Harold. "The Western Tradition." Manuscript. Harvard Law School, 1973.
Horwitz, Morton. Cases and materials in American legal history. Harvard Law School, 1973.
Kendall, Leon T. "The Chicago Board of Trade and the Federal Government." Ph.D. dissertation, Indiana University, 1956.
Lee, Guy A. "History of the Chicago Grain Elevator Industry 1840–1890." Ph.D. dissertation, Harvard University, 1938.
Rothstein, Morton. "American Wheat and the British Market, 1860–1905." Ph.D. dissertation, Cornell University, 1960.
Wilson, Margaret Mary. "The Attack on Options and Futures, 1888–1894." Master's thesis, University of Kansas, 1932.

VI. Cases

Albers v. Merchants' Exchange of St. Louis. 39 Mo. App. 583 (1890); 138 Mo. 140 (1897).
Bailey v. Bensley. 87 Ill. 556 (1877).
Banco Nacional de Cuba v. Sabbatino. 193 F. Supp. 375 (1961).
Barnett v. Baxter. 64 Ill. App. 544 (1896).
Baxter v. Board of Trade. 83 Ill. 146 (1876).
Beveridge v. Hewitt. 8 Ill. App. 467 (1881).
Board of Trade v. Central Stock and Grain Exchange. 98 Ill. App. 212 (1901); 196 Ill. 396 (1902).
Board of Trade v. Christie Grain and Stock Co. 116 Fed. 944 (1902); 198 U.S. 236 (1905).

Board of Trade v. L. A. Kinsey Co. 125 Fed. 72 (1903); 130 Fed. 507 (1904).

Board of Trade v. O'Dell Commission Co. 115 Fed. 574 (1902).

Brine v. Board of Trade. 2 Am. Law Rec. 268 (1873).

Bryant v. Western Union Telegraph Co. 17 Fed. 825 (1883).

Carroll v. Holmes. 24 Ill. App. 453 (1887).

Central Stock and Grain Exchange v. Board of Trade. Cir. Ct. Cook County (1900). Included in briefs to 196 Ill. 396. (Clerk's Office, Illinois Supreme Court, Springfield.)

Chase v. Cheney. 58 Ill. 509 (1872).

Chicago and Alton Railroad v. People. 67 Ill. 11 (1873).

Chicago Board of Trade v. United States. 246 U.S. 231 (1918).

Chicago, Milwaukee and St. Paul Railway v. Minnesota. 134 U.S. 418 (1890).

Christie Grain and Stock Co. v. Board of Trade. 125 Fed. 161 (1903).

Christie-Street Commission Co. v. Board of Trade. 92 Ill. App. 604 (1900); 94 Ill. App. 229 (1901).

Christie-Street Commission Co. v. Board of Trade and Western Union Telegraph Co. No. 204543, Cir. Ct. Cook County (1900).

Clark v. Foss. 5 F. Cas. 955 (1878).

Cleage v. Laidley. 149 Fed. 346 (1906).

Cleveland Telegraph Co. v. Stone. 105 Fed. 794 (1900).

Clews v. Jamieson. 89 Fed. 63 (1898); 96 Fed. 648 (1899); 182 U.S. 461 (1901).

Coffman v. Young. 20 Ill. App. 76 (1886).

Colderwood v. McCrea. 11 Ill. App. 543 (1882).

Cole v. Milmine. 88 Ill. 349 (1878).

Cothran v. Ellis. 125 Ill. 496 (1888).

De Hart v. Coverhaven. 2 Johns. Cas. 402 (1801).

Dickenson v. Chamber of Commerce of the City of Milwaukee. 29 Wis. 45 (1871).

Dickinson v. Board of Trade. 114 Ill. App. 295 (1904).

Ellis v. Marshall. 2 Mass. 269 (1807).

Farmer v. Board of Trade of Kansas City. 78 Mo. App. 557 (1899).

Field v. Clark. 143 U.S. 649 (1892).

Fisher v. Board of Trade. 80 Ill. 85 (1876).

Goddard v. Merchants' Exchange of St. Louis. 9 Mo. App. 290 (1880).

Gregory v. Wendell. 39 Mich. 337 (1878).

Guinard v. Knapp-Stout and Co. 95 Wis. 482 (1897).

Hill v. Wallace. 259 U.S. 44 (1923).

Illinois Commission Co. v. Cleveland Telegraph Co. 119 Fed. 301 (1902).

In re Renville. 46 N.Y. App. 37 (1899).

Jackson v. Foote. 12 Fed. 37 (1882).

Kennedy v. Stout. 26 Ill. App. 133 (1888).

Kinsey v. Board of Trade. 198 U.S. 236 (1905)

Kirkpatrick and Lyons v. Bonsall. 72 Penn. 155 (1872).

Logan v. Musick and Brown. 81 Ill. 415 (1876).

Lyon and Co. v. Culbertson, Blair and Co. 83 Ill. 33 (1876).

Lysaght v. St. Louis Operative Stonemasons' Association. 55 Mo. App. 538 (1893).

Metropolitan Grain and Stock Exchange v. Board of Trade. 15 Fed. 848 (1883).

Miles v. Andrews. 40 Ill. App. 155 (1891).

Minnesota v. Chicago, Milwaukee and St. Paul Railway. 38 Minn. 281 (1888).

Munn v. Illinois. 94 U.S. 113 (1877).

Murphy v. Board of Trade. 20 Chi. Legal News 7 (1887).

National Telegraph News Co. v. Western Union Telegraph Co. 119 Fed. 294 (1902).

New York and Chicago Grain and Stock Exchange v. Chicago Board of Trade. 27 Ill. App. 93 (1888); 127 Ill. 153 (1889).

Oldershaw v. Knoles. 6 Ill. App. 325 (1880); affirmed in 101 Ill. 117 (1881).

Owen v. Board of Trade. Cited in *Bradstreet's* 17 (1889):44.

Pardrige v. Cutler. 168 Ill. 504 (1897).

Pearce v. Foote. 113 Ill. 228 (1885).

People ex rel. Page v. Board of Trade. 45 Ill. 112 (1867).

People ex rel. Rice v. Board of Trade. 80 Ill. 134 (1876).

Pickering v. Cease. 79 Ill. 328 (1875).

Pitcher v. Board of Trade. 121 Ill. 412 (1887).

Porter v. Viets. 19 F. Cas. 1077 (1857).

Public Grain and Stock Exchange v. Baltimore and Ohio Telegraph Co. 1 Ill. Cir. Ct. 558 (1883).

Public Grain and Stock Exchange v. Western Union and Board of Trade. 1 Ill. Cir. Ct. 548 (1883).

Sandborn v. Benedict. 78 Ill. 309 (1875).

Savannah Cotton Exchange v. State ex rel. Warfield and Wayne. 54 Ga. 668 (1875).

Schneider v. Turner. 130 Ill. 28 (1889).

Soby v. People. 134 Ill. 66 (1890).

State of Missouri ex rel. Kennedy v. Merchants' Exchange. 2 Mo. App. 96 (1876).

Sturges v. Board of Trade. 86 Ill. 441 (1878); 91 Ill. 81 (1879).

Tenney v. Foote. 4 Ill. App. 594 (1879).

Trusler v. Crooks. 269 U.S. 475 (1926).

United States v. Jin Fuey Moy. 241 U.S. 394 (1916).

Weare Commission Co. v. People. 111 Ill. App. 116 (1903); affirmed in 209 Ill. 528 (1904).

Webster v. Sturges. 7 Ill. App. 560 (1880).

Wilson v. Commercial Telegram Co. 3 N.Y. Supp. 633 (1888).

Wolcott v. Heath. 78 Ill. 433 (1875).

Wolcott v. Reeme. 44 Ill. App. 196 (1892).

Woods v. Bates. 126 Ill. App. 180 (1906); 225 Ill. 126 (1906).

Wright v. Board of Trade. Ill. Sup. Ct., March 29, 1883. (Clerk's Office, Illinois Supreme Court, Springfield.)

Index